The World's Greatest Secret

This figure of a fish was drawn about the year
150 on the wall of a tomb discovered beneath
Saint Peter's Basilica.

THE WORLD'S GREATEST SECRET

by
John M. Haffert

Revised Edition

Imprimatur: Rev. Msgr. John Torney,
          Vicar General, Diocese of Metuchen

N.B. The Imprimatur implies nothing more than that the
material contained in this publication has been examined by
diocesan censors and that nothing contrary to faith and morals
has been found therein.

It is in the secret ... that man ... must find his
fruitfulness.

John Paul II
L'Osservatore Romano, 1983

CONTENTS

INTRODUCTION

IMPORTANT ADVICE

Because it is a book for everybody, it won't satisfy everybody. It will be too cold for the devotional, too skimpy for the professional, too abtruse for the completely uninitiated. For the latter we strongly suggest use of the **Words and References**, which we have explained at the end in alphabetical order. They are marked with asterisks throughout the text. For a start, for instance, look up **miracle** (p. 288). Whenever a word in the text is marked with an asterisk (a little star), you will find that word explained in the back of the book.

This revised edition contains features that may make it of interest not only to the new reader, but also to the many who loved the previous edition as well. For example, the material covering the reading of the ancient and mysterious graffiti of the catacombs has been expanded, and also, in another section, some little known facts are presented showing the similarities of today's Eucharistic Liturgy with that of the second and third century Christians. Numerous perhaps less noteworthy changes are included as well. It is hoped that this book will be helpful to many Christians of all denominations in discovering more about their common heritage in faith.

THE SECRET: HOPE FOR CHRISTIAN UNITY

There cannot be Christian unity without an understanding and acceptance of the basic secret of Christianity.

Entering the great building of the World Council of Churches in Geneva one is struck by those words of Jesus spoken at the institution of the Eucharist during the Last Supper . . . words which express the thirst of all Christians: *"Father, that they may be one as you and I are one."*

Perhaps by getting back to the roots of Christianity in the catacombs themselves we can find the secret.

And *that secret* for which early Christians died *is the secret to Christian unity.*

As the writer of this book, I am a "nothing person." I prayed (and I asked many others to join me in prayer) that I might be able to write this book with simplicity and objectivity, as though the secret were being told for the first time and being told with discretion and dignity and in such manner that it might be understandable to non-Christians, while at the same time being a call to unity for all those who believe that Jesus was truly the Son of God and that He keeps His promise to remain with us.

Certainly one of the greatest spiritual agonies for saintly, believing Christians is that they are often divided by what they *do not believe,* while they are already spiritually united by what they do believe.

Our unity is felt more and more today as we listen to the great Christian preachers of the "electronic church."

The first of these to whom I used to listen ardently was Dr. Ralph Sockman, whose Park Avenue church was one of the most beautiful in America. I often arranged my time for Sunday morning Mass so as not to miss any of Dr. Sockman's radio broadcasts. And week after week, year after year, *I never once heard him express a doctrine in which I, as a Catholic, did not believe.*

On a trip to Europe in 1946 I sat behind Dr. Sockman on the plane and we spent an hour walking together alone at the Gander Airport in Newfoundland. I was on my way to Fatima and he was on his way to Russia with a study group.

He asked me about Catholic devotion to the Blessed Virgin and wondered why the Miracle of Fatima was not better known, especially because of its importance with relation to Russia. And I answered him almost spontaneously: *"It is the devil's work to keep us divided... to keep us from knowing..."*

Almost thirty years later I wrote this book and had a preliminary small edition published to send to people like Dr. Sockman and other prominent Christian leaders (and also to some prominent non-Christians). I asked them all for their advice.

Several outstanding Protestant clergymen replied. Indeed, some received it with nothing less than enthusiasm.

But there was no letter from Dr. Ralph Sockman who had so long been in my thoughts and prayers. And I wondered if I had alienated him by my reference to Satan as the father of lies and division.

Shortly after the book was published I decided to ask Dr. Stockman if he would appear on a television program with me to discuss it.

To my surprise and joy he replied that he would be glad to do so.

Although he had not written, he had apparently found the book a source of inspiration, and perhaps soul-searching. And, although he had refused many invitations (even from network programs) to appear on television after his retirement, he agreed to appear with me on a program on this all important subject of the Christian secret!

(Unfortunately, Dr. Sockman died before the program materialized.)

Millions of Christians have preceded us to the reward that Jesus promised. They are now united in the many mansions of His Father's house. They are praying for us that together all may finally walk in the unity for which

He prayed on the "night of the Secret."

Certainly this book in itself is not worthy of so sublime a subject. It must be hoped that others will be inspired to treat it in a much more worthy manner.

But it is a beginning. And it is presented with the hope and prayer that those into whose hands it falls will share it with their Christian and even non-Christian neighbors.

Herein lies certainly the world's greatest hope for peace from Jesus Who said: "My peace be unto you . . . behold I am with you until the end of the world."

Above: The author autographs the book at a New Orleans convention while volunteers promoting it look on. The writer forfeits all royalties so that proceeds from the book are used to distribute it further. Personally convinced by the book, groups of volunteers organized in most major cities to help make it known at the time of its first major printing. The book has now gone through five printings since the November 1967 edition. The French edition is published by Téqui, Paris.

CHAPTER ONE

EXCITING DISCOVERY

Near sundown on November 18, 1962, the one-hundred-and-ten ton schooner *Santa Maria* emerged as a speck from the vast sea and splashed her anchor down in twenty feet of water off a tiny island in the West Indies.

The old ship seemed to sense the thrill of her last great adventure as she rolled in the offshore swell.

We had come to find sunken treasure.

We did. Or at least we found the bones of the Spanish galleon which had broken up on this reef before the United States was born. As in one of those strange stories of pirate maps, we had learned of it somewhat by accident.

But we were not alone.

In the first full daylight we gasped at the sight of the shoreline. Vast craters were scattered over the tiny island. Areas of glaring white coral gaped from the palmetto-covered earth. We were even more amazed to find that one lone man had dug all these craters. He had heard of the galleon apparently many months before we did and had left his family to find it. Now half-mad with treasure lust, long since out of dynamite, he continued to dig frantically with his bare hands. He had become convinced that the survivors of the galleon had removed the bulk of the treasure from the wreck, buried it and died without survivors.

We began to dive on the wreck itself. Down on the ocean floor, breathing through hoses from the surface

Discovery in the West Indies wasn't as exciting as discoveries in Rome. Here the *Santa Maria* lies at anchor off Miami Beach after her successful treasure hunt. Insert shows the author who led the treasure hunt as captain and navigator.

we found cannon balls and trinkets and coins of centuries ago. We almost forgot our fear of sharks and barracudas under the pressure of tons of water as we became part of America's past.

Just before sundown we used to move the schooner to a cove at the end of the island. The hours between setting anchor and bedtime were filled with conversations which often had little to do with the treasure. Deeply affected by the sense of solitude, of "other worldliness" experienced together in the silent depths, our thoughts ran to greater things.

The four aboard included a writer who once studied to be a priest; an atheist graduated from Oxford; a professional photographer; and a sailor whose hobbies included weight lifting and skin diving.

The discussions never became angry, but they were often spirited.

"Trouble is," said the Englishman, "you fellows have read too many churchy publications which have prejudiced your judgment. Your church puts the books you ought to read on its Index of Prohibited Books.* You probably feel you'd be contaminating yourselves if you read Frank Harris* or Henry Miller.* You ride through life in a closed carriage of religious views and never get to know what man really is."

The next day a big barracuda met us over the wreck while we were turning over barnacle-encrusted ballast stones. One of us had felt a "presence" in the water, turned around, and there the great lethal fish hung, staring. We could not know when the lightning speed would be unleashed behind those murderous jaws. One of us

* All asterisks refer to *Words and References* in back of book.

signalled that he would watch while the others worked. Finally the sailor motioned that he was going to shoot it and the Englishman took up a side position armed only with a short spear.

"That was a brave thing you did," the sailor said to the Englishman as we climbed back on the deck. But the Englishman was always doing brave things. He was one of the finest athletes and most personable companions any of us had known. And he did not mean to be rude when he challenged the narrowness of our views, as we also did not mean to be rude when we defended the existence of God. Perhaps without expecting to convince each other, we hoped that some thoughts would sink in like seeds disappearing into swallowing soil, finally conquering it in silence.

"Speaking of Frank Harris," the writer said, "didn't he become an atheist just before he was about to be confirmed because a Hindu asked him who had made God? And doesn't his autobiography indicate that he rejected God so easily because he didn't like the Commandments?"

Immediately the Englishman defended Harris: "But Frank Harris was a modern Christian. He acknowledged the historic reality of Christ and of the Gospels. Harris was not like the ignoramuses who say Christ never even existed. Himself a great Latin and Greek scholar, he knew of Christ in the writings of Tacitus and of Josephus, contemporary historians. He has a whole chapter in one of his five autobiographical volumes in which he extols Christ, and yet at the same time proves that He was not divine."

Finally we had to leave the wreck for a time because the writer had to return to New York on business for a couple of weeks. He had not known how to answer the challenge that Harris had "proved" Christ was not divine. So he studied the position of Harris, and then was almost as interested in going back to the schooner to continue those discussions as in continuing the treasure hunt.

Near shipwreck and a host of adventures filled the rest of the voyage, but the discussion at meals and in the few nights of quiet watch still went on. They led to a new and different treasure hunt, and to the writing of this book.

Harris' own words revealed that he first affirmed Christ's reality because of an *archeological* discovery* which he made in Greece and which, in his own words, "had lent an enormous, *a disproportionate influence on my whole outlook and way of reading the past.*"

He claims that while traveling on foot through Attica he began to wonder about the great ruin of a marble lion which was destroyed by the Turks who thought it contained treasure.

The Turks had found the lion solid. It contained no treasure, and no one had solved the mystery as to why it was standing there.

Harris, who possessed an encyclopedic memory, recalled a great battle which took place on this plain in which three hundred young men of Thebes went out to oppose the invading armies of Philip of Macedonia and Alexander. The three hundred young men had taken a solemn oath to stop the invaders or die in the attempt. They were all killed. Plutarch, who described the event, mentioned a river on the plain. Harris says that he studied the area and while there was now no river, a shallow brook flowed not far from the fragments of the lion and a long, grass-grown depression. He reasoned that the lion had been a memorial over the tomb.

He persuaded archeologists* to excavate in that particular spot. They found four stone walls a foot or so broad and six feet or so in height, built in the form of an elongated square, resting on the shingle of an old river bed. Inside there were 297 skeletons. In a corner was a little pile of ashes which they took to be the remains of the other three who had survived longest and were finally cremated. Evidence of the terrible conflict was still discernible in the conditions of the skeletons, one of which had three ribs smashed on one side, while the head of a spear was found jammed between another rib and a backbone; another backbone had been broken by a vigorous spear thrust and one side of the head beaten in as well.

Had it not been for the account in Plutarch, which Harris remembered, the ruin of a lion might still be a mystery.

Previously this description of the battle by Plutarch had been taken by many to be poetic legend.

"I began to read other books," Harris writes, "and notably the New Testament in a different spirit. German scholars had taught me that Jesus was a mythical figure: His teachings a mishmash of various traditions and religions and myths. He was not an historical personage in any way, they declared; the three synoptic Gospels were all compiled from fifty to eighty years after the events, and John was certainly later still."

Harris, although an atheist, now became convinced of the historical reality of Christ because he now knew from personal experience that records of history do not diminish in accuracy because of age. A record of 2,000 years ago could be just as accurate as a description written yesterday. Not only have the facts of Christ's life been told by four different disciples (Matthew, Mark, Luke and John), who even offered their lives in testimony of what they recorded, but the same reality of Christ was confirmed by other contemporary historians such as Josephus and Tacitus.

Now convinced of the fact of Christ, how did Harris, the atheist, react? How did he "prove" Christ was not divine?

Admitting that Christ appeared to hundreds of persons after allegedly dying on the cross, Harris says that Christ had merely fainted, and that afterward because of the care of those who were waiting He was able to be brought back to health and to show Himself to His disciples. Harris says: "If He were dead, He must have been dead for some time, the time at least necessary for someone to go to Jerusalem and see Pilate and return again to Calvary with the order to test the apparent death."

It is remarkable that Harris felt himself to be one of the world's greatest scholars, perhaps because he could memorize whole passages so easily and could speak six languages. *Yet he did not know how far Calvary was from the Fortress Antonia* where Pilate presided that day!

The distance from Calvary to Fortress Antonia is only a ten-minute walk. On horseback around the wall, as it was then, it could have been no more than a few minutes!

Anchored off the island of San Salvador, where Columbus' extraordinary landfall exploded the world into a new age, the writer quietly summed up to the atheist: "You accuse believers of prejudice and ignorance, but it is usually the other way about."

The writer had traveled around the Mediterranean just

before the treasure hunt and he knew of some exciting discoveries, especially in Rome.

"If Harris could be convinced about the facts of Christ because he found a grave in a field in Greece, even as we came alive to early American history when we found pieces-of-eight among the bones of a Spanish galleon, I think we should be able to find something better than a Grecian grave to help good men realize that there is something more glorious than Henry Miller's 'pus and open sewers', something better to which to look forward to than your new prophets like de Maupassant slitting his own throat in his early forties."

So we began to wonder: What is the buried secret of a Spanish galleon when compared to the secrets now being uncovered by scientific, well-equipped treasure hunters of history: the modern archeologists?* When we see the vastness of their excavations spreading around the Mediterranean and get some inkling of the scientific precision with which they work to uncover the secrets of the past, does not the common sea-going treasure hunter seem like a haphazard amateur looking for baubles?

For five years prior to finding the wrecked galleon, our imagination had been captivated by the reported archeological findings around the Mediterranean area, particularly in Rome. Now, with the success of discovering the bones of a Spanish ship, we began to wonder: Why not go to Italy to verify those archeological finds? The Spanish galleon had seemed like a myth until those pieces-of-eight were actually in our hands. And if we could verify a rumor by merely lifting real coin from the bottom of the sea, then why shouldn't we hope to verify that far more precious coin of *the world's greatest secret* which modern archeologists claimed to have discovered?

Forum of Pompeii where Roman power flourished, discovered in the recently excavated city. A German "treasure hunter" had read of Pompeii in old documents. He found the entire city just where it had been buried under volcanic ash nineteen centuries before. It was one of the greatest archeological finds of all time and started a new wave of Mediterranean digging.

So the *Santa Maria* was returned to Miami and her skipper boarded an ocean liner to spend most of the next two years in Europe writing this book.

Those Mediterranean treasure hunters with pick and shovel knew where to look. Their knowledge of history has leaped ahead during recent years. Documents have been founded, catalogued, duplicated on microfilm and made available to them at stations around the world. They found Pompeii. They found Herculaneum and Capernaum and dozens of other ancient cities long since drowned beneath the waves of the changing earth.

Back in that schooner in the West Indies we began to understand the modern archeologists because from old Spanish documents we knew in advance about the galleon whose bones we picked.

Most of the greatest archeological finds of our time have been similarly made because of old documents. It was long known, for example, that probably an important first century cemetery was still uncovered in Rome. And cemeteries, to treasure hunters of civilization, are more exciting than the smell of gold to treasure hunters of the sea. Cemeteries contain tombs, and ancient tombs with their pottery, coins and inscriptions are time-capsules of the past.

Unfortunately, most of the cemeteries of Rome had been emptied before the archeologists reached them. After the Roman Empire crumbled, wave upon wave of invaders pillaged mausoleums and catacombs.

But the catacombs of Vatican Hill, still buried beneath St. Peter's Basilica, were yet to be unearthed. They might still be preserved!

In 1900, by unanimous vote, the International Archeologists' Congress petitioned Pope Leo XIII to excavate beneath the church.

But the Pope refused. The church in question was Saint Peter's Basilica, the largest church in the world!

In 1939, an accident led to discovery.

Pope Pius XII, the reigning pontiff at that time, had ordered a portion of the floor of Saint Peter's crypt be lowered to receive the tomb of Pius XI, and a workman made the amazing discovery. It must have been figuratively a little like Alice's falling through the rabbit hole. He landed in a different world: in a first century cemetery.

With that, the excavation was on.

The expense resembled a U.S. Government appropriation. Several superstructures, though "modern" in comparison to the substructures, had been built long before Columbus discovered America. They had to be shored up. The dome rose above that very spot almost as high as a forty story skyscraper!

This vast structure, almost as tall as the Time-Life Building in New York, with a "wing" so big it could be used for a football stadium, presented problems to the scientists who wanted to dig beneath it. It had taken one hundred twenty years to build. Nobody wanted it to come crashing down in as many seconds, even to probe the secrets of the past!

Painstakingly, the work proceeded. Excitement and suspense mounted. Excavators hit a rich religious lode and began to discover things hidden since Constantine built the first basilica on the same spot back in 315.

They were still tallying the finds when Pius XII died in 1958, twenty years after the first archeological spade sank questingly between the great foundations.

The cemetery they found dated from the time of Christ. Some tombs were found so perfectly preserved that the mosaic and fresco decorations seemed brand new. Excavations from the central floor of the basilica slowly worked toward the spot where tradition said Peter had been buried.

Almost at once two surprising facts came to light:

First, some of the pagan tombs of the first century had been filled in during the fourth century by the then-pagan Emperor, Constantine,[1] to serve as foundations of a Christian church. This was particularly amazing because the pagan Romans had an almost superstitious respect for tombs. In all history only twice did Roman emperors violate the catacombs, even during ruthlessly thorough persecutions. Obviously the pagan emperor must have had a very pressing reason for allowing some tombs to be filled in for building foundations!

Second, as the excavators approached that area where Peter was said to be interred, they found Christian tombs squeezed among the pagan tombs in increasing numbers. They even found some Christians buried in the older pagan mausoleums which were there before Peter's death.

Most amazing was the discovery of Peter's grave.[2]

It was a very poor tomb, lowered in the ground, sealed with a slab of stone. Ordinarily it would never have attracted any attention, squeezed as it was between magnificent pagan mausoleums.

Because of their immense respect for the dead, the Ro-

[1]Constantine, though he declared himself in favor of Christianity earlier, was not himself baptized until shortly before his death, and was therefore a pagan when he built the first "St. Peter's Basilica" on Rome's Vatican Hill.
[2]For an account of the excavations and later positive determination of Peter's remains see John Evangelist Walsh, *The Bones of St. Peter*, (Garden City, N.Y.: Doubleday), 1982.

This vast structure presented no small problem to the scientists who wanted to excavate under it. From the back, (behind us, out of the picture) St. Patrick's Cathedral in New York would fill the space only as far as the top of the curve in the crowd where the Swiss guard blocks the aisle. The church will hold the entire population of a small city (25,000).

It must have been a little like Alice's falling through the rabbit hole. He landed in a different world: in a first century cemetery.

The trap door (above) is the cover of Peter's tomb.

Painstakingly, slowly, the work progressed.

mans had never desecrated Peter's tomb, despite the increasingly bitter persecutions of Christians. They had
done the next thing: They had tried to camouflage or
hide it. They had built a staircase from one level of the
cemetery to an upper level right over this tomb. The date
of this stircase was ascertained from a marked tile in its
foundation. The staircase was built less than a century
after Peter's death, when Christianity was beginning to
spread like a consuming fire through the pagan world.
The red staircase wall, which had been built within the
life span of a single man after Peter's death, was covered
with a maze of inscriptions.

The first archeologist to see this wall found most of
the markings as undecipherable as hieroglyphics had
been before the discovery of the Rosetta Stone.* Pius
XII, who had undertaken the excavations, did not live to
see their major translations. Experts began to identify
these inscriptions with similar ones which had begun to
turn up in excavations all over the Mediterranean area in
Christian tombs of the first and second centuries. These
markings partially lifted the curtain on early Christian
beliefs.

Before the meaning of the red wall markings was deciphered, workmen made other finds. They found three
altars directly below the sixteenth century altar which
visitors see today beneath the dome of St. Peter's. Each
altar is on a different level, one above the other, having
been built at about 500-year intervals. The most recent
had been built by Calixtus, the next by Gregory the
Great, and the last and earliest by Constantine who was
the first of the Roman emperors to recognize Christianity.

The altar of Constantine crowded out still a fourth

Some of the pagan tombs of the first four
centuries had been filled in . . . an amazing
fact because it was a pagan emperor who
ordered it done.

altar, a "trophy," with two columns and a sort of trap
door underneath it. This predated the altar of Constantine by at least 150 years. The "trophy" was built into
the staircase wall which bore many inscriptions.

One of the inscriptions, older than the enclosure of Constantine, reads: *"Peter Lies Within."* [2] The name and
symbol of Peter were found everywhere about. One line
scribbled about A.D. 150 reads: *"Paccius Eutychus
remembered Glykon here."* In the eighteen centuries since
then how many pilgrims to Peter's tomb have written
home:

"I remembered you here."

Why had Pius XII reversed the decision of his
predecessors and agreed, at such tremendous risk and expense, to unearth Peter's tomb? Was he trying to produce
a creditable witness for Christ? Or did he guess we might
find some evidence of Christ's doctrinal legacy for which
Peter had been willing to die? If might help us to understand if we translate what happened to Peter into
modern context.

Rome in its prime, was like Washington or Moscow
today. If our world were pagan and Christ came now,
what would happen if a creditable, intelligent witness
traveled to Washington to testify about Him before a
joint session of Congress?

Since Christ performed great miracles, converting
thousands and thereby upsetting the traditions under-
lying all contemporary life, Congress might listen, and
might even be more tolerant than were Caligula,
Claudius or Nero.

But suppose the witness had been forced to go to

[2]Margherita Guarducci, *The Tomb of St. Peter,* (New York: Hawthorn
Books), 1960, pp. 133-35.

Moscow or Peking? Could he have expected any better treatment than Peter and Paul expected in Rome?

So this digging under the great Roman basilica to the tomb of Christ's "witness" was a dramatic, scientific step into Christianity's infancy. *It was a direct contact with an important witness of Christian faith.*

After all, the writings and the spoken words of Christ's later followers have often been confusing. Over *two hundred* Christian sects have grown out of different interpretations of the Gospels.

So which teachings of Christ most impressed Peter, a man who walked with Christ, learned directly from His lips, and died at last for his belief in what he had heard Christ teaching?

Because they partially answer this question, the inscriptions on the wall over Peter's tomb were truly the *great* discovery made in our own time — a discovery vastly more exciting than a pile of cannon balls and some pieces-of-eight or the remains of three hundred Thebans in an Attican grave.

Mausoleums, or tombs, were discovered to be w
preserved. The second amazing fact was th
clustered around the tomb of Peter were squeez
tombs of Christians, some even inside the pag
mausoleums.

Above: a row of mausoleums bordering an a
cient "street" of the Vatican catacombs.

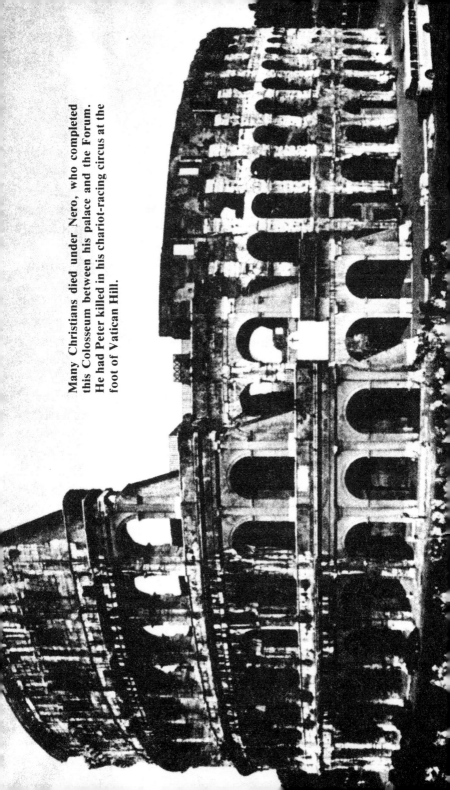

Many Christians died under Nero, who completed this Colosseum between his palace and the Forum. He had Peter killed in his chariot-racing circus at the foot of Vatican Hill.

CHAPTER TWO

WHY THE SECRECY?

The early Christians lived in a clandestine church set against a backdrop of fear. They would move through underground passages, and perform their religious rites deep in the bowels of the earth where pagan eyes could not penetrate.

The reason lies in one terrible word: *persecution*. Only understanding of that terrible word can enable us to grasp why the subject of this book first became the world's greatest secret . . . distinguished in symbols around Peter's tomb and in the catacombs of Rome.

The horrors of early persecutions have been revealed in various documents, beginning with the Bible itself. In the Acts of the Apostles there is a description of the stoning of Stephen, and later St. Paul in his Epistles refers to the persecutions in Rome. At the time that Paul wrote, persecutions were still a comparatively new phenomenon, and they were not quite so thorough as they subsequently became. Paul himself was able to preach openly in the Eternal City (though under custody) for two years before he was beheaded.

Tertullian, writing in the second century, gives us an inkling of the persecutions which Nero inaugurated.

Then the writer Pliny paints a wider picture. It was he whom Emperor Trajan sent to the Province of Bithynia-Pontus to quell "disorder" reported there. He writes that he was amazed to find that a large percentage of the province had become Christian. This caused "disorder" because the members of the new religion no longer bought animal victims for sacrifice to the gods, and dealers in animals felt the economic pinch, as did the pagan priests.

Pliny asked the Emperor how he should handle the matter and Trajan's reply, recorded by Pliny, became the basis for persecution of Christians until Constantine became Emperor in 313, and briefly afterward in the reign of Julian the Apostate. The decree of Trajan demanded that Christians recant and offer sacrifice to the gods or die. Shortly after this the staircase and wall were built over Peter's tomb in the cemetery on Vatican Hill.

Does all this sound like a fantastic tale from some Never-Never Land, only dimly discernible beyond the mists and shadows of time?

To us of the twentieth century, it should seem more real than that. We are no strangers to persecution. It rages virulent, violent and vicious all about us.

Father Leopold Braun, A.A., for many years pastor of the one Roman Catholic church within the borders of the U.S.S.R.[1] said that he did not keep baptismal or marriage records. The Cheka,[2] or secret police, who appeared unexpectedly from time to time to inspect his files, would have visited reprisals on his parishioners had he kept such records.

Then Father Robert Greene, M.M., who was a missionary in the little village of Tung-an in South China, tells his experiences in his book *Calvary in China*. When the Reds took over in 1950, one of their first acts was to paint on the side of the church in huge characters, words

---

[1] Fr. Braun was allowed in the Soviet Union when the United States granted the country diplomatic recognition.
[2] The former name of the Soviet secret police, now known as the KGB (from the Russian name of the organization, which means *Committee for State Security*).

reading "Freedom of Religion."

Seeing this, the happy parishioners thronged to the church as usual for Sunday Mass. As they entered the door Communist soldiers stood aside and watched.

A few nights later, the priest, lying awake in his bed, heard sounds beneath his window. He looked out. Red soldiers were marching by, leading a civilian prisoner.

In the morning he was told: "'Old Lee Tu-pao was taken from his home last night and no one knows what has happened to him.'"

Eventually the church building was used as a prison where Red soldiers questioned the unfortunates and "encouraged" them to "confess." Father Greene describes the glimpse he had of it one day: "Two men strung up by their thumbs to a hook on the wall, their toes barely touching the floor.... I know of one Christian who went eight days thus strung up before he eventually died." [3]

Naturally, the Christians lived in a nightmare of suspense and dread. Father Greene hid the Blessed Sacrament in his bookcase. To make matters worse, he distrusted his own former parishioners, and parents distrusted their own children.

A similar fear and distrust existed in East Germany. The *February 1966* Bulletin of St. Ignatius Church, San Francisco, published an excerpt from a letter written by a priest in East Berlin. A woman came to him and asked: "My son wants to flee to West Germany to study engineering. Should I let him go?"

The priest ponders in his letter: "Is the woman's prob-

[3] Fr. Robert W. Greene, M.M., *Calvary in China*, (New York: G. Putnam), 1953, p. 88.

lem genuine, or does she have 'the task' of exposing me as 'an instigator of defection'?''

Dr. Thomas Dooley tells of the terrible persecution of Christians in Vietnam in his immortal book *Deliver Us from Evil.* And in his book *The Night They Burned the Mountain,* Dr. Dooley tells of his fears when confronted with the thought that he might have to abandon his crew of Asian workers and leave Laos before the Communist invasion:

"I knew that the six or eight of my star pupils would be taken out and beheaded in front of the whole village and their heads, with the organs of the neck hanging down, would be impaled upon stakes. I knew that the Communists would take my Lao crew, stand them in a circle facing inward, and with machetes would deftly cut the tendons in the back of their knees. When the crew would fall to the ground, the Communists would walk around and hack them to pieces. I have seen the Communists do this and just leave the men in the middle of a room or in a field. When the tendons were cut, the Lao would not bleed to death. They would crawl like animals until they were caught and hacked to death. This is what they would do to Chai, to Si, to Ngoan, and to Deng. To the girls on my staff they would do even more dreadful things."

Perhaps *somewhere* in the world we will always have persecution, although that is usually followed by grace and conversion.

But the mind boggles at the hideous facts. We find that we are thinking of them as if they were the stuff of an old Alfred Hitchcock TV skit which had somehow gone awry; we can scarcely realize that they are actual occurrences on this familiar planet, Earth.

Horror is always difficult to grasp whether it is of ancient Rome, of present-day totalitarian regimes, or, for that matter, of yesterday's Nazism which took the lives of hundreds of thousands. Who will forget the awful drama of day-to-day secrecy which fills the diary of Anne Frank, a secrecy which only postponed the agony of the gas chamber?

Only twenty-four hours after the Nazi, Adolph Eichmann, had been hanged, the present writer drove past the chalk walls of the prison in Israel where the hanging occurred. All was quiet. If the wretch had cried out as he fell through the trap, no echo resounded from the quiet hills. It was as though the grisly deed of his hanging and all his own grisly deeds had never taken place. Peaceful green fields lay beneath the shadow of the timeless Palestinian hills. Christ saw those same fields — so the mind darts off on a tangent, seeking a pleasant, romantic thought. We wondered then: "If we find it difficult to realize the monstrosity of an Eichmann who died here *yesterday,* can we ever realize the grim persecutions of *two thousand years ago?"*

However, it helps a little to have the cryptographic writings of the early Christians. The writings are tangible evidence. And we find cryptography* in abundance not only on Peter's tomb, and under the Basilica of St. Peter's, but also in a first century room discovered in 1915 under St. Sebastian's Church beyond the walls of Rome.[4]

The symbols and the writings, meaningless to an outsider, like lightning flash back over the centuries to

---

[4]Although the excavations were not completed until 1956, and are still the subject of study, the original discovery was made in 1915 by Dr. P. Styger. See also Henry V. Morton, *A Traveler in Rome* (London: Methuen & Co.), 1957, p. 144; and Engelbert Kirschbaum, *The Tombs of St. Peter and St. Paul* (New York: St. Martin's Press), 1959, p. 196.

Symbols of Peter combine a P and an E also form image of a key, recalling Christ's words to Peter: "I will give you the keys of the kingdom of heaven; . . . . (Mt. 16:19)

Symbols of Christ using the first, or the first two, letters of 'Christ' in Greek (χριστος).

Combined Latin and Greek symbols of Peter and Christ.

Symbols of the name of Mary.

It took experts several years to "pick apart" the heavy inscriptions, one on top of the other, which covered the red wall over Peter's tomb.

reveal how the early Christians lived.

Looking at the Christians in China under Mao, we know what that meant. The Christians of the little town of Tung-an knew that discovery would lead to the firing squad — or much worse. In some cases, they were in fear not only for themselves but also for the people who sheltered them, so they exercised the caution of hunted animals. They used every form of concealment, reticence, and seclusion; they created every barrier, curtain, purdah, shade, mask or disguise that ingenuity could devise.

Obviously, it was the same for the early Christians. To become a Christian in the first centuries was to choose concealment as a way of life. Fear was a cloak that one donned along with the symbolic white robe of Baptism. The poor creature was henceforth hedged about with countless inhibitions, lest a word, a gesture, or some tiny act of his give him or his friends away.

The catacombs, fetid, cold and damp, were the meeting-places of the brethren. There they could perform their religious rites hidden from hostile gaze, and protected by the Romans' superstitious respect for cemeteries.

In this atmosphere of secrecy the Christians hid their beliefs in symbols, and archeologists today study those symbols for answers. As far back as the fourth century, historians called the Christian life "the discipline of the secret." However, much earlier, before it was called anything at all, it was a deeply ingrained discipline. It was so much a part of Christianity that it could not be shuffled off even after the need for it no longer existed. Secrecy survived in the East until the fifth century, in the West until the sixth. It took time for people to believe that the persecutions were really over and done with. For a long time there was a latent fear of renewal.

When partially trusted strangers or new converts from paganism attended Christian rites, they were allowed to stay only for the first part of the prayers and ceremonies. They were required to leave when the second, more private, part was about to begin. The first part of the liturgical* service was designated for "the catechumens" (that is, for those still learning the catechism of the Faith) and the rest designated for "the faithful" (that is, for those who had proved their steadfastness in the Faith and had been baptized). The great *act* of the liturgy of "the faithful" was perhaps the most carefully guarded secret of all history. *In the Liturgy it was referred to as "the secret" until 1964!*

This secret so filled the hearts and minds of the first Christians that archeologists and historians working all around the Mediterranean keep uncovering the secret symbols day after day. Early Christians had not been afraid to express the secret in symbols and pictures because unless a man knew the secret, the symbols would be meaningless. *The secret was too mystic for mere humans to believe.* Indeed, it was almost too mystic for humans to believe. After Vatican Council II removed the label of secrecy and openly substituted "Liturgy of the Eucharist" for "Secret," the mystery began to creep into interfaith dialogue. The current sound and excitement seems to echo what was heard when Christ first announced it.

At the top of the next page is a *symbol of the Secret* found in a second century catacomb. Similar pictures introduce most chapters throughout the rest of the book.

CHAPTER THREE

BEGAN AS A SECRET

It may have been the most terrible moment that the Apostles ever experienced; more terrible than Gethsemane or Calvary; even more terrible than the moments of their own deaths.

They had left all to follow Christ. They had turned their backs upon their wives, children, their homes, businesses — *everything*. They had thought that nothing mattered except what He did, what He said. They were convinced that He would lead them to reward, to great triumph. They expected Him to establish His kingdom soon, and they, His chosen companions and intimates, wearing purple and scarlet, would be His administrators. Indeed, judging from the crowds, the time was ripe — *now, today*.

They were near the bustling town of Capernaum. Just about every inhabitant of the place had turned out to hear Him speak. The people followed Him with a breathless eagerness all the way up the hill overlooking the lake.

Moreover, since the Pasch was at hand, people on holiday from neighboring hamlets were gathered here for the approaching feast, or they were on their way to the great temple in Jerusalem. The Apostle Matthew, who had been an accountant, estimated that there were five thousand men alone, excluding women and children. The grassy hillside was black with humanity.

Christ did not disappoint them. He spoke to them with greater eloquence than ever; quietly, forcefully, and every man, bright-eyed and intent, leaned forward listening as though his life depended upon the next word.

The meal hour came and went and scarcely a person in that vast throng gave it a thought. Only as He finished His discourse did the people become aware of a gnawing in the pit of their stomachs, and it was then they noticed for the first time that many of the children were crying fretfully and asking for bread.

It had not occurred to the townspeople to bring food with them when they had followed Him up the hill. Perhaps subconsciously they had considered that precaution unnecessary. As long as He was with them hunger, accident, illness, nothing would bother them.

The Apostles were concerned. Though they felt a bit presumptuous to tell Him a fact that He must know, they reminded Him: "This is a desert place. Send the people away so that they can buy their dinner."

Christ's answer was strange:

"Give them something to eat."

Did He mean that they should empty their little treasury and make the round trip to town to buy the scant rations their funds would provide? He asked the Apostle Philip: "Where can we buy bread that these people may have something to eat?"

Philip's answer seems almost impatient: "Two hundred days' wages, which is the most we could muster, wouldn't buy a crumb for everybody here."

"How many loaves have you?" Christ asked.

Of course they had no loaves at all. Nobody in that huge crowd had anything edible but one young lad. Andrew, another Apostle, pointed out the boy: "That lad over there has five barley loaves and two fishes. But," the man added with a shrug, "what is that among so many?"

"Bring them to me," Christ said simply.

When Christ had the bread and fish before Him, He bade the people sit down. Then He looked up to heaven, blessed the food, and handed it to the Apostles, instructing: "Give it to the people."

As the twelve men passed among the huge crowd, serving one hungry person after another, they soon noticed a strange phenomenon: the food they carried never diminished.

There was always plenty for the next person, and the next, and the next. In the end there was more than enough for each one of those many thousands to eat heartily, and when the meal was over, the Apostles gathered up *twelve baskets of left-overs.*

Slowly the people began to grasp the marvel. They understood that this man, this carpenter's son, this Jesus, had miraculously by an act of His will or a wave of His hand or a mumbled prayer or whatever, miraculously multiplied a few scraps of food, making them enough to satisfy the appetites of somewhere between five and fifteen thousand hungry people.

He was a prophet all right, and more than a prophet. He was a Wonderworker beyond their wildest dreams. With Him as their leader there need be no more hunger in Israel. The Romans themselves with all their proud legions would cringe before such power.

As they commented to one another, excitement

mounted. Somebody had scarcely voiced the suggestion
of making Him king when a lusty cheer went up on all
sides. The crowd was of one mind: They would seize
Him where He stood and forthwith proclaim His sovereignty.

But where was He?

He Who wished to be king only of the hearts of men
had slipped away.

It was the next day when they came upon Him again.
They jostled one another in their eagerness to get close to
Him. Expectation was alight on every face, but it was
quickly dimmed by His first words. They seemed almost
a rebuke: "You looked for me not because you have seen
my other miracles or because you seek the things of the
spirit, but only because I fed you."

The Apostles, too, were chagrined and nonplussed by
these words, and did not quite know how to answer. He
went on: "You should strive not for the meat which
spoils quickly, but for the meat which lasts into eternity.
I, the Son of Man, will give you that meat."

That sounded better. But it was still puzzling. Some
people in the crowd, a little bolder than the rest, asked:
"How do we get this food?"

"I will tell you," Christ replied. "Believe in me. I have
been sent by your Father in heaven."

"All right, we'll believe," a number of people
shouted. "But," added a few of them, "show us a sign."

Apparently they wanted another miracle like yesterday's or one even more spectacular. After all, as one
man pointed out, now that he had slept on the matter,
the feat of this Wonderworker with the bread and fish
did not seem so great to him as it had at first. Some prophets of the past had wrought similar marvels. In fact,

the man challenged Christ outright: "Our fathers ate manna in the desert. That was miraculous food, too."

Yes, Moses *had* fed the people for forty years on manna in the Sinai desert, and this Christ had fed them only once. Even the Apostles remembered about that, and they nodded their heads when somebody quoted the scriptural text referring to the patriarch: "He gave them bread from heaven."

Christ's response was: "Moses gave you not the true bread from heaven, not the bread from heaven like the kind my Father will give you. *This new bread which comes from heaven will give life to the world.*"

With these promising words a clamor arose: "We want this bread! We want this bread!"

"I myself am the bread of life," Christ answered. "Whoever comes to me will never again be hungry, and whoever believes in me will never again be thirsty."

A clearly audible murmur ran through the crowd. What was He talking about? He Himself the bread of life? He, the son of Joseph the carpenter, come down from heaven? Didn't everybody for miles around know His father and mother?

"Don't murmur among yourselves. Rather, believe my words," Christ pleaded. "The man who has faith in me shall receive eternal life. It is I who am the bread of life. Though your fathers ate manna, they nevertheless died. But," he went on, repeating Himself as though He were telling them the one thing above all others that He really wanted them to heed and remember, "whoever eats the true bread from heaven shall never die. If anybody eats this bread he will live forever."

He paused as though for dramatic effect, and then said slowly: *"This bread which I am going to give you is my flesh.''*

A gasp went up from the crowd. What a hard saying! It was repellent...disgusting. The Apostles who loved and trusted Him were visibly shaken. They looked at one another as though to ask if they had heard correctly.

But the crowd was in an uproar. The people were arguing noisily, returning time and again to the same refrain: "How can this man give us his flesh to eat?" But they took care lest Jesus should hear their doubts.

In the past He had often restated a point that had been misinterpreted. Now He remained silent. So were they to take Him literally? They could hardly think otherwise, for when He did speak again, it was only to insist solemnly on what He had said before, and indeed to say it more emphatically. "Believe me when I say that you cannot have life, you cannot be alive, unless you eat the flesh of the Son of Man and drink his blood. The person who eats my flesh and drinks my blood will have eternal life and I will raise him up on the last day. My flesh is real food and my blood is real drink. Whoever eats my flesh and drinks my blood lives always in and with me and I in and with him."

This was just too much! The people shook their heads, and then one by one, they turned away. Though a few hours earlier they had been willing to revolt against the established government for His sake, and as revolutionaries had been willing to risk the danger of Herod's armies — not to speak of the Roman legions — now they would not listen to Him another moment. Their great bravery in being willing to hail a king other than Caesar had come to naught. It had been demolished by the mouthings of a mad man.

The Apostles saw the people drift off. It was their

kingdom, too, which was disappearing before it was established — more their kingdom than it was this
crowd's. Again they could not help reminding themselves that they would have been its administrators under
Christ. The glorious prize had been within their grasp.
And now? With each departing figure their hopes sank
lower. Finally they were left alone with Him. Even one
of them should have left also, because he, like the crowd,
had repudiated the Master in his heart. St. John points
out (6:64): "Jesus knew from the first who those were
who did not believe and who it was that would betray
him."

This sensitive person, Jesus Christ, Who was later so
touched with compassion at the sorrow of Martha and
Mary that He wept with them, must have been touched
by the sadness and disappointment that He saw in the
faces of his disillusioned followers. He must have longed
at that moment to explain away this apparently canni-
balistic thing He had said.

But He did not explain it away; He didn't even explain
it. He simply said:

"The words I have just spoken here today are spirit
and life. Do they try your faith?"

Of course — they would try anybody's faith! But like
abashed school boys without the proper answer, the
Apostles stood there nervously shuffling their sandaled
feet on the ground, and not one of them spoke up. Christ
had to put them to the test with another question:

"Will you, too, go away?"

Still they hesitated to speak. But before the silence
lengthened too agonizingly, Peter stepped forward. He
had not understood any better than anybody else, but he
believed in the Master and that was enough. "To whom

could we go?'' he asked. Then, with a stronger voice to sweep away any lingering doubt, he added in a spontaneous burst: "You, Lord, have the words of eternal life. We believe, we know, that you are the Christ, Son of God.''

Whatever the awesome secret Christ implied in His daring statement, apparently no one was ready to grasp it. He let an earthly kingdom slip away rather than yet reveal it.

But the Israelites had many clues. Their Scriptures spoke of a Savior who would come, who would be linked with the mystery of the Passover, and who would reveal all.

Ruins of the Synagogue in Capharnaum where Christ stunned the crowd with His "incredible" statement.

CHAPTER FOUR

THE CURTAIN WOULD FALL

When Harris probed a grave in an empty field in Greece to verify that three hundred Thebans had died there, it was difficult to realize that two thousand years ago this was an important part of the world.

Today, man is spread around the globe. But, then, with the exception of scattered barbarian tribes and a pocket of culture in the Orient, those few countries around the Mediterranean Sea were the world.

And the heart of that world was not so much Rome and Athens, which were cities busy with politics and northern barbarism. Even more, it would now appear, the heart of the world was where civilization seems to have begun: about in the area where Christ made His incredible announcement.

Over three million persons lived around that small Sea of Galilee. It was a major center of population. Famous Greek cities known as the Decapolis extended the Greek civilization down from Asia Minor on one side, and on the other, the richest cultural and social heritage of ancient Egypt was found wedded in the enlightened Hebrews to whom Christ spoke.

What impelled them, even after an entire night during which to ponder the drastic consequences, to proclaim

Him their king? Was it only because He had fed them?

He had no army! Could He defend them in their opposition to the might of Rome? Were not His mere twelve men as poor and inconsequential as the twelve baskets of remains from the bread and fish? Yet they had made up their minds. They wanted Him to be their king.

We know there was an air of royalty about Him, and power. Later, a Roman governor was impulsively to ask, and without humor: "Are you a king?" And the soldiers were not joking later when they felt an impulse to mock him as a king, then blindfolded those eyes that flashed regality and power. He was a man who seemed to fit a description given by one of the most venerable of the Jewish prophets, Jeremiah: *a man of contradiction.*

That same prophet had foretold the captivity of the Jews, their deliverance, and finally the coming of a savior who would make their glorious delivery from Egypt a mere shadow of the deliverance and security he would bring (Jer. 33:7-16): "In those days Judah shall be safe and Jerusalem shall dwell secure." (v. 16).

That day by the Sea of Galilee, they suspected that He was the Savior of whom Jeremiah and their other prophets had spoken.

But would the Messiah, the Savior, speak of giving His *flesh* to eat and His *blood* to drink when they offered to recognize Him, when they offered to proclaim Him king?

And was He not a man, even though He did such wonders? Did not everyone know that His father was a carpenter in nearby Nazareth, that His mother was right here with Him, in the company of some other relatives from His mountain village?

Jeremiah spoke of a Savior. They were expecting a Savior, and one who would be linked somehow with the mystery of the Passover*...the mystery of their delivery from Egypt. That is why this miracle of the bread and fish was significant. The Passover had been marked by a miraculous feeding after the miracle of ten plagues and the parting of the sea.

They said to Him when He promised bread which would enable them to live forever: "We want this bread! We want this bread!"

Each year the Jews relived the Pasch, or Passover. Each year, following their ancient covenant* with God, they girded themselves as for a trip as had their forefathers on that fateful night in Egypt. They slaughtered a lamb, marked the doorposts with the blood, and ate it in a ritual of brotherhood and prayer reminiscent of that night when God showed a final sign to convince the Pharaoh of Egypt to set them free. On that night an angel of death struck down the firstborn in every house of Egypt, passing over those houses marked by the blood of the lamb.

Now this Christ, armed with the lightning of miracles and the gentleness of a lamb and the mystery of a prophet, speaks of giving His *own* blood.

How could this make Him their Savior? They wanted freedom from Rome, and can drinking a man's blood bring freedom? They wanted power, and can eating a man's flesh give power?

There is one disquieting thought:

When the Isrealites had been released from the clutches of Egypt, God had to constantly work miracles to preserve their freedom and their life. He had to destroy armies which the vacillating Pharaoh sent after them. He had to feed them in the desert — and for this it was necessary to *miraculously* let fall each day upon the sands a mysterious bread in sufficient quantity. And that bread was adequate food.

So when Christ said (instead of becoming their king) that He would give them bread to eat which would prevent them from dying, they were not completely incredulous. Their forefathers had eaten manna in the desert.

But was it really possible that this was how they were to be saved — by bread? If so, would He give another sign so they could truly believe something so unbelievable?

Too bad. They would have to wait *two years* to be told of something *far more astounding than mere bread falling on desert sand.* They would have to believe something *so incredible that it would become the world's greatest secret,* kept from all but the "initiated" for hundreds of years and still secret to millions *right into the twentieth century,* when men would still be gasping at the explaination of what He meant.

Understanding would begin only after all the prophecies concerning Christ had been fulfilled: the prophecies of Jeremiah, which described Him as a Man of Sorrows; of David, who said of Him that "They have pierced my hands and my feet, I can count all my bones"; of Isaiah; Ezeckiel; of Hosea, who cried, "Where now is your king?"(13:10); and of Malachi, who prophesied "...from the rising of the sun, even to its setting, my name is great among the nations; And everywhere they bring sacrifice to my name, and a pure offering ..." (1:11).

In the early centuries, Christians formulated this understanding in an act of faith known as the "Nicene Creed" which is still the profession of faith of most Christians in every part of the world today:

"For us men and for our salvation, He came down from heaven: by the power of the Holy Spirit he was born of the Virgin Mary, and became man."

The new Pasch, or Passover, was to provide *a new and saving sacrifice* to revolutionize the world. It would turn the year of His birth into the year 1. It was to distill the good out of all the civilization of the past into a single chalice of incredible love which eventually would transform warring communities into a world governed by fraternal law.

For two years Christ did not explain the "hard saying." He did not destroy His enemies by saying to the people: "Come back, I'll tell you what it means and you can proclaim me King." He gave even His own disciples nothing more than a clue: *The secret was "spirit and life."*

Then came that last night of the Passover. He was finally ready to admit that He was indeed a King. But His kingdom was "not of this world." For the first time He proclaimed clearly that He was the Savior: "For this was I born, for this did I come into the world" (Jn 18:37). Now He was about to explain the hard saying. Now He was about to explain what all the prophets had meant by the "salvation." And He began His whole extraordinary revelation with these words:

"I have greatly desired to eat this Passover with you before I suffer." (Lk. 22:15)

Never before had He "greatly desired" anything. He did not explain that within a few hours He would submit to imprisonment, mockery, scourging, and finally, death by crucifixion. Now, *this moment of passover* was the moment for which He had longed. Everything else, all the teaching of the past years and all of His suffering of tomorrow, was contingent on this moment and this act He was about to perform and for which He had so ardently longed.

Now the purpose of His coming and of His thirty-three years on this earth was to be made clear. Now was the hour when He would explain what He had meant when He said that *He would enable men to live forever by eating His flesh and blood.* Now He would fulfill the Old Law by giving a new covenant* between God and man, a covenant sealed in one final bloodletting that would so far outweigh in value all the bloody sacrifices of the past that the world would henceforth be able to offer "everywhere...a pure offering; For great is my name among the nations, says the Lord of hosts." (Mal. 1:11).

In a few moments, they would know that the relationship between God and man was no longer to be a secret of Israel, but was to be between God and *all* men. And this is how He began that eventful revelation in the year 33, the last night of His life:

Over their protests He washed their feet and said: *"I give you a new commandment: Love one another.* Such has been my love for you, so must your love be for each other. This is how all will know you for my disciples: your love for one another" (Jn. 13:34-35).

But where were they to find such love? He was not asking them merely to love each other person in the room, including the very one who in a few moments would betray them all. He was saying that *anyone* who was to be saved, anyone who wants to follow Him, would have to love all men as brothers the way *He* loved them, unto death.

Now He told them openly that He was *"one"* with God: "If you really knew me, you would know my Father also." He explained a great deal about the very nature of God*: Although of one nature, He was three persons. One Person (the Father) had sent Him; another Person (the Spirit) He would send so they would be able to understand all they had been taught; He Himself was the "Son."

Philip, showing how much the Paraclete was needed, even after three years of listening to Christ and even of seeing Him raise dead persons back to life, said:

"Lord, show us the Father and that will be enough for us."

Jesus replied, with perhaps an air of frustrated weariness: "Philip, after I have been with you all this time, you still do not know me? Whoever has seen me has seen the Father. How can you say, 'Show us the Father'? Do you not believe that I am in the Father and the Father is in me?"(Jn. 14: 8-10).

Thus minute by minute, phrase by phrase, He led them toward that dramatic, climactic moment of the second most historic Passover in history...the moment of the world's greatest secret.

Now He was to reveal the mystery of men eating His flesh and blood. Now He was to reveal how He was Himself to become the ultimate Lamb of Sacrifice, the salvation of the world. Now a new Passover was to begin, of which the old was merely symbolic. Now men were to pass from the slavery of materialism to the freedom of children of God. Now, with the intervention of God "fighting for them" (Ex. 14:14), men would have the daily aid of a miracle *greater* than the manna in the desert. It would be a bread which would enable them to live *forever*. Their passage would not be merely from physical bondage to another land, but from spiritual bondage to freedom of the spirit. They would become one with the Father by becoming one with Him, and thus all men might eventually be one: "as you, Father, are in me, and I in you" (Jn. 17:21). He prayed for them to the Father as He proceeded to the great moment for which He had so long desired.

Saint Matthew (26:26-28) describes what followed in these words: "During the meal Jesus took bread, blessed it, broke it, and gave it to his disciples. 'Take this and eat it,' he said, 'this is my body.' Then he took a cup, gave thanks, and gave it to them. 'All of you must drink from it,' he said, 'for this is my blood, the blood of the covenant, to be poured out in behalf of many for the forgiveness of sins.'"

Now they understood! "At last you are speaking plainly," the disciples exclaimed. Saint John describes the disciples saying, "We are convinced that you know everything.... We do indeed believe you came from God" (Jn. 16:30).

But did they know, really? Or did they recognize only that He was one with the Father, and they would become one with the Father by becoming one with Him — by perpetuating this miracle through which He had just transformed an ordinary Passover sacrifice into the world's first Eucharistic Liturgy?*

There was too much for them to understand without further supernatural aid. First He would have to go through the Passion to show the extent of the love of which He spoke. Next He would have to prove it all again by performing His greatest miracle, *His own resurrection*. Finally, He would instruct them further, then send the Paraclete who "will guide you to all truth" (Jn. 16:13).

Then would fall a great curtain of secrecy.

The Gospels themselves would be written in terms which would in general be understood only by the initiated, by those trusted, instructed, baptized and confirmed. The world at large would not know.

Years of persecution would deepen the secrecy. The ritual of that historic Passover would be called "The Secret" until the twentieth century and Vatican Council II, when excavations in Rome were confirming what some had never dared explain to an unprepared world.

CHAPTER FIVE

DISCOVERY

Guarded in the caves of Palestine and in the subterranean cemeteries of Rome, the sacred rite of the Blessed Sacrament (which made Christians literally blood Brothers) had been found hidden in symbols. Paul said it made them "Of one body, all partaking of one bread." But who, except the initiated, could know the meaning of these powerful words — let alone the symbols of them?

Thus, excavations unearthing Peter's tomb revealed rarities much more intriguing than the scribblings of some ancient pilgrims. Experts who had been studying such enigmas throughout the Mediterranean area from Athens to Rome, from Alexandria to Palestine, worked impatiently to decipher the symbols, *which were an effort at concealment.* But tradition (word-of-mouth knowledge, cherished and passed on intact for at least two generations) was eventually recorded by early Church writers. These documents provided the initial bit of knowledge that Peter was buried in the general area where they found his tomb.

However clear were some of the references to Peter in the Vatican catacombs (e.g., PE, PET, or simply **Petrus**), one particular symbol baffled them, although it had been showing up in excavation after excavation for a hundred and fifty years. It usually appeared on tombs, and usually, too, next to the symbol for Christ. Also, it later appeared in rings, domestic objects and it was often impressed on Roman documents of the fourth and fifth centuries. It too was at last proven to be a symbol for Peter: a P and an E combined in such a way as to form a key.

Dr. M. Guarducci writes: "With the discovery of the symbol's meaning, we now have an idea of the immense popularity enjoyed by Peter during the early centuries of Christianity...."[1]

Also, it would seem to indicate his importance in the minds of Christians as their spiritual leader, and as the first purely human head of the Church. It was so commonly used that it eventually became the symbol for Rome itself. It was found on an epigraph commemorating the restoration of the Colosseum and on coins throughout the Roman world after the first centuries.

Popular though this symbol was, it was less popular than some others, especially those in the other catacombs. Recurring over and over with more frequency than any others are the *symbols of Christ, Mary, and above all, the Eucharist.* *

One symbol for Christ was an X (first letter of "Christos" in Greek) or an X with a P superimposed on it (second letter of "Christos," which is equivalent in sound to the English R). Yet another was an X with a T

[1]M. Guarducci, *The Tomb of St. Peter*, (New York: Hawthorne Books), 1960, p. 109.

Some of the inscriptions spoke of Mary and Christ, together with Peter, but above all they bore witness to a great secrecy.

 Peter and Christ

 Christ and the Cross
(note "T")

 Christ and the Trinity
(note three "A's")

This second graffiti illustration contains symbols representing: Peter and Christ; Christ, the Alpha and the Omega (note that the "✗" surmounts an "O," and is also connected by a line to an "A"); victory (nica) in Christ; and, Christ and Mary.

Dotted line and emphasis provided by interpreter, M. Guarducci. See *The Tomb of St. Peter*, Hawthorn Books, pp. 116, 122.

through its center, representing Christ and the Cross. The symbol for Mary was sometimes just a simple M, sometimes an M on which an A was superimposed. Paradoxically, this second symbol for Mary was not only clearer to the initiated, but it was less clear to the outsider.

Symbols for the Eucharist were multiple: a fish; loaves surmounted by a fish; a bunch of grapes or a vine; a cup often resembling a large vase.

These symbols found around Peter's tomb make his burial place different from most found in the catacombs. The other tombs bear engravings or "graffiti" dealing with death and salvation. The graffiti on Peter's tomb, like those on the walls surrounding an altar table and on the walls of the underground passages and rooms, were hiding something as well as telling something, and here it was that the symbol of the Eucharist dominated. Obviously the Eucharist was the treasure prized and reverenced by Peter and his contemporaries, and it was the *sine qua non* of their religious rites.

Substantiating the cryptography and symbols are many pictures found in the catacombs. Cryptography is for experts. Pictures are for everybody, or at least for everybody who has ever been exposed to Christianity's secret. Naturally the ancient pagans would not have understood even the pictures. What pagan would suspect that a cup of wine and a loaf of bread, the most ordinary and basic of foodstuffs, signified a religious mystery* as deep as the one proclaimed by Christ on that hill by Capernaum? What pagan would ever suspect that a fish served with a few loaves of bread signified a great miracle*; or that a vine symbolized the heart of Christian ritual; or that a woman holding a child with the sun behind

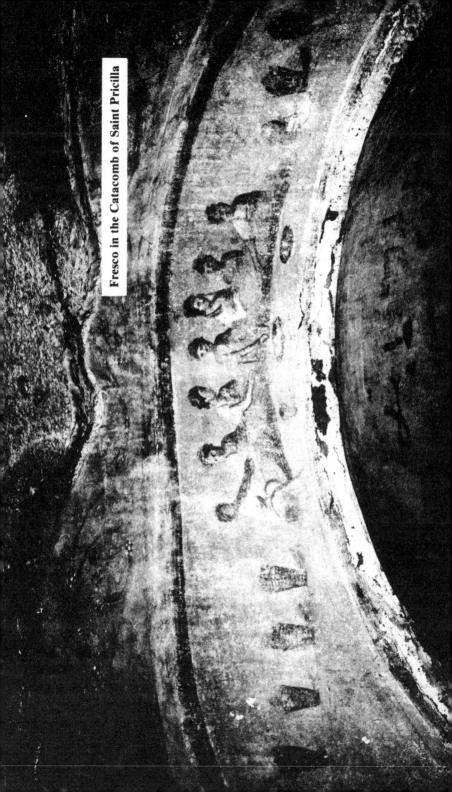

Fresco in the Catacomb of Saint Pricilla

her signified the coming of God to His earth as man?

These are the very pictures found not only near Peter's tomb but in the miles and miles of catacombs* being dug out in our own day under and around the walls of Rome.

One well-preserved fresco was painted within the lifetime of persons directly instructed by Peter and Paul. It was found in the catacombs of the famous Roman martyr Priscilla who is mentioned by Paul in his Second Epistle to Timothy.

Like most of the other pictures from apostolic times, it does not depict baptism or the resurrection, nor a message about faith and good works. It shows seven people reclining at table, eating bread and drinking wine (see p. 52).

The number seven, as we know, is a favorite one in the Bible and it stands for an uncertain quantity. The same number of people, seven, are found in other "Supper-of-the-Lord" scenes elsewhere in the catacombs.

In this particular picture in the catacomb of St. Priscilla, one of the seven persons is a woman. In the place of honor is the person who is breaking the bread. In front of him on a table is a single, two-handled cup.

A fresco painted about the year 190 was found in another catacomb, St. Calixtus'. Again there are seven banqueters breaking bread, but what would appear unusual in this picture, perhaps even to the pagan, are twelve immense baskets in the foreground, standing higher than the table and filled to overflowing with bread.

There is something very joyful about this scene. It is in a subterranean chapel where the pitiful remains of hundreds of martyred Christians have been gathered from the debris of the arena. Yet the aspect of the primitive figures in the fading fresco is of a group celebrating at a great banquet. Now the pagan might well ask, what kind of banquet is this where the guests seem to be eating only bread and have but one cup of wine for all?

Elsewhere in the catacombs the bread is shown with incisions in the form of a cross. One picture found in a catacomb near the Via Appia Antica shows a much more complete account of the Eucharist in a threefold image. In the center Christ is performing the miracle of the multiplication. Then He is shown in the right with His hand raised in a gesture of blessing or thanks or of speech-making, while in the folds of His cloak are five loaves marked with a cross. On the left section of the picture is shown the Samaritan woman drawing water from Jacob's well, the woman to whom Christ promised to give "living water."

Any Christian can understand the picture. The center panel, that of the prefiguring miracle, proved Christ's claim to be God, and so it also proved that He could do the humanly impossible: give Himself as food to His followers. The bread marked with a cross depicted the "holy bread" of His Eucharistic Body by which He did in fact give Himself to His followers; and the raised hand is a gesture of blessing as He speaks the words of transubstantiation. Finally, the Samaritan woman who was an adulterous sinner when she first met Christ could, because she repented, receive from Him the "living water" which is "for the remission of sins."

Few of the early Christian murals contain, as this one does, three sections. In fact, the most commonly seen picture is very simple: it is that of a fish. Sometimes the fish is surmounted by a basket of bread, and sometimes also a glass of red wine is depicted inside the basket and both bread and wine stand over a fish.

In the catacombs of Saint Priscilla (who was known by Saint Paul) archeologists found these sculpted loaves incised with a cross attached to a tomb. They recall the hope of Christians: "If anybody eats this bread he will live forever."

This fresco found in one of the catacombs (Sts. Peter and Marcellinus) shows Christ multiplying bread. It was made about the year 200. In all the catacombs there have been so many discoveries of such symbolic pictures that the photographs fill many albums in the Vatican Archives. The archivist at the Catacomb of Saint Priscilla notes that the frequency of subjects in these early Christian symbols and pictures is: first) multiplication of loaves and fishes; second) the "Breaking of Bread" or the Eucharistic Banquet; third) various other miracles of Jesus.

Most of the symbols found around the tomb of Peter are difficult to see in a photograph. Some are clearer but still require interpretation by experts. Notice "venerosavea" and surrounding graffiti which are illustrated on page 50.

The fish has a double significance. Obviously it represents the miracle of the multiplication as well as the "food from heaven" which Christ promised the next day, the food which was Himself, His body and blood. Also, the letters of the Greek word for fish, *icthys,* are the initial letters in that language for "Jesus Christ, Son of God, Savior" (*Jesous Christos Theou Uios Soter*).

This most famous acrostic* of the early Christian era interchangeably symbolized Christians, Christ Himself, and Christ in the Sacrament of the Eucharist through which Christians and Christ unite in a special way.

The epitaph of Bishop Abercius of Hieropolis in Phrygia can serve as a sort of synopsis of the Christian secret. He went to Rome about ninety years after Peter's death, at a time when the persecutions had already taken heavy toll although the worst was yet to come.

The authenticity of his ancient epitaph was confirmed by the findings of an English traveler named Ramsey, who found an inscribed slab in Phrygia dated A.D. 216, which verified the older text of the epitaph of Abercius. The significance of the words was recognized by scholars. Later research revealed continuing fragments of the same epitaph which had been built into the walls of the public baths in Phrygia. They filled out the complete message which Abercius, for the benefit of posterity, had ordered cut into the stone which was to go above his tomb.[2]

The message begins: *Let the brother who shall understand* pray for Abercius." Thus, announcing that he was

[2]*Dictionnaire d'archéologie chrétienne et de liturgie,* I, (Paris: F. Cabrol & H. Leclercq), 1903-1953, pp. 66-87.
*Christ was particularly identified by early Christians as the "Good Shepherd."

about to record Christian secrets in a manner only Christians could understand, he wrote:

"I am by name Abercius, disciple of the Holy Shepherd[3] Who feeds flocks of sheep on the mountains and plains, Who has great eyes[4] that see everywhere. This Shepherd taught me that the book of life is worthy of belief. And to Rome He sent me to contemplate Majesty and to see a Queen, golden-robed and golden-sandaled[5]; there also I saw people bearing a shining mark."[6] Later he continues:

"Faith everywhere led me forward and everywhere provided as my food a fish[7] of exceeding great size and perfection which a Holy Virgin drew with her hands from a fountain and ever gives this to its friends to eat, wine of great virtue, mingled with bread."

Scholars declare that a mystic or a theologian of today might have difficulty in expressing so much of the doctrine of the Eucharist in so few words, though it might be expressed in less veiled terms. Without secrecy the words could read: "Faith showed me that everywhere I went I received Jesus Christ, Son of God and Savior, to whom the holy virgin Mary had given flesh and blood, and now gives Him to me in the form of wine of great virtue served with bread."

"These writings," the epitaph concludes, "I, Abercius, having been a witness thereto, have told to be written here. Verily, I am passing through my seventy-second year."

---

[4]The all-seeing eye is both a symbol and a definition of God. Thus, here he asserts that Christ is God.
[5]The Church.
[6]Baptism which dogma says confers an "indellible mark."
[7]Symbol meaning *Jesus Christ, Son of God, Savior.*

Sometimes early Christians showed the fish surmounted by a basket of bread, as here in the crypt of Lucina, in the Catacombs of St. Callixtus. Note the glass of wine in the midst of the bread.

A fresco from about the year 190 in the Catacombs of St. Callixtus. There is something joyful about this scene although in a sad place: a subterranean chapel where hundreds of cruelly martyred Christians have been buried. Why a banquet with nothing but bread? And why twelve enormous baskets of bread for seven persons? The latter recall that: "They filled twelve baskets with the fragments. And the number of seven symbolized the Church.

If Abercius' epitaph seems a little abtrusive or even far-fetched to those of us who are neither scholars nor archeological experts, we can turn to other inscriptions. They are legion. In one of the catacombs is found an inscription written by Pope Damasus on the tomb of a young man who was killed while carrying Eucharistic bread. He refused to reveal to those who stopped him what it was he had on his person. His name was Tarcisius and his feast day is kept by the Church on August 15. The inscription on his tomb reads: "Carrying the Sacrament of Christ, he chose rather to suffer death than to betray the heavenly Body to the raging dogs."

Tradition tells us that he was only a boy and that a pagan mob, alerted to the fact that he was carrying the "secret" of the Christians to a co-religionist, tortured him to know what it was. Since they found only "bread" on his person, the boy preferred to die letting them think it was mere bread rather than risk desecration of the Eucharist as the real Body of Christ.

Ours is a blessed age in which these facts of early Christianity are finally brought to light. They reveal what was once considered the secret of secrets, the transcendent Eucharistic doctrine. Together with the infusion of the Holy Spirit, this was the life principle of the Christian Church, or the Mystical Body of Christ, by which Christians "may be made one" as the Savior said to His Father, "as You . . . are in Me, and I in You."

But even as the world in general was not prepared to grasp such a secret after the miracle of the loaves and fishes, would the world be ready to grasp it when the secret began to leak into general knowledge? To what extent would it remain secret even down to the twentieth century when finally Vatican Council II would remove the word "Secret"?

CHAPTER SIX

THE SECRET,
GOSPEL TRUTH

It is little wonder that the fish (meaning *Jesus Christ, Son of God, Savior*) was frescoed into the catacomb walls surmounted by loaves and wine.

When we turn from the discoveries and archeology to re-read the Gospels, we find something we may never really have seen before: *that it was the Eucharist which Christ Himself emphasized.* Not only did He make It the test of faith at Capernaum, but at the eleventh hour, *on the very eve of His death,* He held It up to His followers as His legacy and His pledge of His ever-abiding Presence. At this time, when He knew that these, His last acts and words, would be cherished and remembered more vividly than any which had gone before, what did He do and say?

Though He spoke of love, He did not try to summarize His sermons and His parables. He did not remind His apostles of past miracles or favors. He did not exhort His followers to live up to His precepts nor extract any promises of fidelity from them. Instead, He gave them the Eucharist.

What is more, even though He would die a terrible death in less than twenty-four hours, He identified the institution of the Eucharist with the Passover and with the purpose of His coming. And never before had He said that He ardently desired "this moment," the moment when the secret of the miracle of the loaves and fishes was finally revealed.

Immediately after Christ died, in the short interval before Peter went to Rome, in the interval during which he and all the Apostles remained in Jerusalem, we see that the Eucharist was already considered a sort of trademark for Christ and His followers. It appears in the twenty-fourth chapter of St. Luke's Gospel:

Two disciples of the Lord, Cleophas and his companion, were traveling about seven or eight miles from Jerusalem to Emmaus. Christ had been dead but a scant three days and as they walked along the dusty road, they could talk of nothing else. The terrible, crushing grief which filled their minds and hearts overflowed into words which eddied round and round in repetition as they asked one another time and again: "Were we fooled about this Jesus? Was he really the Christ? Or was the fellow no more than a rabble-rouser seeking to stir up a to-do for his own selfish ends? Or at best was he a good man who was deluded, and so deluded others?"[1]

They shook their heads wearily and the one named Cleophas remarked: "It's beyond all understanding. I know only that all the light has gone out of my life. I feel that a part of me has died with Him."

His companion, whom the Gospel does not name, sighed, "Yes, what have we to hope for now? I

---

[1]Most Scriptural quotations are from the modern translations according to the author's own choice, especially from the translations of Kiest-Lilly, Ronald Knox, Oxford Bible, Confraternity Version, New English Bible and New American Bible.

wish..." He broke off abruptly. "Here comes another traveler along the road."

The newcomer had scarcely greeted them when he noticed their downcast faces and their dejected air.

"What are you talking about? What makes you so sad?" he asked.

"Man, you ask that?" Cleophas exploded. "Are you a stranger in Jerusalem that you don't know what has happened there these past few days?"

"What has happened?" the newcomer asked.

With one voice the two travelers answered: "Jesus of Nazareth is dead...crucified as a common criminal."

But the unnamed one went on: "This Jesus of Nazareth was a prophet, mighty in work and word before God, and before all the people. Our high priests and the princes of the realm delivered him to be condemned to death, and they nailed him to the tree."

"But we hoped that it would be he who would redeem Israel. We hoped that he was the Christ, the Messiah," Cleophas explained.

"And besides all this," Cleophas' companion took up, "this is the third day since his death, and certain women of our company have been saying many strange things. Before the light came out of the east, early in the morning, they went to his tomb and they did not find his body. They said that they saw an angel who told them that he is alive. What are we to think?"

"And others besides the women went to the sepulchre and found it just as the women said. His body *was* gone," Cleophas added quickly.

As their words tumbled out, the newcomer-traveler listened intently. It was only when they came to pause at last that He answered them: "You are really slow to see

CHAPTER SIX

and to believe what the prophets have written. Shouldn't Christ have suffered these things and entered into his glory?''

With that as a prelude, the "stranger" began to talk of the prophecies in the Scriptures. Tracing them all the way back to Moses, He showed how the texts foretold for the Savior of the world just such a rejection by His people and death at their hands.

Cleophas and his companion were silent. Their dark eyes were riveted on the speaker as they drank in His every word. It was all so logical and so convincing, and the stranger was so eloquent and so compelling. They paid no attention to the passing of time as He talked until they suddenly spied from the crest of the hill the squat building of the inn lying in the valley below. It was there that they had planned to stop for the last meal of the day and to rest.

When they mentioned this to the stranger, He murmured something about going on farther Himself.

"Oh, no!" the other two protested. "It is late now. Stop with us."

Obviously they were extremely reluctant to part company and their persuasion soon won over their chance fellow-traveler. He entered the inn with them.

A little later the three men sat at a table and the stranger picked up the bread set before them, held it for a moment in His strong, sun-tanned hands, blessed it, broke it, and gave it to them.

Scarcely had the two disciples of Christ swallowed the morsel when they both sprang to their feet as though propelled by some outside force. This man was no longer a stranger! He was... "Oh, Lord," they cried, and thrust out their arms as though to clutch Him, but

He vanished from their sight.

"Ah, it was He!" breathed Cleophas. "Wasn't your heart burning within you when He spoke...when He explained the Scriptures?"

"Yes, it was He!"

"But we can't sit here," Cleophas said, wrapping his cloak about him and turning toward the door. "We must go back to Jerusalem. We must tell Peter and the others."

Forthwith, leaving their frugal meal upon the table, they rushed out into the gathering dusk and retraced their steps to Jerusalem, back to the place where the eleven Apostles were hiding. Bursting in upon the little gathering, they all but shouted: "We have seen the Lord! It was He and no mistake about it. *We knew Him in the breaking of the bread.*"

After the story of the travelers on their way to Emmaus, other references to the Eucharist appear in the Bible although almost with an air of secrecy.

Saint Paul, in chapter eleven of his First Epistle to the Corinthians, writes of the Last Supper saying: "...on the night in which he was betrayed took bread, and after he had given thanks, broke it and said, 'This is my body, which is for you. Do this in remembrance of me.' In the same way, after the supper, he took the cup, saying, 'This cup is the new covenant in my blood. Do this, whenever you drink it, in remembrance of me.' Every time, then, you eat this bread and drink this cup, you proclaim the death of the Lord until he comes! This means that whoever eats the bread or drinks the cup of the Lord unworthily sins against the body and blood of the Lord. A man should examine himself first; only then should he eat of the bread and drink of the cup. He who eats and drinks without recognizing the body eats and drinks a judgment on himself.''(11:23-29)

Saint Luke writes in the second chapter of the Acts of the Apostles: "And they devoted themselves to the apostles' teaching and fellowship, to the breaking of bread and the prayers" (v. 42). Then in the same chapter, Luke speaks of the Christians "...breaking bread in their homes" (v. 46), indicating that this was the usual procedure when they gathered together. Also in the Acts of the Apostles, we read: "On the first day of the week when we gathered for the breaking of bread..." (20:7).

For years after early apostolic days, fear tied the hands of the Christian scribes and scholars, so that little was written about the Eucharist, or for that matter about any aspect of the Faith. However, knowledge of Eucharistic doctrine and practice of the Eucharistic Liturgy were passed along from generation to generation by what we call "tradition." Happily, tradition is reliable. It is akin to Gospel truth.

It would have to be. No ordinary mortal would come equipped with the inventiveness necessary to make up a story like the Eucharistic one. Or, if some strange being did invent it, no ordinary meal would perpetuate it. For such an idea to have originated and to have endured, it would have to be more certain than surmise in the minds of Christians. They were willing to *die* for it. Moreover, it was not a tenet calculated to recruit new members to the struggling, infant Church. On the contrary! It was a tenet which would repel most people; they would consider it too fantastic for belief and an insult to their common sense. Nevertheless the little band of Christians stuck to it and passed it on to their children, and their children to their children, through the years. And they *did* die for it.

It was tradition* alone which held together the chain of teaching in unbroken sequence through the years of persecution and secrecy. As a matter of fact comparatively few people in pagan Rome could read. The Gospels and the whole collection of sacred writings that we now call the Bible were not assembled and compiled into one book until after the periods of the persecution. The deposit of Faith then was handed down orally from one Christian to another for almost four centuries until the Bible was compiled and until other manuscripts and books of all sorts could publicly record it.

Today, thanks to the ever-advancing science of archeology, we are beginning to find evidence which corroborates the writings as well as the tradition. But we may never find corroboration of all details. Nor have the writings themselves recorded every detail. We still must look to tradition to flesh out the skeleton of the written word which wasn't filled out until after the time of secrecy.

At a luncheon meeting of some prominent men, somebody asked: "How did Lincoln pronounce those words of his address '... of the people, by the people, for the people'?"

All answered: "... *of* the people, *by* the people, *for* the people."

But one person added: "Actually I suppose we can never know for sure. *It has never been recorded.*"

"Anything about the address is important," remarked another man who happened to be Naval Attache to the United States Embassy in Rome, "for it is the epitome of the American doctrine, and certainly one of the most significant documents of all time."

Then the writer of this book, who had first broached

the subject, said: "Lincoln stressed '... a government of the *people,* by the *people,* and for the *people.*' My English teacher was corrected on this point by his teacher *who heard Lincoln say it.*"

Perhaps no one ever thought to record Lincoln's inflection in these past one hundred years. Our grandparents or great-grandparents knew many, many persons who were contemporaries of Lincoln. They had not appreciated the importance of the address at Gettysburg when it was delivered. It was but a small fragment from a war which marked a black and baneful passage in their lives.

Yet any one of hundreds could have written a note to correct the countless school children who emphasized the wrong words. Apparently nobody ever bothered to write it ... *until now, a hundred years later, in this book.*

So it must have been with early Christianity. Only tradition saves some small facts. Because of secrecy caused by persecution, only tradition saved even important facts until the day when, comparatively free of persecution, the so-called "Fathers and Doctors of the Church"* could record them in writing. In the fourth century these hardy souls began to defend Christ's teaching against the objections of the non-Christian world and to put Christian teaching down in legible black and white.

Though one "Father" wrote in Africa, another in Athens, another in what is now Istanbul, another in Rome, *they were all found to agree in their teachings and writings.* This is another proof (if we need it) for the validity of the tradition they recorded.

What these first writers (now called Fathers of the Church)* taught about the Eucharist is just as amazing and just as "unbelievable" as what Christ Himself (according to the Gospel account) told the crowd which turned away from Him in Capernaum. It was an explanation after three hundred years of experience.

CHAPTER SEVEN

SCIENCE AND THE SECRET

In the *Introduction* of this book we mentioned that a preliminary edition was used for a survey to test whether or not the book held interest throughout and, if not, where interest lagged. Many said they found this one chapter "difficult."

By contrast, a Teilhard de Chardin enthusiast answered that this chapter was "the high point of the book."

So we did two things: 1) We tried to make it easier to read; 2) We asked one of the nation's top experts on the atom, Dr. Francis J. Heyden,* to give his advice.

The world's greatest secret would be better left secret if it were to appear as ridiculous to many in the modern world as it appeared when Christ first announced it in Capernaum, causing thousands who had previously hung on His every word to be repulsed and to turn away. How, for example, will those millions behind the Iron Curtain who know a great deal of science and little about Christ, react to this central secret of Christianity?

To the believer, no explanation is necessary. To the non-believer, a great deal of explanation is now possible.

First, let us remember that even after fifteen hundred years the impact of Christ's miracles was so great that *all* Christians believed in the Eucharist. Even Martin Luther,* who set in motion the world's first wave of disbelief, himself believed. In *Wider Etliche Tollen*

Geister (1532), he testified that "the whole of Christendom accepts the doctrine of the Real Presence."* In *This is My Body,* published in 1527, he wrote: "These words of Christ, still stand firm against the fanatics" (See *Luther,* p. 286).

So it must be evident to any intelligent person that apparently the Eucharist is really credible because millions upon millions of persons — indeed those who have given us most of our present culture — almost *unanimously* believed it. And there were even geniuses among them.

It is evident that they believed primarily because, as one of the greatest intellects of the Middle Ages concluded: "Christ told us so."

After the Fathers of the Church had explained it, one man named Paschasius Radbertus questioned it in the ninth century but never got a following. Then a man named Berengarius, of Tours, raised a question which gave the Church its first occasion to defend the belief in a dramatic, official manner. Berengarius made a sincere retraction at a Synod held in Rome in 1079, and so it was not until the time of Martin Luther, that is, until almost our own day, that this early secret of Christians became a basis of division.

Now, for the first time, the Church found it necessary to *define* the belief.

So the bishops of the world were convened in Trent,* less than twenty-five years after Luther nailed his theses on the door of a church in Wittemberg. What they proclaimed was taken almost verbatim from the Fathers of the Church:

"Jesus Christ, our God and Savior, although He offered Himself once and for all to God the Father on the

altar of the cross by His death, there to work out our
eternal redemption, yet (since His priesthood was not to
end with His death) He left to His Church at the Last
Supper a visible sacrifice. This sacrifice, the Eucharist,
was what our nature required. The Eucharist presents
the Sacrifice of Christ to the Father, once and for all
wrought upon the cross. Through the Eucharist, the
memory of the cross will abide to the end of the world.
Moreover, its saving power of grace will be applied for
the remission of those sins that we all fall into day by
day. Declaring Himself to be a priest forever 'according
to the order of Melchisedech' Christ offered His body
and blood to God the Father under the appearance of
bread and wine, and gave them under the same appearance to His apostles. He then made these men and their
successors priests of the New Testament by the words,
'Do this in commemoration of me.' So Christ gave the
command to offer the Eucharist as the Church has
always understood and taught."

The Council of Trent document, written in 1545, then
went on to say that even as the Christian community
consists of many Church members, "of this union nothing is more strikingly illustrative than the elements of
bread and wine, for bread is made from grains of wheat
and wine is pressed from many clusters of grapes. Thus
they signify that we, though many, are closely bound
together by a bond of this divine mystery and made, as it
were, one body."

Unbelievable! Thus do many Christians exclaim after
reading this definition of the Eucharist formulated at
Trent. It is not borne out by our senses. We moderns
who fancy ourselves scientific shy away from anything
which cannot be put into a test tube and proved by

laboratory experiment.

We look at what we call the Host. It seems to be bread of cracker-like consistency. Is that Christ?

Isn't the whole idea incredible, not to say absurd?

This is where modern science comes to our aid. Now, with some understanding of the *nature of matter,* the miracle of the Eucharist (aside from the greater mystery of the Incarnation and considering only the fact of transubstantiation)* appears plausible. This does not mean that reason alone, aided by science, can *explain* it. But it means that much of the mystery as to *how* transubstantiation takes place is stripped away.

Especially for those who may find the following explanation a little difficult, we cannot overstress the fact that ultimately one pierces through the mystery of the Eucharist only with the force of faith.

It we could understand the mysteries of God, we would be no longer merely human; we would be what our first parents wished to be: as gods.

One is reminded of the tale told of the great "Doctor" Augustine who wanted to write about the Trinity* and of course met great difficulty in finding words for such ineffable truth. The more he thought the more baffled he became.

One day as he was walking along the seashore pondering his problem he saw a little boy playing in the sand. The child was digging a hole and pouring water into it from a tin pail. To give himself a brief respite from his vexing thoughts, the theologian stopped to speak to the child. He asked, "What are you doing, lad?"

The boy answered, "I'm going to empty the whole ocean into this hole."

Augustine suddenly realized that it was no more ridic-

ulous for the child to be trying to pour the ocean into a
hole than it was for him to be trying to pour understanding of the Infinite into his human brain.

While acknowledging our inability to explain the inexplicable, we can consider some of the findings of modern
science which may have a tangential relationship to the
Eucharist. If we can understand matter itself we can perhaps understand how the Eucharistic miracle happens.

To the modern scientist, matter is nothing more than
plain energy. It is as though positive electricity and
negative electricity were counterbalanced to give quantity to substance.*

This is not difficult to understand. Atomic energy has
been harnessed as the direct result of this hypothesis
which is now taught as a matter of course to most school
children.

Even before the atom bomb this hypothesis was held
by many scientists. Twenty-five years before writing this
book (that is, a few years before the atom bomb), the
author presumed to write in another book[1]: What makes
a table or a wall or a stone *resist* pressure? We believe it to be nothing more than positive points of *force,*
held in place by correlative negative points of force.
Electricity has not quantity because it is merely points of
force in the pure positive or negative state. And the
proof that something *without* quantity could *constitute*
quantity is found in the fact that a bolt of lightning can
split a giant tree as though it were a mighty steel axe.

Naturally, between a positive point of force and a
negative point of force there is an electrical *field.* Since
all the world is fundamentally constituted of these pos-

[1]John M. Haffert, *The Brother and I,*(Washington, NJ: AMI Press),
1960. First published in 1942 as *From a Morning Prayer.*

itive and negative points of force, this field is universal. The undulations of this field constitute light and sound. Some undulations pass through most densities of the universal field, but there are certain densities through which they cannot pass. For example, light passes through the field that exists between the planets, but it is 'undone,' as it were, by the field in a piece of wood. Radio can transmit sound and television light and sound by reducing them to a strange undulation that is not undone by most fields, and then reproducing and undoing the original undulations in a receiving set.

"We would imagine that the five senses work similarly. It is not an electrical impulse that rushes to the brain when a man sees something. The optic nerve is merely a receiving set, undoing the undulation of light to which it is sensitive and reducing it to a new undulation: the type of undulation to which the sense of touch reduces tactile sensation...the same undulation to which the ear reduces sound...the same undulation that causes all things sensed by man to seem *one* sensation and to be thus the tool of his active intelligence."

So it would appear, from the apparent confirmation of this theory by radio, television, X-ray, and finally atomic power, that matter is indeed merely *forces* in juxtaposition.

This suddenly opens a possibility of understanding the mode of the Eucharist. Before this men had to accept only on blind faith that the Body of Christ — without changing, and remaining entire — became contained in a tiny space and under new appearance. They had to believe only because Christ told them so (confirmed by miracles). Now we can accept the possibility that the *effect* of the forces of Christ's body merely become *sus-*

pended with relation to the forces of a piece of bread.

Essentially this is not much different than the miracle witnessed by hundreds of reliable persons during one of the apparitions of the Virgin Mary to Saint Bernadette: the saint's hand strayed into the flame of a lighted candle during her ecstasy, but did not burn. After the ecstasy a doctor reached the flame again to her hand. She cried out.

It is logical to conclude that her hand did not cease to be a hand, and the fire did not cease to be fire. But the *effect* of the fire was *suspended* with relation to Bernadette's hand during the ecstasy.

Similarly we may presume that the effect of the "matter" or body of Christ ... which scientific experience tells us may be pure force ... is suspended with relation to the absolute accidents* of bread and wine.

Can we state positively that Christ's physical presence under the appearance of bread and wine would mean that *the points of force in His physical quantity* were present *but their effect was withheld by divine power?*

We can say this much: The energy concept of matter is accepted today as a working fact, and that seems to make the mystery of the Eucharist, though still supernatural and miraculous, not quite so covered with misty clouds.

Indeed, in the pre-Einstein era, when the energy concept of matter ($E = mc^2$) was still no more than an exciting but much shakier hypothesis, Dr. J. Pohle, the celebrated Professor of the University of Breslau, Germany, wrote in his book *Lehrbuch der Dogmatik*: "Assuming a real distinction between force and its manifestations, between energy and its effects, it may be seen that under the influence of the First Cause, **the energy**

(substance) necessary for the essence of bread is withdrawn by the virtue of conversion, while the effects of the energy (accidents) in a miraculous manner continue."[2] (Emphasis ours.)

Conversely, according to Pohle, when Christ becomes present in the Eucharist it is merely the *effects* of His physical energy (impenetrability, visibility) which are suspended. This explanation, at least in the opinion of some, adequately explains away the most apparent contradiction of the whole Christ — in the fullness of His manhood and of all His human and divine faculties — contained in such small space. If the *effect* of "points of force" of any body could be suspended, *the body could be contained in almost inconceivably small space.*

This is what our new discoveries about matter must lead us to believe.

Even long before help from modern science, geniuses of the Middle Ages began to shed great light upon the Christian "Secret" through the development of rational philosophy. Even some early Greek philosophers (as though anticipating the discovery that matter might be energy) drew a fine distinction between "modal" and "absolute" accidents. Modal accidents were those which could not be separated from their substance without involving a metaphysical contradiction, like the form and motion of a body. On the other hand, absolute accidents were those accidents which could be separated from substance without involving metaphysical contradiction. Size (quantity of a body) they considered an absolute accident.

Aristotle, one of the greatest pre-Christian philosophers,

---

[2]"Eucharist," *Catholic Encyclopedia,* (New York: Robert Appleton Co.), V, 1909, p. 582.

taught essentially this. He defined substance as the *heart* of matter; accidents as the *modifications* of matter.

The accidents of the Eucharist are bread whiteness, bread taste and bread size; the substance is Christ. The physical reality of the whiteness, of the taste and of the size of the Eucharist cannot be questioned. In other words, philosophers could reason that Christ does not destroy the accidents of the bread and replace it with a mirage suddenly created at the moment of transubstantiation.

Aristotle also taught that quantity is not a corporal substance, but only a phenomenon of substance.[3]

This is precisely what the scientists are trying to prove today in using the working hypothesis that matter is merely contained energy.

However, despite new evidence from centuries of thought and discovery, matter (or substance) is especially difficult to understand when it becomes *alive,* and for many is understandable only on the basis of authority and supernatural providence.

What, for example, causes a tiny speck in a woman's womb to grow into a being so complex that we produce more scientific books on this one subject than on any other, and still have not scratched the surface of understanding? What is that "something" contained in a uterine speck so small that it is invisible to the naked eye, yet it multiplies millions of times to the complexity of man?

We give it a name. We often call it *entelechy.* * Yet giving it a name does not help us to understand all that follows the moment of conception: an intricate unfolding of modifications of energy to fill out the "sub-

---

[3]Aristotle, *Metaphysics,* ed. Immanuel Bekker, 3rd ed, vol. VI, p. 1029, a. 13.

stance" of man.

In any event, when we realize that a man is potentially contained in a tiny cell, it no longer seems quite so difficult to believe that Christ could be wholly, substantially present in a wafer consecrated for us to consume.

Yet if He had not told them so, if they had not heard it from His lips or read His own words in the Bible, and if the testimony of two thousand years of Christian experience did not confirm it, how could Christians ever believe it?

Faith alone conquers all objections like that of the little girl in the story. Her father gave her a crucifix and asked: "What's the difference between the figure on the cross and the Host held up at the Consecration of the Mass?"

The child did not hesitate. She answered: "I look at the figure on the cross and I see Jesus, but He's not there. When I look at the Host, I don't see Jesus, but He *is* there."

We who lack the simple faith of children feel the need to know all we can because this secret of primitive Christianity is also a secret of life. So far its ultimate discovery by all Christians in the modern sweep of ecumenism must take us back to the words written by Christ's own disciples: Matthew, Mark, Luke and John.

Einstein, whose theories contributed greatly to the discovery of atomic power, was afraid the explosion of even one bomb would set off a chain reaction which would cause all the earth's quantity to disintegrate, since matter is now believed to be nothing but energy. This very understanding of matter perhaps sheds light on Christianity's greatest secret . . . and deepest mystery.

CHAPTER EIGHT

BOOK OF THE SECRET

We often see just a loaf of bread marked with a cross in the Mediterranean excavations.

Generation after generation of the ancient Jews told their children that the great one, the Messiah,* would be born in "the house of bread," or as the name is in Hebrew, Bethlehem.

"Where is he who is born King of the Jews?" was the question that was asked by certain foreigners newly arrived from the distant East. Following a strange star in the heavens, they had traveled over misty mountains, through arid deserts, across broad valleys, until they came at last to Israel and to its capital city, Jerusalem.

The chief priests and the scribes there had an answer for the Easterners. The Holy Scriptures foretold that the expected of nations was to be born in the town known as "the house of bread."

From the moment that Christ lay like a kernel of wheat restored to the straw of the manger, one scene and one circumstance after another seems to tie in by symbolism and analogy with His future Eucharistic life. It was as though all His coming and all His days were

80

directed, like the entelechy of living cells, toward the Eucharist.

Indeed, we can go back before His birth. At the moment of the Incarnation nine months before His birth we see a correlation between God-man in embryo* and God-man in bread. Surely His hiddenness in those nine months and His sanctification of John the Baptizer suggest his hiddenness in the Eucharistic bread and his sanctification of all who approach him there.[1] He might have been expected to materialize in some dazzling, glorious manner. But He chose to come as a speck of matter in a human tabernacle.

One could review His whole life as recorded in the Gospels and continue finding these connections and looking for this symbolism with marked success. His very first miracle, the one which inaugurated His public life, was the changing of the water into wine at the marriage feast of Cana. In the Eucharist He changes wine into His blood.

Let us try an experiment. Let us open the New Testament at random and by the spot-check method see how closely Christ's Palestinian life relates to His Eucharistic life.[2]

The first opening falls upon the tenth chapter of the Gospel of John. The first verse to meet our eyes reads:

"And they once again took up stones to stone him. Jesus answered them: *'I have showed you many good works from the Father; for which of these do you stone me?'*

"The Jews answered him, *'It is not for a good work*

---

[1]See *Presanctification*, p. 302.
[2]This is an honest experiment. We will put on these pages whatever passages we find as we open the Bible.

The star above marks the place where Jesus was born in the cave of Bethlehem.

Think of it!

"Bethlehem" means "House of Bread," and hundreds of years in advance the prophet foretold that the Savior was to be born in the House of Bread although it would still be hundreds of years later before we would begin to understand why.

And He was placed in a *manger* ... a *vessel for eating.*

And, at the moment of coming into our world as our Savior and our Eucharist, He was not to be placed in the cradle made by the skilled hands of His carpenter father and on the soft mattress prepared by His loving Mother, but in a manger on *straw* ... stems from which wheat had been threshed for bread.

From the tabernacle of the Immaculate He was placed there apparently *helpless* and *speechless* although the angels sang of His glory and a star led Kings to adore Him.

O Mystery of the Eucharist! Emmanuel! Jesus in the Blessed Sacrament with us ... proclaimed *in almost every word* and symbol of Scripture.

that we stone you but for blasphemy, because you, being a man, make yourself God.'"

A few verses later, we read: *"Again they tried to arrest him, but he escaped from their hands."*

Two facts strike us here: Christ claimed to be God, and at the moment of His choice He became invisible.

In this day of militant atheism stones still threaten Him in churches and in tabernacles where we assert His Divinity. But He constantly escapes and constantly renews His Presence. Just as He became invisible on the occasion of the Gospel story, so He becomes invisible now, hidden under the appearances of very ordinary looking bread. Heroic missionaries who consecrate the bread sometimes slip behind the Iron or Bamboo Curtains *and no enemy detects the Lord Whom they bring with them.* He is both human and divine, yet He becomes invisible.

If you have a Bible handy, you might like to follow the experiment. This time the sacred book opens on Mark's tenth chapter. James and John have just asked Christ for a place on His right and left sides when He is glorified. He replies that they do not know what they are asking and He challenges: "Can you drink the cup I shall drink...?"

Eagerly they say that they can. But He goes on to tell them that their request is not His to grant them, and He admonishes them for seeking so high a position. He says: *"...whoever would be great among you must be your servant, and whoever would be first among you must be slave of all. For the Son of man also came not to be served but to serve...."*

How completely these words find fulfillment in the Eucharistic state of subjection. *He makes Himself dependent on men.*

Next our Bible falls open on the tenth chapter of St. Luke.

Here we find Christ in Bethany visiting the home of the sisters Martha and Mary. At the moment their brother Lazarus is out. Mary sits as the Master's feet listening to His words. Martha asks Christ to speak to Mary and bid her to help with the cooking. Christ answers: *"Martha, Martha, you are anxious and troubled about many things; only one thing is required. Mary has chosen the better part and she shall not be deprived of it."*

In this passage, again the dual nature of Christ is asserted, with emphasis on personal conversation with Him.

Where can we meet Christ in person? Of course we can find God anywhere, wherever we happen to be at the moment, whether in a crowded subway, on a lonely mountain pass, in a bustling newspaper office, in a hospital bed. God is everywhere and we can always seek His Presence in prayer, in love and in the turning of our mind and heart to Him. He is at hand. Martha must have known and lived this truth and it is emphasized by many today who do not believe in the Eucharist.

But we can, according to the doctrine of the Eucharist, actually sit at His feet as Mary did in Bethany by walking to the nearest tabernacle.* The truth that He is everywhere is not always enough to evoke prayer. Even the truth that He dwells within our very souls is not always enough. It is sometimes too nebulous an idea for us to grasp solidly.

The secret of Christianity reveals that God had pity on us. He comes to our human weakness in human form as well as with His divinity. He comes in His own flesh and blood in the Eucharist. He is there in a set place, at a set time, *under the appearance of a visible and tangible thing* that we can see, and feel, and taste.

Patiently today He waits in the tabernacles throughout the world, hoping that a few Marys will stop to sit at His feet. Sadly today He addresses the millions upon millions of Marthas who, though they are good and just people, are so caught up in a whirlwind of activities and business that they rarely, if ever, find time for prayer in His Eucharistic Presence.

And He is so available! Could He have made Himself anymore so than by entering thousands upon thousands of tabernacles in every city and hamlet in the world?

If it might appear that some of our interpretations of the Bible passages we chose at random were contrived, let it be quickly admitted that many lessons can be drawn from the life of Christ. During the survey made before publication of this book, many tried the same experiment with varying success. Some came upon passages more apt than the three we quoted. But those passages in particular which assert His divinity, His power of working miracles, and His desire for physical intimacy with us are obvious confirmations of the climactic events of the Last Supper. And what if we deliberately chose the passages from the Evangelists which we considered *appropriate* instead of opening the Bible *at random?*

Once we know the secret of Christianity, all that Christ did and said has new meaning. But even more, our present relationship with Him leaps to new life, wherever we may be, in any corner of the world. That house in Bethany is no more honored than a place He has chosen in my own town. He wept outside that house in sympathy for the grief of two sisters; and a few moments later He called their brother back from the tomb. He demonstrated in those few minutes how completely He was both human and divine. He showed His delight to be with the children of men, to share in their sorrows and to be their joy.

So we find in almost every gospel passage that the same Christ who walked, talked, prayed, forgave and wrought cures in Palestine is just as meaningful in the Eucharist. Indeed, the Eucharistic life of Christ is at once the fulfillment and the extension of His life in Palestine. He is as close as the nearest tabernacle.

In a sense the world's first stone tabernacle is in Jerusalem on Mount Zion,* in the ruins of the house of Caiaphas, the high priest in the year 33 A.D. It is the recently discovered security prison where Christ spent the last hours of the night on which He instituted the Eucharist.

These tombs in the valley of Chedron saw Christ pass by that night...and they witnessed Him dragged back up Mount Zion by armed men to the prison hole which became the world's first tabernacle, a stone's throw from where He had just fed His disciples with bread turned into Himself.

Prison of Christ

This prison is a box-like structure about twelve feet in diameter and about twelve feet deep. Access was through a hole in the ceiling. The prisoner was lowered into this stone box and the only way to get Him out was with a rope. While the fact of the prison's existence was long known, the actual prison itself was not discovered until the twentieth century, together with the scales to weigh the "sin offerings" and other items which identified the prison area as belonging to the high priest. A staircase has now been cut into the prison so that the Eucharistic Liturgy can be celebrated in this subterranean hold where on the very night after the institution of the Blessed Sacrament He, by His Presence, made the place a tabernacle. Hidden here, between the hours of the first Mass and its culmination on Calvary, He prayed for us.

To receive the Eucharist in such a holy place could be a special experience. Nonetheless there is hardly a Christian who would not agree with the pilgrim who said: "I spent so much to come to the Holy Land, which seems scarcely to have changed since Christ's day, and it was here I learned what I should have known before I started. He left here places and memories. Himself He left in the Eucharist."

And what about His miracles? Does He still perform them in London and New York, in Berlin and Des Moines, in Bangkok and Athens, as He did in Bethany?

CHAPTER NINE

"PROOFS"

Of the thousands of frescoes, drawings, and inscriptions found in the catacombs from the first centuries of Christianity, *most* refer to miracles* related to the Eucharist. The miracle most frequently depicted is that of the Multiplication of the Loaves and Fishes. Pictures of this miracle are even more frequent than the "Breaking of the Bread" (see pp. 53, 55), which is the second most recurring image. Next the catacombs reveal other miracles of Jesus in the following order of frequency: the cure of the Paralytic who was let down through the roof of a house; the resurrection of Lazarus; the cure of a woman with an issue of blood; the cure of a blind man. The fourth most frequently found subject is the adoration of the Magi at Christ's birth, again a miraculous occurrence.

As we mentioned before, miracles were a basis for Christian faith in the "incredible secret." Our Lord Himself had often told them: if they could not believe, they had only to remember the miracles He performed. Hence we can particularly understand the frequency of the pictures of the resurrection of Lazarus because, just before summoning the four-day corpse to life, Christ cried out before the tomb: "...but I have said this for the sake of the crowd, *that they may believe*..." (Jn. 11:43).

And there is the touching incident, also related by Saint John, of the man born blind. When the Pharisees angrily questioned the parents, the latter were afraid to explain what happened but affirmed that the man had been born blind and that now he saw. When the Pharisees questioned the man, saying Christ was a sinner and "...we have no idea where this man comes from," the man answered, "Well, this is news! You do not know where he comes from, yet he opened my eyes.... It is unheard of that anyone ever gave sight to a person blind from birth. If this man were not from God, he could never have done such a thing" (Jn. 9:29-30, 32-33).

But who of us is not made a little edgy and uncomfortable by the word "miracle"? We usually prefer to satisfy ourselves with descriptions and analogies.

When it comes to saying flatly *"I believe in this miracle"* (beyond human comprehension and possible only to God), we are left with only the supernatural. We may feel like a child walking into the sea and suddenly finding only water beneath his feet.

Sometimes we argue: If He were really there in that bit of bread stuff which people receive, He could and would give sight to the blind, hearing to the deaf and perform other miracles just as He did in Palestine. Why the one big miracle of His Presence without the others?

To ask that question is not at all preposterous. Moreover the answer is that He *does* perform miracles through the Eucharist. Indeed in the light of modern facilities of communication and objective medical tests, it seems that Christ performs *more miracles today in His Eucharistic life than He did in Palestine.* But the Space Age is conditioned to publicize only miracles of science. Real miracles rarely make headlines.

Even those of us who do not deny the *possibility* of miracles may hesitate to recognize that miracles *are* an integral part of the Gospel fabric. Though we see that we cannot reject miracles unless we also reject Him and the veracity of the Scriptures, we may murmur the trite phrase: "But the age of miracles is past."

Back in the fifth century, Saint Augustine wrote: "Miracles are still worked in His Name or by means of the Sacrament . . . *but they are not so popularized or made known as to have the same glory as those first ones.*"

Now, fifteen hundred years later, in the twentieth century, those words apply even more aptly. Some miracles He performs today are so striking that if we examine them with an open mind, they leave no room for skepticism.

Although this train of thought may make some readers uneasy, there is no help for it. It would be more comfortable to present the Eucharist in a general and vague light, with soft drapings of sentimentality, without the glaring light of reality to reveal the embarrassing anomaly of miracles.

But the fact is that as Christ performed miracles in His Palestinian life, *so He performs them in His Eucharistic life.* As we mentioned above, it seems certain that if we add up all the evidence for miracles, we find that He performs many more miracles in His Eucharist-life now than He did in Palestine.

One reason these miracles today are not so "popularized or made known," as Augustine puts it, is because they are not witnessed in the same way as they were in Palestine. Five thousand men, not counting women and children, were on the mountain by the Sea of Galilee when He created matter from nothing. But today the Eucharistic Christ is approached by single persons, one by one. The meeting between Christ and man now is *personal.* Only in such places as Lourdes and Fatima do we see the Eucharistic Christ today surrounded by vast throngs who cry out "Lord, that I may see!" — "Lord, that I may hear!" — "Son of David, have mercy on me!" There, of course, is where we are most likely to witness Christ the Miracleworker.

But even miracles at great Eucharistic gatherings are scantily publicized. The press gives short space to Lourdes or Fatima or any other such place, despite the fact that millions of people visit these shrines, thousands have been cured there, and non-partisan medical commissions have judged the miracles.

An invalid coming to Lourdes usually registers at the *Bureau des Constatations Medicales.* If he does register upon arrival, and if he subsequently claims a cure, his before-and-after state is examined and assessed. The examining doctors are unpaid, independent men. The President is the only medical man permanently attached to the Bureau. Any doctor of any nationality, of any belief, or of no belief, is free to enter the Bureau, make whatever inquiries he chooses, and be present when any case or alleged case is being investigated. Pious people who imagine cures, or hysterical people who are cured by suggestion, are quickly dismissed. Despite all this, there are cures which no natural cause whatever is capable of producing.

Lourdes being a place where the Virgin appeared is of course a center of devotion to her. But it is consequently, and above all, a center of devotion to Christ's Presence in the Eucharist. Most cures occur during the procession of the Eucharist.

It would take more than the extent of this book to report even the most outstanding Eucharistic miracles, so rather than enumerate many we may at least give details

"Son of David, have mercy on me!"

of one witnessed by Dr. Alexis Carrel, the first American to win the Nobel Prize for physiology and medicine. His biography fills the better part of a page in *Collier's Encyclopedia*. He was particularly distinguished as an experimental surgeon and biologist and he won the Nordhoff-Jung Cancer Prize in 1931, the Newman Foundation Award in 1937 and the United States Distinguished Service Medal.

In a day when less was known about the human brain and heart than is known today, he kept a heart alive for years outside an animal's body. He pried deep into secrets of man, into the very nature of the brain and the coordination of the symphathetic and parasymphathetic nervous systems as the bases of temperament and disease; into nutrition, disease, mental illness, motivation, habit and conditioned reflexes.

Withal he found the time to write a number of books. One of them, *Man the Unknown,* won him international renown not only as a surgeon but as a writer. Published simultaneously in Paris and New York, it soon became a best seller. Among his other books were *Anastomosis and the Transplantation of Blood Vessels, The Preservation of Tissues, The Transplantation of Limbs, The Transplantation of Veins and Organs.*

At one time, for what he called "purely scientific reasons," Dr. Carrel decided to go to Lourdes, and he quoted himself as saying just before his departure for the shrine: "If God exists, miracles are possible. But does God exist objectively? How am I to know? *To the scientific mind a miracle is an absurdity.*"

When somebody asked him what kind of miracle he would have to see to be sure that God existed, Carrel answered: "An organic disease cured...a cancer disappearing, a congenital dislocation suddenly vanishing."

On his journey to Lourdes he proposed to be "entirely objective," and he did not think it likely that he would admit a miracle even if the many sick people on the train in which he traveled were suddenly cured, because most of them probably were suffering from nervous and traumatic hysteria.

However, one patient obviously was dying from organic disease. Her name was Marie Ferrand. "If such a case as hers were cured," wrote Dr. Carrel, "it would indeed be a miracle. I would never doubt again."

With permission of *Reader's Digest* and of Harper & Row, publishers of Dr. Carrel's account of his trip entitled *Journey to Lourdes,* here is what the surgeon wrote after he went to the infirmary at Lourdes to examine Marie Ferrand.[1] In the account he refers to himself by name, spelling Carrel backward.

"Her head, with its white emaciated face, was flung on the pillow. Her wasted arms lay flat at her sides. Her breathing was rapid and shallow.

"'How are you feeling?' Lerrac asked her gently.

"She turned her dim, dark-circled eyes toward him and her gray lips moved in an inaudible reply.

"Taking her hand, Lerrac put his fingertips on her wrist. Her pulse was excessively rapid and irregular. Her heart was giving out. 'Get me the hypodermic syringe,' he told the nurse. 'We'll give her an injection of caffeine.'

[1]Condensation of Alexis Carrel, *The Voyage to Lourdes,* (New York: Harper and Row), 1950. Reprinted with permission. This version appeared originally in *Reader's Digest,* (Plesantville, NY: Reader's Digest Assn., Inc.), Sept. 1950, pp. 147-62.

"Pulling back the covers the nurse removed the cradle that held up the bedclothes and the rubber ice bag which hung over the patient's abdomen. Marie Ferrand's emaciated body lay exposed again, her abdomen distended as before. The solid masses were still there; at the center, under the umbilicus, he could still feel the fluid. As the caffeine entered her thin thigh, Marie Ferrand's face contracted suddenly.

"Lerrac turned to A.B. 'It's just what I told you,' he added, 'advanced tuberculosis peritonitis. She may last a few days more, but she is doomed. Death is very near.'

"As Lerrac turned to leave, the nurse stopped him. 'Doctor, is it all right to take Marie Ferrand to the pool?'

"Lerrac looked at her in amazement. 'What if she dies on the way?' he asked.

" 'She is absolutely determined to be bathed. She came all the way for this.'

"At that moment Dr. J., who practiced in a town outside Bordeaux and had accompanied his own patients to Lourdes, entered the ward. Lerrac asked his opinion about having Marie Ferrand carried to the pool. Once again the covers were removed and Dr. J. examined Marie Ferrand. 'She's at the point of death,' he finally said in a low voice. 'She might very well die at the Grotto.'

" 'You see, mademoiselle,' said Lerrac, 'how imprudent it would be to take this patient to the pool. However, I have no authority here; I cannot give permission, or refuse it.'

" 'The girl has nothing to lose,' said the Mother Superior. 'It would be cruel to deprive her of the supreme happiness of being taken to the Grotto, though I fear she may not live to reach it. We shall take her there now, in a few minutes.'

"'I will be at the pool myself in any case,' said Lerrac. 'If she goes into a coma, send for me.'

"'She will certainly die,' Dr. J. repeated as they left the ward."

Dr. Carrel's account then goes on to describe the pools of Lourdes, and he says that he was standing outside the pools when Marie Ferrand was brought to be lowered into the waters. His narrative continues:

"For a moment, before going to the pool, they lowered the stretcher to the ground. The sick girl was apparently unconscious. Lerrac put his hand on her wrist. Her pulse was more rapid than ever, her face ashen. It was obvious that this young girl was about to die. He wondered how it would affect the pilgrims if she died in the pool. What would they think of miracles then?"

Marie Ferrand was not cured. But neither had she died. Nothing had happened. Many dramatic cures at Lourdes follow exactly the same pattern.

Dr. Carrel remarks this fact and then describes the ceremonies which followed, leading up to the great moment when all the sick are assembled at the Grotto to receive *the blessing of Christ in the Eucharist.*

He tells how he "walked past the little carts and through the crowd toward the Grotto. Pausing for a moment at the edge of the stream he observed the crowd. A young intern from Bordeaux, Mr. M., whom Lerrac had met the day before, greeted him. 'Have you any cures?' Lerrac asked.

"'No,' replied M. 'A few of the hysteria cases have recovered, but there has been nothing unexpected, nothing that one can't see any day in a hospital.'

"'Come and look at my patient,' said Lerrac. 'Her

case is not unusual but I think she is dying. She is at the Grotto.'

" 'I saw her a few minutes ago,' said M. 'What a pity they let her come to Lourdes.'

"It was now half-past two. Beneath the rock of Massabielle, the Grotto glittered in the light of its thousand candles. Beyond the high iron grille was a statue of the Virgin, standing in the hollowed rock where Bernadette once saw the glowing vision of the lady in white, the Immaculate Conception. In front of the iron grille and almost touching it, Lerrac recognized the slender figure of Marie Ferrand's nurse. He and M. made their way through the crowd and, stopping near Marie Ferrand's stretcher, leaned against the low wall. She was motionless, her breathing still rapid and shallow; she seemed to be at the point of death. More pilgrims were approaching the Grotto. Volunteers and stretcher-bearers came crowding in. The little carts were being wheeled from the pools to the Grotto.

"Lerrac glanced again at Marie Ferrand. Suddenly he stared. It seemed to him that there had been a change, that the harsh shadows on her face had disappeared, that her skin was somehow less ashen. Surely, he thought, this was hallucination. But the hallucination itself was interesting psychologically; hastily he jotted down the time in his notebook. It was twenty minutes before three. But if the change in Marie Ferrand was an hallucination, it was the first one Lerrac had ever had. He turned to M. 'Look at our patient again,' he said. 'Does it seem to you that she has rallied a little?'

" 'She looks much the same to me,' answered M. 'All I can see is that she is no worse.'

"Leaning over the stretcher, Lerrac took her pulse

again and listened to her breathing. 'The respiration is less rapid,' he told M. after a minute.

"'That may mean that she is about to die,' said M.

"Lerrac made no reply. To him it was obvious that there was a sudden improvement in her general condition. Something was taking place. He stiffened to resist a tremor of emotion, and concentrated all his powers of concentration on Marie Ferrand. He did not lift his eyes from her face. A priest was preaching to the assembled throngs of pilgrims and patients; hymns and prayers burst out sporadically (the Blessed Sacrament was reserved in the Grotto), and in this atmosphere of fervor, under Lerrac's cool, objective gaze, the face of Marie Ferrand slowly continued to change. Her eyes, so dim before, were now wide with ecstasy as she turned them toward the Grotto. The change was undeniable. The nurse leaned over and held her.

"Suddenly, Lerrac felt himself turning pale. The blanket which covered Marie Ferrand's distended abdomen was gradually flattening out. 'Look at her abdomen!' he exclaimed to M.

"M. looked. 'Why yes,' he said, 'it seems to have gone down. It's probably the folds in the blanket that give that impression.'

"The bell of the basilica had just struck three. A few minutes later, there was no longer any sign of distention in the girl's abdomen.

"Lerrac felt as though he were going mad.

"Standing beside Marie Ferrand, he watched the intake of her breath and pulsing of her throat with fascination. The heartbeat, through still very rapid, had become regular.

"'How do you feel?' he asked her.

" 'I feel very well,' she answered in a low voice. 'I am still weak, but I feel I am cured.'

"There was no longer any doubt: Marie Ferrand's condition was improving so much that she was scarcely recognizable...

"The crowd at the Grotto was not even aware that it had happened.

"It was the resurrection of the dead; it was a miracle!

"Lerrac went back to his hotel, forbidding himself to draw any conclusions until he could find out exactly what had happened...

"At half-past seven he started for the hospital, tense and on fire with curiosity. One question alone filled his mind: Had the incurable Marie Ferrand been cured?

"Opening the door of the ward of the Immaculate Conception (Hospital) he hastened across the room to her bedside. With mute astonishment, he stood and gazed. The change was overpowering. Marie Ferrand, in a white jacket, was sitting up in bed. Though her face was still gray and emaciated, it was alight with life; her eyes shone; a faint color tinted her cheeks. Such an indescribable serenity emanated from her person that it seemed to illuminate the whole sad ward with joy. 'Doctor,' she said, 'I am completely cured. I feel very weak, but I think I could even walk.'

"Lerrac put his hand on her wrist. The pulse beat was calm and regular. Her respiration had also become completely normal. Confusion flooded Lerrac's mind. Was this merely an apparent cure, the result of a patient's stimulus of auto-suggestion? Or was it a new fact, an astounding unacceptable event — a miracle? For a brief moment, before subjecting Marie Ferrand to the supreme test of examining her abdomen, Lerrac hesitated.

Then, torn between hope and fear, he threw back the blanket. The skin was smooth and white. Above the narrow hips was the small, flat, slightly concave abdomen of a young undernourished girl. Lightly he put his hands on the wall of the abdomen, looking for traces of the distention and the hard masses he had found before. They had vanished like a bad dream.

"The sweat broke out on Lerrac's forehead. He felt as though someone had struck him on the head. His heart began to pump furiously. He held himself in with iron determination.

"He had not heard Doctor J. and M. entering the ward. Suddenly he noticed them, standing beside him. 'She seems to be cured,' he said to them, 'I cannot find anything wrong. Please examine her yourselves.'

"While his two colleagues carefully palpated Marie Ferrand's abdomen, Lerrac stood aside and watched them with shining eyes. There could be no doubt whatever that the girl was cured. It was a miracle, the kind of miracle which took the public by storm and sent them in hordes to Lourdes. And the public was justified in its enthusiasm. Whatever the source of these cures, the results were not only breathtaking but positive and good. Again it swept over Lerrac how fortunate he was, that among all the patients at Lourdes that day it was the one he had known and studied carefully whom we saw cured!"

Then follows a description of the scientist-doctor's personal reaction. What would his fellow-scientists think of a man who believed in miracles? Would any one of them believe who had not seen it for themselves? Dr. Carrel concludes: "When a scientist tried to apply his intellectual techniques and convictions to metaphysics, he was lost. He could no longer use his reasoning, since

During the Ecumenical Council many Bishops joined the throngs before the Eucharistic presence in the grotto of Lourdes. Although identical to the same presence in churches all over the world, here there is accurate record kept of miraculous cures like that seen by Dr. Carrel.

reason did not go beyond the establishing of facts and their relations to each other. In the search for causes, there was nothing absolute, there were no signposts along the way, there was no proof of right or wrong. All things in this mysterious realm were therefore possible. Intellectual systems no longer seemed to count. In the face of life and death, the mere theories were void. It was not science that nourished the inner life of man; it was the faith of the soul. He had to reach a conclusion. He was certain of his diagnosis. It was incontestable that a miracle had taken place. But was it by the hand of God? Some day he would know. Meanwhile, it was safe to say it was a cure; that much he could guarantee. Yet deep within himself, he felt that was not all...

"He climbed the steps of the church in the glitter of lights while the organ boomed and a thousand voices chanted. He sat down on a chair at the back near an old peasant. For a long time he sat there motionless, his hands over his face, listening to the hymns. Then he found himself praying: '...I believe in Thee. Thou didst answer my prayers by a blazing miracle. I am still blind to it, I still doubt. But the greatest desire of my life is to believe, to believe passionately, implicitly, and never more to analyze and doubt.... Beneath the deep, harsh warnings of my intellectual pride a smothered dream persists. Alas, it is still only a dream but the most enchanting of them all. It is the dream of believing in Thee and of loving Thee with the shining spirit of men of God.'"

The notes which Dr. Carrel made are still on record at the Medical Commission in Lourdes.

If the great scientist, Carrel, had not been at Lourdes that day, who would ever have heard of Marie Ferrand

and her cure? One of the most significant facts in the entire account is in the two sentences: "The crowd at the Grotto *was not even aware* that it happened. It was the resurrection of the dead; it was a miracle!"

Many of the miracles Christ performs now in His Eucharistic state are even more dramatic than that of Marie Ferrand. There was a worker from Belgium with a piece of bone missing in his leg, his ankle and foot dangled, suspended only by flesh and tendons, so that it could be turned a hundred and eighty degrees. That missing bone *was instantly created in his leg*. The doctors had before-and-after X-rays. When the man died, an autopsy showed where the new bone had come to unite with the separated bone. The full documentation and X-rays can be seen at the office of the Medical Commission at Lourdes, together with the affirmation of many witnesses.

Dr. Carrel was so deeply moved because he was a *witness*. The writer can add the account of two apparent miracles which he himself witnessed, which partially explains his desire to write this book.

The patient in the first case was a man in Lisbon, Portugal, who suffered from Parkinson's disease. As the creeping paralysis rose from his lower limbs, advancing closer and closer to the heart, the patient was plunged into deep melancholy. His wife pleaded with him repeatedly to go only ninety miles away to Fatima. In mockery, because he knew that, like himself, his attending physician did not believe in miracles, he said to his wife in the doctor's presence: "I'll go if he does."

It occurred to the doctor that a trip to the church at Fatima* might cheer his patient, or at least it would be a temporary distraction, so he surprised the ill man by say-

When this American bishop blessed the sick at
Fatima, May 13, 1950, a paralytic was cured.

ing: "All right, let's go."

The six apparitions of the Virgin Mary at Fatima took place on the 13th day of six consecutive months, so that day is particularly celebrated at the Shrine. As this was the 13th day of October there was a large crowd of pilgrims. The non-believing doctor and his non-believing patient were among the first in the rows of invalids. I (the writer of this book) was carrying the canopy over the Holy Eucharist as It was raised by the priest to bless the patient.

The man suddenly pushed himself up in his wheelchair. Trembling, he began to move and feel his legs. Then he cried out to those around him: *"I'm not dreaming, am I? I am not dreaming?"*

This writer's reaction was something like the reaction of thousands of television viewers in the first moment they saw the murder of Lee Harvey Oswald, during a live news program following the assassination of President Kennedy in 1963, or of hearing the news that Pope John Paul I had died of a heart attack in late September, 1978, or that his successor, Pope John Paul II, had been shot in an assassination attempt in St. Peter's Square on May 13, 1981. *It did not seem real.*

The doctor's mouth fell open in amazement as he slowly sank to his knees. Tears began to roll down his cheeks. "This was not for you," he exclaimed through sobs. "This was for me."

Some years later I witnessed another apparent miracle in the same place. The patient this time was a woman twenty-two years old named Arminda dos Campos. She had been ill for nine years and had undergone seven major operations. She had a greatly distended abdomen, total paralysis and an opening in her side cut by a surgeon's scalpel to drain purulent matter. Again I was standing very close to the patient. In fact, I was standing directly in front of her at the moment of her cure and saw the blankets flatten on her body, saw her sit up, and within two hours *I saw the scars which had instantaneously formed in the place of the incisions.*

In another book[2] I recorded my own reactions to seeing the scars within two hours of the cure: As I stood near the side of the table opposite the Bishop,[3] the cured girl was introduced from the end of the table by one of the nurses. The Bishop of Fatima listened patiently. In his twenty-six years as Bishop he had heard many similar stories. He had gone into sheaves of endless details about cures.

Then I heard the nurse saying: "Show the Bishop the scars where the fistulas were."

There, on the upper part of the thigh, at a spot revealed with careful modesty, were two clear, dry scars. They were not red as a freshly-healed wound usually is. They were clear (like a little scar on my own hand... more than thirty years old). One of them was so deep that it would have been possible to insert the tip of one's little finger where the opening had been.

After staring at the healed tissue, wondering if it could have been possible that there were really awful sores there just a few hours before, I saw the face of the nurse. Tears were streaming down her cheeks. With an open-arm gesture and trembling hands, suddenly she exclaimed: "And Your Excellency, to think that this morning I put bandages there on large, running openings!"

[2]*Russia Will Be Converted,* (Washington, NJ: AMI Press), 1952. Out of print.
[3]The bishop referred to here is the first Bishop of Leiria, Dom Jose Correia da Silva. Because Fatima is within the Diocese of Leiria, the bishop of the diocese is commonly referred to as "the Bishop of Fatima."

It was only in that final moment — looking into the tear-stained face of the nurse — that the miracle made its full impact. In that moment I believed with all my heart that we in that room were experiencing the same wonder experienced when Christ healed the ten lepers, or when the blind man shouted out that suddenly he could see. We were, I felt absolutely sure, seeing it with our own eyes — not two thousand years ago, but *now*. We were objectively experiencing the reality of the Eucharist, *the reality of Christ among us.*

But what of the many other miracles? Few are so strongly confirmed. And yet, the Eucharistic Lord remains in the reach of all, in all the tabernacles of the world, waiting to be asked for His graces and assistance.

And He gives them in abundance.

In Santarem, Portugal there is a consecrated Host which took on the appearance of bleeding flesh and which has remained incorrupt. An American group made a stop at this important Eucharistic shrine during their 1984 World Peace Flight. Archbishop Pearce, chaplain of the group, told them: "Don't be afraid to ask for a miracle."

Just before entering the Santarem "Church of the Holy Miracle," Archbishop Pearce, chaplain of the 1984 World Peace Flight, told the pilgrims:

"Don't be afraid to ask for miracles."

One of the pilgrims, Muriel Thornberg, had a diabetic sister, legally blind for twelve years, and during the past six years had open suppurating sores on her legs and feet which obliged her to use a wheelchair. Doctors said she would probably never walk again. Adding to her sorrows was the fact that she was a widow, living alone, with just about enough money to get by.

So Muriel Thornberg, as she kissed the monstrance containing the mirculous Host in Santarem, begged at least for the miracle that her sister's feet would be healed.

She says: "Somehow, as I was thus embracing Our Lord in the Blessed Sacrament in this extraordinary manifestation of the 'Bleeding Host,' I felt surely that my prayer was answered."

When Muriel returned from the World Peace Flight she could hardly wait to call her sister to ask about her condition.

One foot was healed. But on the other there was still a hole nearly an inch across and more than an inch deep, filled with pus. Muriel knew that the Jesus to whom she spoke in that miraculous Host in Santarem was the same Jesus in any tabernacle. So she hastened to Church to remind Him of what He had done when she had had the privilege of embracing Him by kissing the monstrance in Santarem. It was Ascension Thursday and she prayed with fervor that the cure would be complete.

The very next day (Friday, June 1, 1984) the doctor examined the foot. "He had a strange expression on his face," Muriel reports, "and suddenly asked if someone had been praying for her."

The foot was completely healed and the doctor said he did not now how it could possibly have happened.

"When my sister then told him about my prayers for her before the Blessed Sacrament the doctor said that this was the only possible explanation for her recovery."

Muriel had taken the exhortation of Archbishop Pearce to heart:

"Do not be afraid to ask for a miracle."

And from Whom could she more certainly expect a miracle than from Jesus Himself in the Blessed Sacrament, especially at Santarem where a bleeding Host has remained incorrupt for several hundred years as a visible, extraordinary proof of the words of Our Lord Himself: *"This is My Flesh, this is My Blood."*

"I think God may have been testing my faith when both feet were not healed right away," Muriel Thornberg says. "But could it not also be that Our Lord had cured one foot, and then called me back to the tabernacle before curing the other to remind me that He is the same Jesus, truly present, in the Blessed Sacrament everywhere?"

To understand this reality we keep returning to the miracle of the Last Supper.

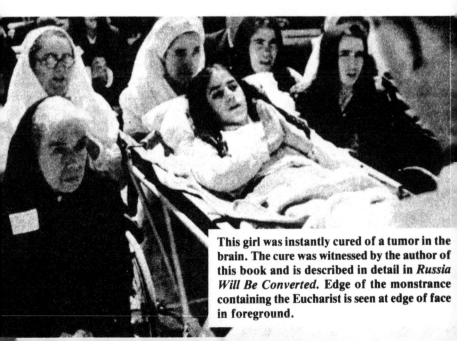

This girl was instantly cured of a tumor in the brain. The cure was witnessed by the author of this book and is described in detail in *Russia Will Be Converted*. Edge of the monstrance containing the Eucharist is seen at edge of face in foreground.

CHAPTER TEN

WHY WE HAVE
THE SECRET NOW

Waterpots are often seen in catacomb pictures. They may indicate the miracle of Cana or they may be meant to recall the great act of humility and love with which Christ began the Last Supper.

Just before that meal was to begin, Christ laid aside His outer garments. He girded Himself with a towel. Then He poured water in a basin and went from one Apostle to another, washing each man's feet and drying them with the towel which hung from His waist.

On Holy Thursday* of 1964, while this book was originally being written, Pope Paul VI performed the age-old ceremony as it is performed every year. He removed his outer vestments, descended the papal throne in the apse of St. John Lateran* to wash the feet of certain people present. They happened to be five Mexicans, one Cuban, one Chilean, one Paraguayan and others from Latin American countries, a total of thirteen.[1]

[1]The number thirteen is not a mistake. The number was originally twelve, but on one occasion in the early days of the Lateran church when the Pope began to wash the feet of the deacons who had been chosen, he counted thirteen men instead of twelve. To the amazement of all it was an apparition of Christ, Who, after the washing, disappeared. So now thirteen are selected in the Lateran church to commemorate the event.

111

Many find this washing a moving sight. It strikes them as dramatic that the Pope, the supreme pontiff of Christendom, should kneel to perform such a menial task for them. And yet, how faint a picture this is of what Christ did.

The feet of modern men are usually clean. In fact, since the men to be washed by the Pope are selected in advance, they carefully scrub their feet to prepare for the ritual. The washing is not physically necessary.

But the feet of the men at the Last Supper were dirty. How could they be otherwise? The Apostles had been walking all day along the dusty roads leading to Jerusalem and also over the spittle and dung strewn city streets. In short, it was a nasty job that Christ undertook, a job quite different from the ceremonial ablution which the Pope annually performs in Christendom's first church.

Why did Christ do it?

Peter protested the act. He thought it unseemly, even shocking, that Christ, the Son of God, should minister to them in such a lowly manner.

Admittedly the job had to be done. In those days when people reclined at table, the couches would have become soiled from dusty feet. But usually people washed their own feet unless they were affluent enough to pay a servant to do it for them.

Christ gave His reason. He washed the feet of the Apostles to show them that they must love one another and be humble in their attitude toward one another. He spelled it out in exact words: "If then I, being your Lord and Master, washed your feet, you also ought to wash one another's feet. For I have given you an example that as I have done to you, so you do also."

A few minutes later He expatiated: "A new command-

ment I give you: that you love one another as I have
loved you.... This is how all will know you for my
disciples: your love for one another."

Christ had a second reason also: He did it because He
Himself loved them so much that He yearned to express
His feeling in any way that presented itself. After all,
service is love made manifest. Christ became the servant
to show that nothing was too insignificant, nothing too
great for Him to do for them.

Love filled Him. "Having loved His own, He loved
them to the end." He loved until His last few hours on
earth, until His very death on the cross. Then this love
burst forth into soaring words which have haunted the
world like an unforgetable melody ever since: *"As the
Father has loved me, so I have loved you. Live on in my
love."*

Yes, love was the theme song of His every act and
word that night: love of the Father for Him, His love for
the Father in the Holy Spirit, His love for man and men's
love for one another.

*All this was the prelude to the great Act of Love, the
giving of Himself under the appearance of their ordinary
foodstuffs.*

**"Jesus took bread, blessed it, broke it, and gave it to
his disciples. 'Take this and eat it,' he said, 'this is my
body.' Then he took a cup, gave thanks, and gave it to
them. 'All of you must drink from it,' he said, 'for this is
my blood, the blood of the covenant, to be poured out in
behalf of many for the forgiveness of sins.' " (Mt.
26:26-28)**

Early Christians were able to accept this because they
saw love as the key to God's relationship with man. The
Apostle John had written that God *is* love. They saw that

love, especially divine love, tends to share and to give, and that every action of God, indeed His very Being in Trinity, is an expression of love and of giving. *One wants to consume the beloved.*

Modern man, for reasons too profound and too ramified to explore here, often has become alienated from God. There seems to be a general feeling that God is not interested in the affairs of man, and in this atmosphere the acceptance of a divine love which would go to the point of a sharing such as Christ declared is simply out of grasp. For this reason many Christians, although believing in Christ and accepting the Bible as an honest and believable account of all that Christ did and said, take refuge in the idea that He did not mean His words literally. They think that He meant to say this *represents* My Body, rather than what He *did* say: "this is" My Body.

As mentioned in the last chapter, we must have the assumption that the reader either believes and wants to understand more of the world's greatest secret, or that he does not believe, *but for the sake of understanding is willing at this point to take a position of belief.*

Since the Eucharist, and all other mysteries of Faith, fit like the spokes of a wheel into the central mystery of the Triune God's loving nature, the Eucharist cannot be grasped even remotely without some understanding of God Himself. Most Christians who find difficulty in believing Christ's words about Himself as food probably do not disbelieve God's ability to perform such a miracle, but cannot believe *that He loves man that much.*

During that historic Last Supper, Christ told His disciples about this. He revealed to them the nature of God.* He told them that God is love, and that love is the explanation of His being with them. He even demonstrated it.

He washed their feet, like a servant, before telling them unequivocally that "I and the Father are one...when you see me, you see the Father also."

Every word Christ spoke at that first Eucharistic Liturgy was a word of love. The disciples felt it, even though they could not understand. Today, many of us understand but do not feel.

Theologians today use the word "circumincession" to express the complete and reciprocal interchange of life and love which flows between the three Persons without beginning and without end — an interchange reflected in the Eucharist which Christ revealed to us that night.

Each of the three Persons, possessing the loving nature, took a distinct part in the institution of the Blessed Sacrament. The Father gave the Son: "the Father sent me," Christ said. The Son gave the Eucharist: "This is my body." And the Holy Spirit reached out to men and made possible their mental and spiritual acceptance of such a mystery: "It is better for you that I go ... whereas if I go, I will send the Paraclete to you."

So the reason for the Eucharist is found in the nature of God: *God's love*. This alone ultimately makes the world's greatest secret understandable. *The loving nature of God desired to give us His very Self.*

Love can be given in half measures from man to man, but God gives all: Himself.

He unites with us; He united us to Him. Love always tends to union. Through the Eucharist we are joined to God, and through Him to our fellow Christians. "That you may be one even as the Father and I are one," was the way that Christ expressed it.

Father Walter Burghardt[2] describes a day during World War II when "A tremendous event took place over the face of the earth. That day Christ, our Lord, hiding His Godhead and His manhood under the appearance of bread, pillowed His head on the tongue of a child in Baltimore's Cathedral. The same day the same Christ slipped past bursting shells and past the lips of a Marine in the Marshalls. The same day Christ braved the beaches of Normandy to rest His brow beneath a British helmet. The same Christ made His home next to the throbbing heart of an Italian peasant woman and bent low to a bomb shelter in Berlin. The same Christ rode with a pilot in the cockpit of a Japanese Zero fighter and fed the brave on a Burma road. Even the barbed wire could not keep the same Christ from lighting up a brown face in the Bataan."

Christ came that day also to the pope, to presidents of nations, labor unions, corporations. He made all these people one in the love which is Himself, the Giver of the Eucharist, the Sacrament of Love.

Yes, only love — *an infinite love* — can explain it.

[2]Fr. W. Burghardt, *All Lost in Wonder,* (Westminster, MD: Newman Press), 1960, p. 93.

CHAPTER ELEVEN

THE SACRIFICE

Early Christians even found a way to symbolize the identity of the Eucharistic Liturgy with sacrifice: An altar with three legs as traditionally used for the bloody sacrifices of old.

Today there may seem little resemblance between the Eucharistic Liturgy and the liturgy that the Gospels describe as the Last Supper. Nonetheless, it is only the "trimmings" which have changed. In the essential part, there has been no substantial change whatever.

From the beginning Christians let their enthusiasms and their inspiration of the moment guide them in the peripheral parts, that is in the parts of the liturgy before and after the "Secret." The secret part, celebrated in a similar manner wherever Christians gathered for worship, was a repetition of what Christ Himself had given the Apostles that last night. It is the same today, and it was the same in the first years of Christianity. We see this fact confirmed again and again by the many symbols and pictures which have come to light in the recently unearthed catacombs.

On that night of nights before Christ died He asked them to do as He was doing then "in commemoration" of Him. So His followers made the Eucharistic Liturgy a fulfillment of that, His final request. Acting for the great High Priest, Christ, the priest pronounces in His name the identical words that Christ used: *"This is my body...this is my blood."*

117

In the Catacombs of Sts. Peter and Marcellinus in this very early "breaking of bread." Notice the altar with three legs in front of the banquet table . . . the same kind of altar used for bloody sacrifice before the Eucharistic Liturgy.

The Eucharistic Liturgy, as a renewal of the Last Supper, must be the most sublime form of worship to be found in today's world because the participants do not worship alone; they worship "through Him, with Him and in Him." Prayers of one's own invention said from now until that day when Gabriel's horn shall sound in the heavens, even if numbered in astronomical figures, could not be as sublime as one celebration of the Eucharistic Liturgy. Obviously the Mass* is Christ's prayer; it is His sacrifice; it is His worship. It is of an order different from any purely human act; it is Divine, and the Christian's faith assures him that he actually participates in it!

Throughout history the Eucharistic Liturgy (or the Mass) has been understood to be a universal form of worship, even though it is said in local languages. It has always included "all Christians, living and dead," particularly "all true believers" as well as "us sinners." It has been and is like a huge symphony orchestra in which all join to make harmonious melody for and to and through God.

To some people since the Reformation the official character of the Eucharistic Liturgy may seem to have become too stylized. So Vatican Council II gave great attention to a tendency to use private prayers even during the Mass. Too many had lost sight of the fact that the *official* character of the Eucharistic Liturgy lends weight to the prayer and to the worship of the Christian community together, with Christ.

Perhaps an analogy may help clarify this.

If a man's barber were to present him with a medal in the name of the United States Congress, would not the presentation be taken as a joke? But if this barber were authorized by Congress to present the medal, even in the Capitol building, it would be a great official honor.

The official Eucharistic Liturgy is solemn to Christians because Christ authorized it. So is it not fitting that the most solemn breaking of the bread be set in a fairly elaborate framework of prayers, hymns, sermons, scriptural readings and so on, not unlike the setting given by Christ Himself the night before He died?

To some readers who know the Eucharistic Liturgy the following description of it will seem unnecessary. But to others it may seem the most significant part of this book because it describes the Last Supper rite as the central religious act of millions of persons around the world today.

Presented with a questionnaire to evaluate this book before publication, one non-Christian said of this section:

"Being a non-Christian I found myself becoming quite engrossed; it made me understand this rite which is actually very secret outside of the Church."

As we might expect, the explanation begins in the New Testament.

In the second chapter of the Acts of the Apostles, St. Luke speaks of the brethren devoting "themselves to the apostles' instruction and the communal life, to the breaking of bread and the prayers" (2:42). In the First Epistle to Timothy (1 Tim. 4:13) as well as in the First Epistle to the Thessalonians (1 Thes. 5:27), St. Paul exhorts the brethren to read his epistles and "to attend to reading and to doctrine" in connection with the Eucharistic feast. Also we see in the Acts of the Apostles (20:7) and in St. Paul's epistles to the Corinthians (1 Cor. 14:26) and to the Ephesians (Eph. 5:19) that when Christians gathered together for worship and to celebrate the Eucharistic feast, there were psalms, hymns and sermons. The famous passage from St. Paul's first letter to the Corinthians (1 Cor. 11:20-29) actually gives an outline of the breaking of the bread in thanksgiving that followed the earlier part of the service. Then in his letter to the Hebrews (Heb. 13:10) he speaks of the table of the Eucharist being an altar.

So Dr. A. Fortescue, Ph.D., S.T.D., the great liturgical scholar of England, could write ''we have already in the New Testament all the essential elements that we find later in the organized liturgies: lessons on the psalms, hymns, sermons, prayers, consecration, communion.''[1]

As we said above, the Eucharistic Liturgy was more fluid than it is today. Some scriptural readings were probably a matter of choice of the individual priest. Those with a Jewish background might naturally have stressed what was read in the synagogues, and among the Gentiles the letters of Peter, Paul and James were certainly read over and over.

Today parts of all these readings have been standardized into the present liturgy.

Fortunately the Apostle John has left us a detailed, eyewitness account of what Christ did at the Last Supper, as we described in Chapter Four.

That Passover Supper was an offering by Christ to the Father, through the Holy Spirit, of His Body and Blood. Also it was the giving of His Body and Blood to men and for men for the remission of sins, for salvation.

A moment's thought shows that the same definition also fits the offering of Calvary.

[1]*Catholic Encyclopedia*, V. 9, 1912, p. 307.

That, too, was a love offering by Christ to the Father, through the Holy Spirit, of His Body and Blood and an offering made for men for the remission of sins.

Thus Christian theologians from the very early days of the Church, from the very time of the Apostles themselves, saw that on Calvary Christ was the High Priest Who made the offering or sacrifice, and that in the Eucharistic Liturgy He again becomes the High Priest Who makes the offering or sacrifice. On Calvary, the "victim," or the offering was Christ Himself, His Body and Blood; in the Eucharistic Liturgy, the "victim" or thing offered is also Christ Himself, His Body and Blood. The very word "host" means sacrifice.

A single point of difference made by Christians between Calvary and the Eucharistic Liturgy is the manner in which the offering is made. On Calvary Christ's body and blood were visibly offered. There was a death which bystanders could witness, an offering reminiscent of the Old Testament immolations; the lamb was slaughtered and destroyed. In the Eucharistic Liturgy Christians knew that Christ did not die again, but offered Himself, the Lamb of God, and thus immolated or sacrificed His Body and Blood in a mystical (hidden) manner under the appearances of bread and wine.

On Calvary Christ died for men's sins. He offered Himself in atonement that men might then, through His atonement or redemption, have a chance to try for heaven, a chance which primeval sin had lost for the human race. In the Eucharistic Liturgy His death applies to men's souls the graces that He has won for them in proportion to their spiritual capacity.

Pope John Paul II, in his message of June 15, 1983 concerning the Sacrament of Reconciliation, said:

"Those who participate in the Eucharistic Sacrifice receive a special grace of forgiveness and reconciliation. Uniting themselves to the offering of Christ, they can more abundantly receive the fruit of the immolation which he made of himself on the Cross."[2]

By receiving the Eucharist Christians believed they were intimately united with Christ and offered themselves with Him to the Father through the Holy Spirit. In Peter's words (1 Pt. 2:9) we are "a royal priesthood," for we are then co-offerers. Through the robed priest at the altar who speaks for us, and through our High Priest the Lord and Savior Jesus Christ, we make the offering He makes to God the Father. Through Him Whom we receive into our hearts and souls in the Eucharist, we offer ourselves. If we give ourselves to Him as completely as He gives Himself to us, sincerely desiring to retain nothing of ourselves, He will lavish His grace upon us so abundantly as to make us into His image, into saints, "for this is the will of God, your sanctification."

Some argue as to which is more important in the Eucharistic Liturgy, sacrifice or Communion. St. Thomas Aquinas argued for the latter. Vatican Council II reasserted the importance of participation in the entire Eucharistic Liturgy and confirmed communion as its high point.

"...if you do not eat of the flesh of the Son of Man and drink his blood," Christ said, "you have no life in you." (Jn. 6:54)

Saint Thomas states that *no one* possesses grace before he receives this sacrament at least in desire, "his own in the case of an adult, that of the Church in the case of

[2]*L'Osservatore Romano,* 20 June 1983, p. 3.

infants''[3]

Thus Saint Thomas, who was singled out by Pope John XXIII before Vatican Council II as the chief authority to be considered in this matter, stresses that *all* other sacraments are dependent upon this one. To receive Christ in this sacrament we are baptized and confirmed. To make it possible, priests are ordained. Even marriage, as an element in the visible structure of the Church, serves to represent communion in human terms.

Furthermore, at the moment of the Consecration the whole Church (triumphant, suffering, and militant) is united in a particularly efficacious way. Vatican Council II turned the altars around and drew the communities into active participation in this sublime, incomprehensible Event.

Since this time Communions have increased, but still millions miss Mass altogether.

For this reason there appears urgent need for increase of private devotions and especially of sacramentals. Such is the burden of the Message of Fatima.

Saint Thomas says that sacramentals (such as the Rosary and the Scapular) play an *essential role* in the liturgy by helping to establish this ideal condition for the reception of the sacraments.[4]

It is worth recalling here the declaration written at the Council of Trent as a summation of what Christians had always believed about the Eucharistic Liturgy from the time of Christ up to the mid-sixteenth century when it was written. It describes exactly what is believed today by a

---

[3]*Summa Theologica*, III, q. 79, art. 1, reply 1.

[4]See also: Colman E. O'Neill, O.P., *Meeting Christ in the Sacraments*, (New York: Alba House), 1964, pp. 334-35.

majority of Christians without any change whatever. The declaration, which we quoted earlier, goes like this: "Jesus Christ, our God and Savior, although He was to offer Himself once and for all to God the Father on the altar of the cross by His death, there to work out our eternal redemption, yet since His priesthood was not to be extinguished by His death, He at the Last Supper, on the night that He was betrayed, wanted to leave to . . . the Church a visible sacrifice. The exigencies of our nature demand it. The sacrifice of God once and for all wrought upon the cross, should be reenacted and its memory abide to the end of the world, and its saving power applied (anew to each generation) for the remission of those sins into which we all fall day by day . . . He offered His Body and Blood to God the Father under the appearances of bread and wine, and gave them under the same appearance to His apostles. These men He then appointed priests of the New Testament — they and their successors — by His words, 'Do this in remembrance of me.' So He gave the command to offer the sacrifice as the Church has understood and taught."

Now, in comparison, here is how the latest Ecumenical Council* affirmed it in 1964:

"At the Last Supper, on the night He was handed over, Our Lord instituted the Eucharistic Sacrifice of His Body and Blood to perpetuate the sacrifice on the Cross throughout the ages until He should come, and thus entrust to the Church, His beloved Spouse, the memorial of His death and resurrection: A sacrament of devotion, a sign of unity, a bond of charity, a paschal banquet in which Christ is received, the soul is filled with Grace and there is given to us the pledge of future glory." (Vatican

Council II)[5]

A modern ecumenical writer puts it well: "At His death on Calvary, Jesus gave back to the Father His bodily members nailed to a cross and covered with blood as a visible expression of His sacrifice for our sins. Christ gives us His own Body and Blood in the Holy Eucharist to be offered as a sacrifice commemorating and renewing for all time the Sacrifice of the Cross. In Holy Communion He draws to Himself all the members of His Mystical Body, the Church, in order that He may give them as a sacrificial gift to the Father. Thus, by the great power of His love, He wishes to join us in a living union with His Mystical Body as one sacrifice, so that Body may grow..."[6]

Sometimes externals of religious practice have caused apparent difficulties among Christians to seem more profound than they really are. The 1966 meeting of the World Council of Churches in Geneva saw strong intervention of the Orthodox* to draw all Christian churches to unity by turning back to the essential belief of early times. The Orthodox themselves, with valid Sacraments, may well be the provident bridge to ultimate ecumenism,* *even though the peripheral elements of their liturgy are quite different from almost all others.*

More and more we are coming to understand that the outer trappings of the liturgy are of little importance. Vestments for the liturgy were at first the everyday dress of the apostolic era. When styles subsequently changed, this original form of dress remained and became the ap-

[5]*Constitution on the Sacred Liturgy,* ch. 2, n. 47; Rush, A.A.S.. LVI, 1964, p. 113.
[6]See: Lawrence G. Lovasik, S.V.D., *The Eucharist in Catholic Life,* (New York: Macmillan), 1960.

Pilgrims participate in a Mass celebrated in the catacombs where Peter and Paul said Mass, where one is surrounded by tombs for first martyrs, where the first symbols of the Eucharist are frescoed into the walls. Not much has changed except the costumes of the community.

proved garb.

Modern ceremony has evolved. Action performed a certain way for a number of times often became traditional. Other ceremonies used temporarily were later dropped. One such was the "spiritual exercises" in which people moved by the Holy Spirit prophesied and so on.[7] Another was the agape* or feast of altruistic love, before the Liturgy began. In the beginning this probably derived from a desire to duplicate the Last Supper which Christ ate with the Apostles before He gave them the Sacrament.

Communion at one time was usually given under both forms throughout the entire Church, that is, under both the bread and the wine. The Church, however, from its earliest years has believed, and theologians agree that Christ is wholly present, Body, Blood, Soul and Divinity, under *either* form. Therefore, for convenience sake, and also to emphasize this, the custom of giving Communion under bread only was adopted by most of the Western Church. Some Christians still commonly use both forms and almost all Christians today (especially after the Ecumenical Council, Vatican II) use them on occasion. Christ used both bread and wine to emphasize the identity of the Eucharist with Calvary, as we have already explained.

But because this is so important, let us interrupt our thought for a moment to emphasize this again.

[7] These "exercises" can be found within the scope of Eucharistic Liturgies celebrated at the larger gatherings of the Catholic charismatic renewal. This movement within the Church began in 1967 and has received the approval of Pope Paul VI and Pope John Paul II. See *The Spirit and The Bride Say, "Come!" — Mary's Role in the New Pentecost,* AMI Press, 1982.

Imagine yourself in the hospital being shown your own X-ray, with bones, heart, and shadows of tissue. You might say: "These are my bones! This is my heart!," etc. This is the way we may consider that Jesus spoke at the last supper (and what He does at every Mass) when he says: "This is My Body! This is my Blood!"

His Body is not separated from His Blood when He says: "This is My Body," or when he says, "This is My Blood." But as before a hospital scanner I might speak of parts of my body as though they were separate, we exclaim before the separate species used in the miracle of transubstantiation: This is His Body! This is His Blood! (although we know well that He is *whole* and *entire* under *both* species).

And Jesus has a special reason for presenting Himself whole and entire under two different species.

Just as a doctor would want to draw attention to our heart or lungs if there was a problem, Jesus wants to draw attention to His blood because the world had a problem...and *He shed His Blood for it*. And the fact of that shedding of blood is *made present to us in every Mass*.

At Fatima* the Archangel communicated the eldest child with the Host and the younger children with the Precious Blood. But all three received Our Lord completely...and at the same time they became deeply aware (because of the two species, with the host bleeding into the chalice) of the Sacrifice Jesus made in order to save us and to communicate Himself to us.

Oh! How awesome to hear those words: "This is My Body! ...This is My Blood!"

To counter the heresy that Jesus was not wholly

present in both species, the Church began to communicate Him to the faithful only under the species of
bread.

It was the custom in the days of the early Church to
use a single loaf of bread. Small particles were broken
off for each communicant. Today usually separate
hosts* are used and only the one which the priest con-
sumes is necessarily broken.

Parenthetically it also might be noted, though this has
nothing to do with the Liturgy proper, that in the first
centuries because of the danger of attending liturgical
services, the initiated or baptized were sometimes allowed to carry the Consecrated Bread home with them.
The next day they could communicate themselves without running the risk of going out to the Mass.* The actual "breaking of the bread" or the Mass, would take
place only once or twice a week. After the persecutions
ceased and the celebration of the Mass became a daily
event, the practice of taking hosts to private homes was
gradually abolished.

All through the centuries some changes or evolution
continued. Different languages have been used. In the
earliest days of Christianity, Greek rather than Latin was
the usual language. Today, the sole remaining fragment
of Greek in the Roman or Latin liturgy is the *Kyrie
Eleison* ("Lord, have mercy") prayer.

Very ancient usages generally remain in the Mass. The
basic outline of the liturgy as it is today existed in
liturgies as early as 150 A.D. (For example, readings,
homily, a Eucharistic prayer, and communion.) Other sup-
porting elements had taken form by the third cen-

tury,[8] It is notable that among these ancient liturgical practices, some have been restored to the Mass in the recent liturgical reform. The interaction between the priest and congregation at Mass, the offertory procession, and the "Second Eucharistic Prayer" (see p. 135), were derived from these ancient liturgies.[9]

Also, as mentioned earlier, since the days of the persecutions when the catechumens were excluded from the breaking of bread and permitted to stay only for initial prayers, the Mass has been divided into two parts. There still remains the definite breaking point in this part of the Mass where the Liturgy of the Word ends and the Liturgy of the Eucharist begins. (Formerly this marked the end of the so called Mass of the Catechumens and the beginning of the Mass of the Faithful.)

Incidentally, since the most solemn and secret part of the Eucharistic Liturgy was heralded by the dismissal of the catechumens, it is easy to see how the word "Mass" evolved. It is derived from the Latin word for dismissal.

But to return to the discussion of changes. Recently many prayers formerly recited in Latin by a majority of Christians are now recited in the vernacular. When the priest actually distributes the Host* or "the Blessed Sacrament" to the people, he now says simply "The Body of Christ" and the communicant acknowledges with the simple profession of faith: "Amen." (But let us repeat what we said just a bit earlier that the Christians believe they receive not only the Body and Blood of

[8]Joannes H. Emminghaus, *The Eucharist: Essence, Form, Celebration*, (Collegeville, MN: Liturgical Press), 1978, pp. 37, 45-46.
[9]Emminghaus, *The Eucharist,* pp. 43, 62, 163.

Christ, but the whole living Christ, the Person of the Savior with His Soul and Divinity.)

Variations of the Christian Liturgy include not only these already mentioned but also the Liturgy of the Eastern Church, which was for a thousand years markedly different from that of the Western Church. The so-called Roman Rite, though it has become most widespread, is far from unique. As a matter of fact, the Roman Rite more closely resembles the Protestant Episcopal service than it does some Eastern Rites which are actually included in the membership of the Church of Rome.

None of these variations of liturgy, as we have reiterated, touches the essential sacrifice.

From the very first days of Christianity there were cyclical changes repeated in the liturgy each year. In the first centuries it was seen that prayers and scriptural reading should logically reflect the season or the feast being celebrated. So one section of the Eucharistic Liturgy, called the *Proper,* was made to vary each day while the rest the of the Liturgy, the *Ordinary,* was the same for every day of the year. For instance, the Proper of Easter was and is different in spirit and in wording from that of Christmas. Through the year the Liturgy follows Christ's life and that of His Mother and the other saints.

The so-called "Liturgical Year" begins four weeks before Christmas with Advent. The first four weeks are a period of preparation for the coming, or the advent, of the Lord. We are reminded of the final judgment for our sins and the priest wears the somber purple vestments of penance. But always the essential sacrifice is unchanged. Always and in all actions the words are the same: "This is My Body; this is My Blood." When Christ does come at Christmas, all explodes in light and joy. This great feast is followed by such major feasts as the Solemnity of Mary, Mother of God, on New Year's Day, then by His first manifestation to the non-Hebrew world, Epiphany or the Feast of the Magi.

After a period of rejoicing lasting some weeks, there follows another somber period, Lent, in which we are asked to do penance. This leads to Palm Sunday and Holy Week in which we recall Christ's first breaking of the bread, His suffering and His death, and finally to the triumph of the Resurrection on Easter Sunday.

After Easter Christians celebrate the feast of the Ascension, followed nine days later by the birthday of the Church, the feast of Pentecost or the feast of the Coming of the Holy Spirit upon the Apostles in the form of tongues of fire.

In these variations of the daily Eucharistic Liturgy, or the Mass, Christians relive the life of Christ as He passed it in Palestine. Pope Pius XII called the liturgical year: "Contact with His Mysteries."[10]

Also there are saints' days throughout the year. St. Patrick's Day and St. Valentine's Day may be among the best known, but these are only two out of over two hundred.

Then occasionally there are Masses for special needs and occasions such as Nuptial Masses, Masses for the dead, for peace and justice, etc. There are also Votive Masses which can be offered in honor of a saint or a Divine truth.

Aids in following the Church's liturgical life are easily obtainable. Among these are Church calendars which give ongoing information concerning the current

---

[10]The encyclical *Mediator Dei,* CTSE ed., 176.

liturgical themes. And in most parishes missalettes are available which help one to fully participate in the Liturgy. They include the "program" of the liturgy in its entirety, including, for example, readings for Sundays, prayers of the Mass, and responses. Some choose to obtain their own "Mass book," a Missal, which is a miniature version of the same book used by the priest. This is designed to help anyone to appreciate the Liturgy, and contains readings for each day of the year. Also we might recommend *The Eucharist: Essence, Form, Celebration,* 229 pp. (see p. 131).

The Eucharistic Liturgy in the Roman Church opens with the *Introductory Rites* which include an *Entrance Hymn, Greeting, Introductory Remarks* and the *Penitential Rite* (assisted by the deacon if there is one present), which is an acknowledgement of unworthiness and a prayer for forgiveness. Next comes the *Glory to God,* a magnificent hymn of praise, and the *Opening Prayer*.

The *Liturgy of the Word* follows. This consists of readings (usually by the laity) from the Old Testament, psalm verses, readings from the New Testament, and finally, the Gospel reading proclaimed by the deacon (or priest).

On Sundays and sometimes weekdays a homily (or sermon) is given after which there is a solemn *Profession of Faith* (the Nicene Creed) and the *Prayer of the Faithful*. This completes the Liturgy of the Word, formerly called the Mass of the Catechumens. The ancient "secret" part will follow.

The Mass of the Faithful, now called the *Liturgy of the Eucharist,* opens with an *Offertory Song* or *Prayer* which contains expressions of love, oblation and praise.

During this time, members of the congregation bring the gifts of bread and wine to the altar in a formal *Offertory Procession.*

The priest then offers the bread to the Father in preparation for the Eucharistic Sacrifice and then the wine (to which he has added a few drops of water to symbolize our union with Christ). He washes his hands, calling to mind the need for purity before offering the sacrifice.

The Prayer over the Gifts is followed by the *Preface,* a great hymn of praise and thanksgiving which commemorates Christ's giving thanks before the consecration of the bread and wine.

The *Preface* ends with the Holy, Holy, Holy... (Sanctus), a beautiful hymn of praise repeating the word "holy" three times to honor the Most Holy Trinity.

Next comes the essential part of the Mass, the *Eucharistic Prayer* or *Canon,* which has as its high point the *Consecration.** This most solemn moment is immediately preceded by prayers (which when listed, sound more lengthy than they are) for the Church, the Pope, the bishop of the diocese, all the living, all believers and all present. There is also a remembrance of the saints in Heaven, particularly the Apostles, the first popes and the martyrs. The celebrant then continues with the remaining Eucharistic Prayer.

The culmination of the Mass comes with the *Consecration.* At this time, the priest says the sacred words of Christ and then lifts the Host and the Chalice so that all present can see. The faithful adore their God.

This august act is followed by a prayer in remembrance of the dead, a plea for ourselves and for all sinners. Then this most solemn part of the Mass is brought to a close with the prayer: "Through him, with him, in him, in the unity of the Holy Spirit, all glory and honor is yours, almighty Father, forever and ever," to which the congregation responds, *"Amen."*

The *Lord's Prayer* follows. Then an offering of peace to one another (usually a handshake) and further prayers of love, humility and desire for the coming of Christ lead up to the *Communion*. The priest partakes of the Eucharist and offers it to the deacon; together they then offer it to the congregation. Following *Communion* the Sacred Liturgy begins to draw to a close with prayers and hymns of thanksgiving. The deacon dismisses the people, sending them forth to continue the celebration of the Eucharist through charity among all the people of God.

Today there is considerable emphasis on the Liturgy as a certain means of uniting with Christ. The Ecumenical Council, Vatican II, was much preoccupied with the subject, and authorized the use of the vernacular so that the people could participate more actively by reciting the prayers in their native tongue.

However, as has been said so often, the essence of the Mass still remains what it has always been: not the prayers that are said, but the offering or the sacrifice, and a person can unite with that without understanding all the prayers. Moreover, although the recommendation is to go to Mass whenever we can, we can unite with the Mass even if we cannot go. After all there are people behind the iron and bamboo curtains who can never get to Mass. There are mothers of small children and mothers of handicapped or subnormal children who cannot stir from home except on the rare occasions when they can make arrangements for someone to watch over their households. There are people on sickbeds in hospitals and asylums.

Is it not commonly admitted that God takes circumstances into consideration, and takes sincere desire for the act? In other words, if you or I truly cannot go to Mass and Communion on a special day or days, we can offer ourselves, our wills, and our hearts, spiritually in union with Christ's offering in the Mass. Also, we can ask that Christ come to us spiritually in Communion. Whenever we honestly cannot go to Him, will He not come to us, if we want Him? Many children in grade-school learn the prayer: "Since I cannot now receive You, dear Jesus, in Holy Communion, come spiritually into my soul, and make it Your own forever and ever."

Even when we go to Communion daily we can say this prayer at odd moments throughout the day. Surely, it can multiply graces in our souls and give us an awareness of our Guest, Who abides with us spiritually from birth to death provided we do not drive Him away.

Who can measure the grace of God? A spiritual Communion reverently made by a man in a slave-labor camp, or on some distant battlefield, could win more grace or a greater increase of love and awareness of God than another person's Mass and Communion in church.

Some extremists say that since the Eucharistic Liturgy is "official prayer," more sublime than other forms of divine worship, lesser devotions should be eliminated. But this is like saying that only food sustains life, therefore do away with eating and inject food directly into the bloodstream.

The Eucharistic Liturgy, high point of Christian experience, lasts only thirty or forty minutes. How can anyone in those few moments attain profound union with God without the aid of supplemental devotion? For many it is impossible. This is confirmed not only by experience but also by the messages of Fatima and Lourdes.

One theologian said he could not believe in Fatima, despite the miracles and the approval of the Church, because of the prophecy that entire nations will be annihilated if people do not pray the Rosary. But a colleague explained it this way:

The salvation of the world is Christ, actually present through the Eucharist. He is man's "Food of Life," and is All-sufficient. But so many men have strayed from any contact with Him that they starve to death, hopelessly. It is as though all the food they needed were on a table, but they lie helplessly on the floor, too weak to reach it. They need help not only of the intercession of a fellow human being close to God, but also of the first step toward Christ, that humiliating step of acknowledging weakness and therefore crying out for forgiveness and aid. Millions might read this book, for example, and even find it credible. But how many as a result could actually experience fulfillment of the wonderful promise of the Last Supper?

We hasten now to introduce the events of Fatima because they have been scientifically examined[11] and constitute perhaps the most important Eucharistic manifestation of our era.

[11] See *Meet the Witnesses,* AMI Press, 1961.

Ecumenical Council Vatican II restored some parts of the Eucharistic Liturgy to early Christian form, although the heart of the Secret has never changed.

CHAPTER TWELVE

POWER OF THE SECRET

The miracles of Christ, as we mentioned before, are the subject of most of the first century frescoes brightly adorning the tombs of those who died for Him.

But it is doubtful whether any of those first Christians, except those actually in Palestine with Our Lord, saw anything as dramatic and convincing as what happened in our own century at Fatima.

Paul Claudel described it as *"an explosion of the supernatural."*

Three children claimed to receive a message from Heaven in a country whose capital had been proclaimed "the atheist capital of the world." They predicted that *a miracle* would take place *at a certain time, in a certain place,* "so that all may believe."

Such a thing had never before happened in history.

And the first important vision which these children claimed was that of an angel* holding a Host over a chalice. Blood dripped from the Host into the chalice and the children were struck with awe and fear.

Leaving the Host and the chalice suspended in mid-air, the angel prostrated himself (in the Islamic manner of forehead to the ground) before the Holy Eucharist and three times repeated the prayer which begins: *"O Most Holy Trinity, Father, Son, and Holy Spirit, I adore Thee profoundly. I offer Thee the most precious Body, Blood, Soul and Divinity of Jesus Christ, present in all the tabernacles of the world, ... "*

Finally the angel arose, took the Host and the chalice and gave the children Communion[1] while saying: *"Take the Body and Blood of Jesus Christ, horribly insulted by ungrateful men. Make reparation for their crimes and console your God."*

Then the angel vanished.

Subsequently the Virgin* appeared to the children. She extended her hands from which rays of light streamed upon them and they felt "lost in God," and they found themselves praying: *"O most Holy Trinity, I adore You! My God, my God, I love You in the Most Blessed Sacrament!"*

Five other times the Virgin appeared to the children. She told them that men must change their ungodly ways of living or World War I would be followed by World War II and that even "further wars" and "annihilation of entire nations" would follow the provocation of international Communism. (This was in 1917 when the children in this remote Portuguese hamlet had never heard of Communism and Russia was not considered a threat to the world at large, by anybody, anywhere.) She ended by saying that the revelation was from God, and that a public miracle would occur on October 13th to prove it.

As far as we know, *this is the only occasion in history when the exact time and place of a public miracle was predicted "so that all may believe."*

That miracle, a phenomenon described by some one hundred thousand witnesses as something like the sun falling toward earth, was seen over a radius of thirty

[1]One child was communicated with the Host, the other two from the chalice. The nine-year old boy did not understand and when his ten-year old cousin explained, he said: "I knew that God had entered into me, but I did not know how."

This statuary group stands on the spot where the three children saw the angel.

square miles. All who saw it thought they were about to die. No natural explanation was found.[2]

When we ask what the miracle proves, what *"everyone may believe"* — we are left with the whole revelation of Fatima which began with an apparition of the Eucharist before which an archangel fell in adoration, an exclamation of adoration to God in the Eucharist, a message of reparation practiced through devotion to the Immaculate Heart,* and some remarkable prophecies: World War II, the spread of atheistic Communism through the entire world, further war, even annihilation of entire nations. Many of these prophecies made in 1917 came true, and the others appeared imminent before the world celebrated the Golden Jubilee of the apparitions in 1967 (as was also the case when Pope John Paul II went to Fatima on May 12-13, 1982 to publicly thank Our Lady of Fatima for saving his life in an assassination attempt). But in addition to the dire prophecies were two great promises (if the Message of Fatima is heeded):

"Russia will be converted, *and an era of peace will be granted to mankind.*"

It is remarkable that in 1967 His Holiness, Athenagoras I, Patriarch of the Orthodox,* the religion which is predominant in Russia, said: "I often see a beautiful hand holding the chalice of Our Lord over a nearby hill, and I hear secret voices that speak of love between humanity and peace among men." And on April 22, 1967, the forty-two-year-old daughter of Stalin arrived

---

[2] Some of the witnesses of the "miracle of the sun" are still living. The historic facts can be verified by anybody who is interested. The present writer interviewed hundreds of witnesses and wrote a book from the testimony given by scientists, journalists, photographers, priests, and even by persons who up to the time of the miracle were atheists. (*Meet the Witnesses,* AMI Press, 1961.)

These are actual photographs taken during the miracle which had been foretold at Fatima by the children.

The Miracle itself could not be photographed because of its brilliance.

Even for an eclipse of the sun, photographers use special equipment and "setup" in advance. Yet this was a phenomenon more brilliant than an eclipse. Photographs of the crowd seem as though taken at high noon. The light was visible thirty miles away, and appeared as a great red flash sixteen miles down in Leiria (where the angle of view was such that the climax of the miracle, the "falling," was not seen.)

The colors have been characterized as "monochromatic sectors" which appeared to revolve and to subsist without any known support. In other words, the colors were not prismatic, but individual rays of brilliant color.

Note especially the enlargements, right and below.

in the United States for "self-expression" denied to her so long in Russia. She said: "It was impossible to live without God..." and from that moment of her belief in Him "the main dogmas of Communism lost their significance for me." There were "no longer capitalists or communists... only people, the same everywhere in their hopes and ideals."

In a series of television programs which the present writer produced in the late 1950's and the early 1960's on the possibility of the conversion of Russia, he interviewed a former captain of Soviet Intelligence who testified that not only was personal belief in God becoming common in Russia but that it often reached points of moral heroism. George F. Kennan, former U.S. Ambassador to Russia who helped Stalin's daughter come to the U.S., appealed to Americans to welcome her and to recognize that "a new era is dawning." At Fatima, Portugal, the Blue Army of Our Lady, primarily through its five million U.S. members, built a Russian-style chapel near the place of the apparitions as a gesture of welcome to the great people of the East. Here every day the Eucharistic Liturgy is celebrated in the same manner as in Russia. The Blessed Sacrament is reserved in this "Russian" chapel and simultaneously in a Latin chapel beneath it. Perhaps history will judge the modern story of Christ with us, in the Blessed Sacrament, in a light similar to that of the first centuries from which came the great era of the Middle-Ages-faith that bore the fruit of modern progress. The triumph of East-West union, after more than sixty years of persecution and literally millions of martyrs (far more than in all the first centuries of Christianity) may well bring the greatest age of man, greater than most would even dare to dream. (See **Fatima,** pp. 276-79.)

Logically enough, we may ask why God seems to concentrate so much of His miraculous activity in certain places, such as Lourdes and Fatima. We cannot read His mind, but we can speculate. Perhaps this concentration is a means of calling men's attention and allowing proof to build up, as it were, under proper and objective observation. The secular press gives them little space, but it does not and cannot fail to report them when they gradually come to world attention. Miracles can be ignored only when they are isolated occurrences.

However, other Eucharistic miracles occur constantly all over the world. After all, it is the same Christ in the Eucharist whether He be in Lourdes or Alaska, in Fatima or Finland.

We need not believe in any one of them. On the face of it, some seem credible; others seem like pious fables which appeal, we think, only to simple folk. But on second thought, aren't all miracles a sort of baby-talk that God uses to reach us, His childish earthlings, we who strut about pretending to be so grownup, so independent, and so sophisticated and self-reliant?

There is a story told about Saint Louis IX of France. Once he was working in his study when a courtier burst in exclaiming: "Sire, come quickly! Come to the chapel! The Infant Jesus is appearing in the Host in the monstrance."

The saint did not move. "I could not believe more firmly in Christ's presence in the Eucharist if I were to see a miracle," he answered and went back to his writing.

But few are like Saint Louis.

One of the oldest and best verified miracles of the

Blessed Sacrament is that of Lanciano, Italy.

A doubting priest saw the appearance of bread in his hands turn into that of bleeding flesh. The appearance of wine in the chalice changed to that of five separate drops of blood. *And this Flesh and Blood has remained incorrupt since the eighth century.*

The most recent investigation, authorized by the Archbishop of Lanciano, Mons. Pacifico Perantoni, took place
in 1970. The results were remarkable. Not only did they
reveal that the Host and Blood were still incorrupt but that
the flesh of the Host is *heart tissue*. The report in *l'Osservatore Romano* of April 3, 1971, reveals:[3]

> The investigation began with an histological study into the
> "Flesh," and carried out microscopical, microchemical and
> chromatographic tests of the "Blood." Immunological tests were
> made in order to find out the species the same Blood and Flesh
> belonged to, and to determine the blood-groups of both the Flesh
> and the Blood. Moreover, in order to get a more certain and
> inconfutable scientific certitude, laboratory analyses and
> electrophoretic tests of the proteins were made to determine the
> calcium, chlorides, phosphorus, magnesium, potassium and
> sodium contained in the Blood.
>
> What were the results?
>
> 1) The blood of the Eucharistic Miracle is real blood and the
> Flesh real flesh; 2) the Flesh is composed of cardiac muscular
> tissue; 3) the Blood and the Flesh belong to the human species;
> 4) both bloodgroups of the Flesh and of the Blood are the same
> (so they came from the same person); 5) the proteins in the Blood
> have been found to be normally fractionated with the same
> percentage ratio as they are found in the serotherapeutic table of
> the fresh and normal human blood; 6) in the Blood there are also
> chloride, phosphorus, magnesium, potassium, sodium in a
> reduced amount, while calcium is in a larger quantity.

The report ends with a photographic documentation
and one of the scientists, a professor from Arezzo,
writes:

> "Supposing the heart had been drawn from a corpse, I think
> that only a hand with great experience in anatomic dissection
> would have been able to get a 'slice' of the heart of such a uniform

---

[3]This report is available in its entirety in English in *Eucharistic Miracle* by
Bruno Sammaciccia, published by Francis J. Kuba, C.P., 22 Fairview
Ave., Trumbull, Conn. 06611.

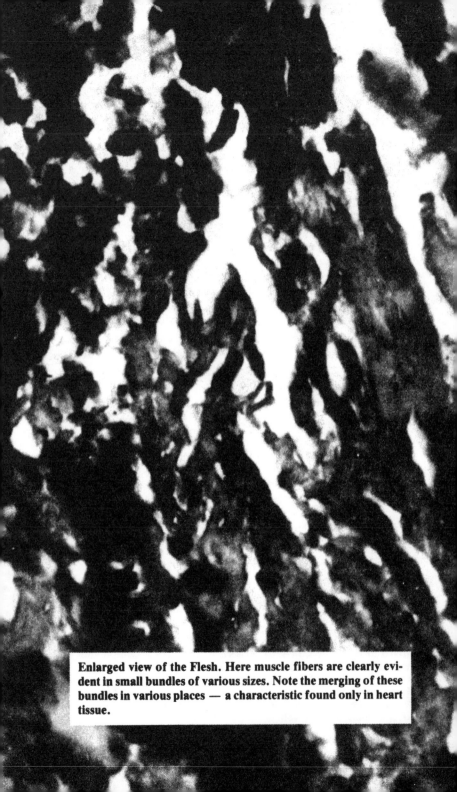

Enlarged view of the Flesh. Here muscle fibers are clearly evident in small bundles of various sizes. Note the merging of these bundles in various places — a characteristic found only in heart tissue.

size (as it is still seen in the Flesh), and tangentially to its surface, as it is evident in the prevalently longitudinal course of the fasciae of the muscle fibers, which is visible through the histological examinations. Moreover, the blood in a corpse becomes deliquescent and decomposes rapidly. In connection with this I must repeat that salt or other substances used even in the old times to embalm were not present in the histological sections. Lastly, though it is true that some proteins have been found in 4,000 or 5,000 year-old Egyptian mummies because of the preservation used, our case is quite different. A slice of myocardium, left in the natural state throughout several centuries and exposed to the biological and physical agents, was inevitably bound to decompose.''

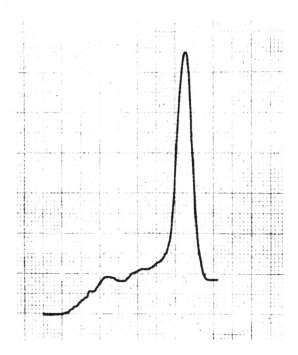

The (electrophoretic) tracing of the Blood is superimposable on that of a serum of fresh blood.

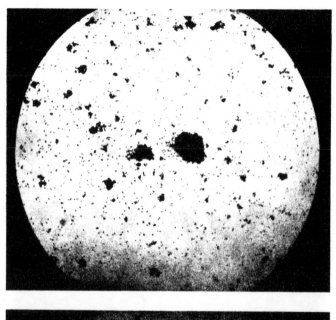

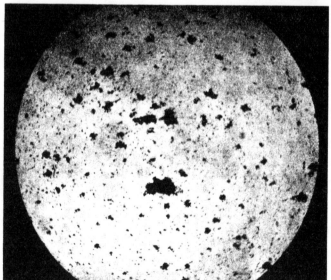

The presence of agglutination in two test tubes of the Blood indicates that it is type AB.

Scientific illustrations courtesy of Bruno Sammaciccia, *The Eucharistic Miracle of Lanciano, Italy*, (Trumbull, Conn.: Rev. F. J. Kuba, C.P.), 1976.

The writer has carefully examined this miracle at close hand and has seen the magnifications (four hundred times) of the muscle tissue. What is most surprising is the graph made from rehydrated blood serum from the Eucharistic miracle which shows each of the serum proteins to be present in the same percentages as in fresh human serum. And to think that this miracle has been perpetuated, minute after minute and hour after hour in our midst *for over eight hundred years!* It causes us to recall with ever greater wonder the words of the priest who showed us the incorrupt Host of Lanciano: *Living Bread!''*

There are many stories of miracles connected with some outrage against the Blessed Sacrament. To list just a few places where, and times when, such miracles were said to occur: Slavings, Moravia, 1120; Excelles, on French-Italian border, 1453; Poznan, Poland, 1599; Breslau, Germany, 1831; Orthez in the Upper Pyrenees in 1845, and many, many others.

A recent account of profanation of the Blessed Sacrament and Christ's dramatic manifestation was published in the mid-1960's in the Montreal weekly *Patrie.* The event took place in Bui Chu, China.

Most Eucharistic-minded persons (frequent communicants) tend to regret such miracles on the periphery of the major miracle of transubstantiation. They admit that in some instances miracles have been necessary because of blasphemy, lack of faith, or need of reparation. But they rarely express interest in hearing about them. And that seems to be pretty generally the official Church attitude.

The miracle of Bolsena-Orvieto is a notable exception because the Pope personally conducted the investigation almost "on the spot" and thereupon commissioned Saint Thomas Aquinas to write the Mass of the "Body of Christ" (Corpus Christi), for a new feast in the Church. The first time a Pope ever traveled in a helicopter was in August of 1964 when Pope Paul VI flew from the Vatican to Orvieto for the anniversary of the miracle. And even one of the famous "Seven Altars" of Saint Peter's Basilica in Rome commemorates the somewhat gory episode.

The story concerns a man known as Peter of Prague, a Bohemian priest of the thirteenth century who supposedly doubted the Real Presence. While celebrating Mass at St. Christiana's tomb in the lake town of Bolsena, Italy, he broke the Host after the Consecration and was stunned to see blood flowing from it and dripping onto the corporal (or the square of linen on which the Host and the chalice are placed during Mass) and onto the marble beneath.

Later the corporal was taken to the Cathedral of Orvieto, where to this day it is preserved.

Another strange story concerns a citizen of the United States, Frances Allen, daughter of Ethan Allen, soldier-patriot of the American Revolution. When she was twenty-one she persuaded her mother and stepfather to send her from her home in Vermont to Montreal where she could complete her education at the convent school of the Sisters of the Congregation of Notre Dame.

Once there she soon made herself *persona non grata*, for she took every occasion to mock the Eucharist. For the sake of peace and harmony among the students the Mother Superior decided to ask the girl to leave. One of the nuns, however, begged the Superior to give Frances another chance.

It was of no avail. So for a second time it was decided to send her home.

On the afternoon of her departure, she happened to be helping one of the nuns arrange some flowers for the chapel. On impulse the Sister turned to Frances and said: "Would you mind taking them in for me and putting them on the altar?" Then the Sister added, again on impulse: "Be sure to adore the Lord while you are there."

The girl reached the sanctuary gate just a few steps from the altar and suddenly found herself unable to move farther. Her legs seemed paralyzed.

A moment later she fell to her knees, babbling words of faith.

The following year she entered the cloister of Hotel Dieu in Montreal as a postulant, and later she went on to become the first nun from the thirteen original colonies.

Perhaps emotion rather than the direct intervention of God caused a seeming paralysis, but in view of the outcome, isn't it logical to suppose that God may well have had a hand in what happened?

This incident occurred back in the early 1800's.

There are similar happenings in our own day. Sr. Mary Claude of the Holy Cross[4] (who wrote of this herself for the present writer) had gone with another sister to visit a sick parishioner. By mistake they called at the wrong house. But the woman who greeted them at the door invited them in and began to ask questions about the faith. Finally, she asked if she could have formal instructions. In the weeks that followed she accepted the doctrine of Christianity eagerly, with one exception: She could not bring herself to believe in the Eucharist.

[4]Member of the Congregation of the Holy Cross, Montreal (1967).

The corporal from Bolsena, now reserved in the Cathedral of Orvieto. The red stains have somewhat faded with age and the corporal is opened to view only on rare occasions.

Pope Paul VI celebrates Mass in Orvieto Cathedral where the corporal from Bolsena is reserved. On August 8, 1976, His Holiness returned to Bolsena to speak by television to the 41st International Eucharistic Congress in Philadelphia. The Pope said that the miracle of Bolsena (with the bloodied corporal in Orvieto) still revives in the Church today an inner awareness of the Eucharist... "a Mystery great and inexhaustible..." (Osservatore Romano, n. 34, 438.)

The Sisters suggested that she attend Benediction of the Blessed Sacrament and they recommended: "When the Host is held up in the monstrance,* ask God to help you believe in the Real Presence."

The following week the Sisters visited their protege again and inquired how she had liked the ceremony of Benediction.*

"He was beautiful!" came the instant and glowing response.

Nonplussed, the Sisters began asking questions, and the neophyte explained that she had seen the Lord leave the monstrance to bless the people and then go back again when the priest returned to the altar. "I saw His wounded side through His pure white garment and the marks of the nails on His hands and feet," she added, and was surprised to know that her experience had been unusual.

Imagination? Possibly. But to the day of her death some years afterward the woman stuck to her story, and she refused to be satisfied with any picture of Christ that she saw. "He was much more beautiful than that," she insisted.

But this book is not meant to be a recital of the unusual or the quaint or the fantastic. Aside from the cures of Lourdes and Fatima, little scientific effort has been made to verify any of the so-called miracles, so we cannot speak of them with much assurance. However, every Christian knows that the most important Eucharistic miracles are not miracles at all in the sense that they can be outwardly perceived. In the Eucharist this morning Christ enabled a man to overcome his unruly passions; He strengthened a woman against the undertow of her malicious resentment; He calmed a storm of hatred and healed a soul in grief. Miracles of this type happen every day, everywhere, and they are the important miracles of the Eucharist.

Here we have Christ dwelling among us; and "power goes forth from Him." *What was a secret of early Christians becomes a secret of personal force, now, everywhere.*

That is perhaps the lasting and most exciting impression we get of the Eucharistic Christ, the effects of the "forces" that are His Body suspended in relation to those of bread: *Power.* One need only experience it for a moment, or see it as Doctor Carrel did, and the whole world changes. No longer are we alone. No longer does life seem meaningless. No longer do crosses weigh. No longer is there room for anything but surging, glorious hope!

CHAPTER THIRTEEN

THE SECRET
MADE PERSONAL

Nothing in the catacombs cries more eloquently from the past than an inscription written on the tomb of Tarcisius: "Carrying the sacraments of Christ, he chose rather to suffer death *than to betray the heavenly Body* to raging dogs."

That inscription and a boy's skeleton were all that remained to tell the modern world, when the archeologists found them, of a faith in the Eucharist and a heroism that makes fifteen hundred years of united faith in the Eucharist understandable.

We can easily recreate what happened.

In those early centuries, Christians had to assemble in stealth to celebrate the Eucharistic Liturgy. And between celebrations the Eucharist was carried to the sick, to the imprisoned, to those about to face martyrdom, to those in hiding. Tarcisius had the Blessed Sacrament on his person. He was probably taking it to someone in prison, or perhaps even caught in the act of approaching a Christian soon to be put to death. He was seized and beaten to reveal the Christian Secret.

What was it he was carrying? Why was he coming to see a Christian who looked forward to receiving him so eagerly that it was evident that he carried something important, something that gave him away?

Rather than permit that they should know, and therefore perhaps dishonor Our Lord in the Blessed Sacrament, Tarcisius let them beat him to death. And all they found was what looked like a piece of bread...

"This is the bread that comes down from heaven," Our Lord had taught them (Jn. 6:50). Tarcisius had never seen Christ. He had never seen the miracle of the loaves and fishes or the resurrection of Lazarus, or perhaps even the glorified Christ Himself. He died almost two hundred years after the Last Supper. So where did he get such faith out of a world of secrecy and persecution?

Again, we do not have to study back two thousand years. We have the evidence in persons all about us.

To write this one chapter, the writer scanned the biographies of more than a hundred canonized saints.* Each book, without exception, proved to have two chapters: One on the saint's "outstanding" or "heroic" or "unique" devotion to the Eucharist; the other on "special" devotion to the Blessed Virgin. And most of the chapters were written in such a way that the author seems to feel that these devotions were the *distinguishing* characteristics of the person of whom he was writing.

It is safe to say that there is not a single canonized saint* who has not shown special devotion to the Eucharist, even though some saints manifested the devotion more markedly and obviously than others. We can call them Eucharistic saints (though the term is a bit misleading), or saints who were very particularly devoted to Christ in the Eucharist.

To describe all the Eucharistic saints would take hundreds of pages and but a few examples will do.

St. John Chrysostom, Bishop of Constantinople, lived back in the fourth century when Christianity was first daring to break its three-and-a-half centuries of stark secrecy, a thousand years before the Reformation.

In his homily no. 50 on the subject of the Eucharist he writes: "Believe therefore that now the same supper is being celebrated as that one at which He presided. This one is no different from that one. And when you see the priest who stretches out (his hand) to you, do not think it is the priest doing it, but the hand of Christ Himself."

One of the saint's homilies of the Gospel of St. Matthew, no. 82, is dedicated to the Last Supper. To those who ask why Christ instituted the Blessed Sacrament during the feast of the Pasch, he replied that the events of the Old Testament, of which the Pasch was one, were only shadows and figures of that mystery. He established the reality where the image alone had been.

Then he argues that whereas Christ's word cannot err, our senses can and do easily err. Explaining about the bread and wine of the Eucharist, he writes that if we had not been created bodies, He would not use material things to transmit His graces. But "since the soul is united to the body, He gives you spiritual graces by means of sensible things."

In preparing for Communion, says the great Bishop, strive "to be purer than the rays of the sun," and "think what an honor has been given you, what a banquet you have on hand! That what the angels dread to look on, nor gaze at without fear for the splendor which It emits, such is the food with which we are nourished, with which we mingle ourselves, and for which we are made one body and one flesh with Christ."

As Jesus was born of the same substance as ourselves and entered into our nature, thus did He come to all of us, but He likewise comes to each of us separately and in particular. St. John puts it this way: "Jesus unites Himself to each one of the faithful, and He with Himself nourishes them and does not trust them to others. In this manner He proves that He has received your flesh."

Then leaping over the centuries we can choose a modern example: Saint John Neumann, Bishop of Philadelphia.

Loving his Eucharistic Lord and wishing to dramatize the Blessed Sacrament and to center spiritual life in his diocese around Him, he dreamed of bringing the Forty Hours Devotion[1] to the United States.

At first the idea was received coldly. People on all sides told him: "You can't do that! If you left the Blessed Sacrament exposed in churches for over forty long hours, don't you know what would happen? The ignorant and the impious would profane and dishonor It."

The idea might have died there except for what happened one night. The Bishop had been writing letters for hours and he grew so weary that he fell asleep at his desk. When he awoke an hour or so later his papers were a charred mass. Whether a puff of wind had blown a letter into the flames of a candle, or whether the candle had overturned, he could not tell. Only one letter remained intact, except for charred edges. Picking it up, he saw that it was the only letter he had written that evening about the Forty Hours Devotion.

[1]During Forty Hours Devotion the Blessed Sacrament is "exposed" or exhibited in the monstrance on the altar for forty consecutive hours (that being the approximate time that Christ lay in the tomb) while continuous adoration is maintained by relays of devout people. Usually the practice is taken up by one church in a diocese after another, so that the "exposition" is continuous if possible within a diocese.

At this discovery he dropped to his knees. It seemed to
him that a voice was telling him: "As this writing was
saved from the flames, so shall I preserve My Son, present in the Blessed Sacrament, from profanation and dishonor. Wait no longer. Carry out your plans."

The Bishop again eagerly took up his pen. Letter after
letter he wrote on through the night, ordering the
celebration of the Forty Hours Devotion in every church
of his Philadelphia Diocese. The custom spread and
today the devotion is practiced throughout the entire
United States.

Having almost at random chosen two Saint Johns who
are centuries apart, may we now turn to two Thomases?

The great thirteenth century philosopher and theologian,
Saint Thomas Aquinas, has sometimes been called the
Eucharistic Doctor, for he is known not only for his
monumental theological work on the Eucharist in
Summa Theologica, but also for incomparably beautiful
hymns to the Blessed Sacrament. It was he who was
chosen to write the Proper parts of the Mass and the
Office (or official prayers) for the feast of Corpus
Christi, the feast on which we honor the Body of the
Lord and celebrate, as on Holy Thursday,* the institution
of the Blessed Sacrament.

The learned doctor used to go to Christ in the Blessed
Sacrament whenever he had a special problem. On his
deathbed he made a profession of faith which should be
recorded whenever the Blessed Sacrament is discussed.
He who is bracketed with Aristotle and Plato as one of
the greatest philosophers of all time, said just before he
died: "If in this world there be any knowledge of this
mystery keener than that of Faith, I wish now to affirm
that I believe in the Real Presence of Jesus Christ in this

Sacrament, truly God and truly man, the Son of God, the Son of the Virgin Mary. This I believe and hold for true and certain.''

The second Thomas we chose is Saint Thomas More. When he was Chancellor of England some of his friends reproached him for going to Communion so often. With all his duties and responsibilities they thought that this piety took up too much of his time. He answered their objections with these words: ''Your reasons for wanting me to stay away from Holy Communion are exactly the ones which cause me to go so often. My distractions are great, but it is in Communion that I recollect myself. I have temptations many times a day; by daily Communion I get the strength to overcome them. I have much very important business to handle and I need light and wisdom; it is for this very reason that I go to Holy Communion every day to consult Jesus about them.''

Now, let us choose two men named Francis. We can begin with Saint Francis Assisi. Even when as a young man he was more interested in feats of chivalry than in spiritual matters, his devotion to Christ in the Blessed Sacrament led him to send expensive chalices to poor priests. Later, when he turned from worldliness, his Eucharistic devotion grew. Christ had spoken to Francis from a crucifix and said: ''Mend my Church,'' so the young gallant, with scarcely a backward glance at the old life, rushed off to restore the literally crumbling parish church of St. Damian. He begged enough oil for it to keep a light burning night and day before the Blessed Sacrament. Soon afterwards, God called Francis to found his Order of friars, which today we call the Franciscans.

As the leader of his little group of men, Francis wrote

letters giving advice and instructions.

Five of eight letters of Francis of Assisi which have come down to us treat of the Blessed Sacrament, either entirely or in part. In one of them he exhorts the clergy: "Keep churches clean, altars and everything belonging to the celebration of Mass and the administration of the Sacraments... how wretched are the chalices, corporals* or other linens where the Body and Blood of Our Lord Jesus Christ is sacrificed... Our Lord is loving enough to entrust Himself to our hands and we handle Him and receive Him on our lips day after day."

He taught his friars that whenever they saw a church they should bow low to salute the Presence inside, and whenever the Blessed Sacrament was being carried anywhere, he added: "Let all the people on bended knee render praise, honor and glory to the Lord God, living and true."

In yet another letter he said: "Let everything in man halt in awe, let all the world quake and let heaven exult when Christ the Son of the living God is there on the altar in the hands of the priest."

Then he writes: "In this world I see nothing bodily of the most high Son of God except His most holy Body and Blood," and he reminded his priests to preach the reception of the Sacrament. Meanwhile *he himself would never become a priest because he did not feel worthy of such a high state.*

Often he speaks of the reverence in which priests should be held, even bad ones. After all, he says, "their hands have touched the Lord." He deemed no dignity greater than that of the priesthood, "because of its sublime privilege of consecrating the Body and Blood of Christ."

To priests themselves he urged dedication and devotion because they are "chosen by the great King to bring to the nations of the earth what they themselves have learned and gathered, especially before the tabernacle."

His own devotion to the Real Presence was extraordinary and his first biographer, Thomas de Celano, writes: "Every fiber of the heart of Francis was aglow with love for the Sacrament of the Body of Christ."

One could go on and on about Francis of Assisi, but we turn again to another Francis, separated by centuries of time: Saint Francis de Sales. This gentle, courteous French bishop is described as "one of the finest bishops and most attractive men that Christianity has ever produced."[2]

In his book *Introduction to a Devout Life* he writes: "When you have received It (the Host) excite your heart to come and render homage to this King of salvation; speak to Him of your most intimate affairs; contemplate Him within you where He has come for your happiness; finally give Him the best welcome possible and behave in such a manner that by all your acts it may be known that God is with you."

Of frequent Communion he said: "If worldly folk ask you why you communicate so often, say it is in order to learn to love God, to purge yourself of your imperfections, to free yourself from your miseries, to console yourself in your afflictions, to support yourself in your weaknesses. Say that there are two kinds of people who should communicate often: the perfect, because being so well-disposed, they would do great wrong if they did not approach the Source and Fountain of Perfection, and

[2]Donald Attwater, *A Dictionary of Saints,* (New York: P. J. Kennedy & Sons), 1958.

the imperfect with the end of being reasonably able to aspire to perfection; the strong, that they may not become weak, and the weak to become strong; the sick that they will be cured, and the healthy that they may not fall sick; and that you, imperfect, weak and sick, need to communicate often with Him Who is your perfection, your strength and your doctor... *Say that you receive the Holy Sacrament in order to learn how to receive it,* for one never does well that in which one has not had practice.''

However, does such stress on the Eucharist in the lives of holy persons imply that the Eucharist is the one means of grace and the only mark of Christian heroes? No, because if this were true the only Christian saints would be those who have access to the Eucharist. And Christ did not promise to say: ''Possess the kingdom, for you have received Communion often.'' Rather He will say ''Possess the kingdom... for I was hungry and you gave me to eat; I was thirsty, and you gave me to drink...''

But during twenty centuries of Christian history we find greatest devotion to the Eucharist in those who did feed the hungry heroically, those who visited the imprisoned, those who gave their own lives to save others, those who truly loved their fellow men as Christ taught. And this is so universally true, of those Christ-like persons who had access to the Blessed Sacrament, that almost any of them might be singled out for *exceptional* love of Christ in the Sacrament of His Love.

Pope Leo XIII remarked of Saint Paschal Baylon: ''Of all the saints who have been known for their extraordinary devotion to the Most Blessed Sacrament, Saint Paschal occupies first place.'' In his Apostolic Letter *Providentissimus Deus,* Leo declared Saint Paschal the patron of Eucharistic Congresses* and associations. But what about Saint Peter Julian Eymard, Saint John Eudes, etc.? It almost seems that Pope Leo had chosen at random.

We have not yet mentioned women who were outstanding Christians.

One of the most famous was Catherine of Siena. Known principally for her ambassadorial missions and her part in persuading the Pope to return from Avignon to Rome, she deserves rather to be known for her exceptional devotion to the Eucharist. It was closeness to Christ in the Eucharist which made all her feats possible.

Then again leaping the centuries we come to Elizabeth Bayley Seton of the United States who, as a young Episcopalian widow visiting Italy attended Mass with Italian friends and heard an Englishman mutter at the Elevation of the Host: "This is what they call their Real Presence." She was deeply disturbed by the remark and later wrote in her diary of the "unfeeling interruption."

Shortly afterward she wrote her sister-in-law: "How happy we would be if we believed what these dear souls believe, that they possess God in the Sacrament and that He remains in their churches and is carried to them when they are sick! Oh, my! When they carry the Blessed Sacrament under my windows, while I feel the loneliness and sadness of my case, I cannot stop my tears at the thought: My God, how happy I would be, even so far away from all so dear, if I could find You in the Church as they do... The other day, in a moment of excessive distress, I fell on my knees without thinking when the Blessed Sacrament passed by and cried in an agony to God to bless me if He was there, that my whole soul desired only Him."

When she returned to New York she attended her own church as usual, but chose a side pew which faced the Catholic church opposite. She records that she constantly found herself speaking to the Blessed Sacrament there.

Later, after her subsequent conversion, she burned with faith at no time more strongly than when she was about to receive Communion.

She wrote: "God is everywhere, in the very air I breathe, yes everywhere, but in His Sacrament of the Altar He is as present actually and really as my soul within my body; in His Sacrifice daily offered as really as once offered on the Cross."

Mrs. Seton later founded the beginnings of the Catholic elementary school system in the United States, and also a community of sisters, later united with the Daughters of Charity founded by Saint Vincent de Paul in France.

On New Year's Day, 1821, Mother Seton was near death. To receive Communion in those days, one had to abstain from food and drink from midnight, and when a nurse requested the dying saint to take a beverage, she said: "Never mind the drink. One Communion more and then eternity." Thus in the face of death she reminded us that only on this earth is Eucharistic union with Christ possible... *an honor even the angels cannot enjoy.*

It is a union not to be compared to the beatific vision, but it has the merit of being voluntary. To see God is to love Him, but the average person who receives the Eucharist sees nothing but the appearances of bread and wine.

Women who have become Eucharistic saints are like the stars, innumerable. Some of them lived miraculously on no other food but the Eucharist. Saint Catherine of Siena whom we just mentioned was one who lived for months on the Eucharist alone. Saint Angela of Foligno was another, and in her case this miraculous state lasted twelve years. In our own day, Alexandrina Maria da Costa, who died in 1955, lived for 167 months with the Eucharist as her sole food.[3]

Who can doubt the promise made nearly two thousand years ago: "Behold, I am with you all days, even to the end of the world"? Aren't those who cannot believe prompted to cry out like Saint Elizabeth Ann Seton[4]: "Jesus, bless me if You are really there, for my whole soul desires only You!"?

In our introductory remarks to this book, we noted that because it is for everyone, it cannot satisfy everyone: "It will seem too skimpy for the professional." And perhaps this is nowhere more evident than in the chapter on proofs (or miracles) and in this chapter. Well over a hundred miracles were prepared. Only three were used. In the end, the truth of one miracle should be as strong as that of a hundred, and the example of one saint should be as compelling as those of a hundred.

But there is one miracle and one final example of a completely Eucharistic life which we feel compelled to include.

[3]Alexandrina was hospitalized and closely watched day and night for forty days by doctors and nurses. Her subsistence solely on the Eucharist was certified as scientifically inexplicable. Her mission paralleled that of the apparitions of Fatima. She died October 13, 1955. Her last words: *Do not sin. The pleasures of this life are worth nothing. This sums up everything. Pray the Rosary every day.* " The Cause of her Beatification and Canonization are now in Rome (1983).

[4]Saint Elizabeth Ann Seton was canonized September 14, 1975 in St. Peter's Square by Pope Paul VI. She is the first native born U.S. citizen to be raised to the glory of the altar.

High up in the mountains just to the north of Beirut, Lebanon, is the body of a priest which exudes what seems to be a mixture of blood and water. When his tomb is opened each year, the body actually is floating in the liquid which in twelve months has accrued to a depth of about three inches. The body itself, as described in an official doctor's report witnessed by this writer, is as though it had been dead only a few days. Miracles performed at the tomb are so startling and so numerous that they remind one of the miracles of Lourdes.

We ourselves visited there in the spring of 1967 to examine the evidence and talk with witnesses. It was our conclusion, after journeys around the world and more than fifty trips to Europe, that this was perhaps the greatest single phenomenon of our time.

One of the unusual aspects of this phenomenon is the very fact that this priest, on a mountain almost 5,000 feet straight up from the sea, was never heard of at all in the outside world during his life. He was a Maronite monk whose life was his daily Mass. Near the monastery was a hermitage where the monks could go for several days of quiet retreat. It had no heat, very small cells, and a tiny chapel. This priest asked frequently to spend days at the hermitage and finally obtained permission to remain there constantly for twenty-three years. Other priests took turns sharing the hermitage with him. They never recorded anything very extraordinary except that he chose to say his Mass about eleven o'clock in the morning so that he could have all the morning to prepare for the Mass, and then have the rest of the day for thanksgiving. And at the elevation of the Host, since He was of the Oriental rite, he had permission to add the words: "O most Holy Trinity, receive Thy Divine Son for the conversion of sinners!''

It was while he held the Host elevated, his heart speaking this prayer, that he collapsed at the altar in 1898. A priest assisting at the Mass had to pry the Blessed Sacrament from the saintly monk's clenched fingers. Eight days later, after suffering which seemed to be a perpetuation of that moment of Calvary, he died on the bare floor in a room behind the chapel.

Like all the other monks, he was buried in the general cemetery. It was to be expected that he would soon be forgotten. But a light was seen around the tomb. Finally, in 1950, the monks asked permission to have the body exhumed.

During the subsequent years the body has been exhumed and buried several times until finally a part of the old monastery was set aside where the tomb is now above ground. Previously, although the body remained absolutely incorrupt and constantly exuded liquid, the very coffins themselves disintegrated. Even the bottom of an exterior zinc coffin split beneath the feet of the body. Attestations of the various doctors which were placed in the tomb after each examination remained intact until the exhumation of 1976. The very paper, which normally would have yellowed, remained fresh even though iron boxes in which these attestations were placed disintegrated.

The monastery began to keep records of miracles performed through the intercession of this priest from 1950 onward. Within two years they recorded *over twelve hundred.*

Obviously God had a special reason for performing miracles to call the attention of the world to this obscure priest of the mountain whose whole life centered in and around the Eucharistic Liturgy.

Pope Paul VI declared him Blessed on May 12, 1965, prior to the final session of the Ecumenical Council. His body had been exhumed and found incorrupt for the first time only fifteen years before. In 1977, Pope Paul VI canonized this priest of the Eucharist. He is now Saint Sharbel Makhlouf.*

The miracle of Saint Sharbel reminds the world of the center of this man's entire life: the Eucharist. It is noteworthy that he stands at the bridge of the world between the East and the West, himself of an Eastern rite and Semitic race, in that part of Asia where the East and West truly meet. The actual prayer which Father Sharbel recited at the time of the elevation probably was longer than given above but it is as Father Ciade quoted: "The essence of Saint Sharbel's thought... the offering of the Eucharist to the Trinity for sinners."

CHAPTER FOURTEEN

MOTHER OF THE SECRET

As we draw near the end of this very much condensed version of the most dramatic and repercussive belief in history, the writer dares to intrude a personal reaction as a prelude to what must now follow.

Many amazing things came to light during the seven years of this book's preparation, but to the writer the most amazing of all was the frequency of a symbol around the tomb of Saint Peter that was rarely mentioned and is little known. The greatest expert on the *graffiti* around Peter's tomb says that this one frequently repeated symbol was usually found in conjunction with the symbols of Christ and the Eucharist.

It was the symbol of the Virgin Mary.

And this is surprising because there is hardly any mention of her in the Gospel. True, she had remained behind after the Ascension and was perhaps the center of the new Church on the stunning day of Pentecost. And she must have meant a great deal to the early Christians because of her intimacy with Christ and because He performed His first miracle (the one which prefigured the Eucharist) at her request: It was the transformation of water into wine at the marriage at Cana. And He performed that first miracle even though He said that His time had not yet come.

But it must be evident that if we could speak of "Eucharistic Saints," as we did in the last chapter, beginning with the boy-martyr, Tarcisius, then the Blessed

175

Virgin must be explained as the Eucharistic Saint *par excellence.*

This attitude of the early Christians is borne out by the inscription on the tomb of Abercius found in Hieropolis in Asia Minor: "Faith everywhere led me forward and everywhere provided as my food a fish of exceeding great size and perfection which a Holy Virgin drew with her hands from a fountain and ever gives this to its friends to eat, wine of great virtue, mingled with bread."

From the whole inscription it is certain that the fish is used acrostically and means "Jesus Christ, Son of God, Savior." The fountain is the Church. And of the conclusion there can be no doubt: the Holy Virgin gives the Eucharist.

Even today few Christians would place this much emphasis on the Blessed Virgin in relation to the world's greatest secret.

Apparently something, over the centuries, has been lost. . . . Something that was contained almost entirely and exclusively in tradition. (See pp. 66-68.)

At first glance she may not seem a Eucharistic saint at all. Her role in God's plan is closely bound up with other mysteries of Faith, notably the Incarnation. Yet she is *the* Eucharistic saint above all others for one big reason: she gave the Lord a body. It was she who gave Him flesh and blood, the very same flesh and blood which comes to us in the Sacrament. She can truly be called "the Mother of the Eucharist."

Since the embryo she conceived was of the Holy Spirit, she, as no other mother of the human race, could say as she held her Infant in her arms: *"This is my body."*

Saint Peter Julian Eymard, through whose intercession have occurred miracles as great as any recorded in previous pages, called her *Our Lady of the Most Blessed Sacrament.** And Saint Pius X, "the Pope of daily Communion," called this "the most theological of all Mary's titles after that of the Mother of God."

Saint Peter Julian's Congregation received the privilege of celebrating a feast on May 13th in honor of Our Lady of the Most Blessed Sacrament. Subsequently, Our Lady appeared at Fatima as though to verify the title. Rays of light streamed from her hands upon the three children who saw her, and illumined by God's grace, they exclaimed: "O Most Holy Trinity, I adore Thee! My God, my God, I love Thee in the Most Blessed Sacrament!"

Later the children said that as the light from Mary's hands engulfed them they felt "lost in God" and they felt impelled to give the Eucharistic prayer of praise mentioned above.

The authenticity of the Fatima vision, as we mentioned previously, was confirmed by a public miracle performed at a predicted time and place and witnessed by some 100,000 persons *"so that all may believe."*

May 13th, Feast of Our Lady of the Blessed Sacrament, is now also the Feast of Our Lady of the Rosary of Fatima, celebrated in Fatima. In 1967, Pope Paul VI flew to Fatima on this day and prayed in the company of hundreds of thousands for world peace. And in 1982 Pope John Paul II did the same.

It would seem that the Popes were anxious to fulfill within their own century the great and consoling prophecy of St. John Bosco* that following an Ecumenical Council great storms would arise, but when the Sovereign Pontiff succeeded in anchoring the barque of Peter to the twin columns of devotion to the Blessed Sacrament and to the Blessed Virgin, the storms would subside and the great era of unity and peace would follow.

By 1967 Pope Paul VI had made five historic journeys all related directly to devotion to the Eucharist, to the Blessed Virgin, and to Unity and Peace. He was the first Pope to ride in a helicopter when he flew to Orvieto for the Centennial of the Miracle of the Bleeding Host. He was the first Pope after Peter to go to the Holy Land and beyond into India to participate in a Eucharistic Congress.* His major encyclical on the Eucharist is appended to this book, and on the occasion of his pilgrimage to Fatima on May 13, 1967, he issued a major encyclical on the true meaning of the devotion to the Blessed Virgin whom he had proclaimed during the Ecumenical Council to be "Mother of the Church."

Pope John Paul II, closing his address on the Eucharist at a seminary in the Archdiocese of Milan on May 21, 1983, prayed: "May the Virgin Mother, who through the action of the Spirit formed the physical body of the Saviour and, as Mother of the Church, accompanied the establishment and development of the Mystical Body, help all priests and seminarians to learn deeply the [Eucharistic] secret of the life of the Son who became our brother.

"This is the reason for faith and for hope for the near future of the Church and of the world."[1]

To understand Mary's role better, a diagram might help. Admittedly, it is only a slight help for it is only a remote analogy. After all, we cannot draw pictures of God.

First God existed alone. We draw Him as a triangle.

[1]L'Osservatore Romano, 20 June 1983, p. 4.

Then outside of Himself He created man "in his own image," giving him free will and allowing His light to flow freely to him. We represent man attached to the triangle, full of divine light.

Man, wanting to be equal to God, decided to disobey Him. This sin of futile and prideful defiance must have been the greatest evil of all time, because man in his pristine state of enlightenment was able to see the disruptive horror of the evil more clearly than any man has since been able to do. Also he was closer to God than perhaps any saint (with the exception of Mary) has ever become since, and yet he chose to separate himself from God. So now we draw him separate from God, separate from his source of light. He was in lonely darkness.

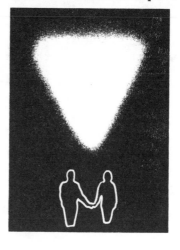

Foreseeing her extraordinary fidelity, God then preserved one member of the human race from the black shadow of the first sin by the merit of the redemption to follow. This preservation and this privilege we call the Immaculate Conception of Mary.* We draw her attached to the triangle, full of light and giving forth light.

One of the human race (Virgin Mary) is preserved free from sin in anticiption of Redemption.

Hail Mary, full of grace, the Lord is with thee (Lk. 1:28)

Through this immaculate person faithful to God where Eve had been faithless, the second Person of the Blessed Trinity was united to human nature. He came on earth and spent thirty-three years enlightening man — "The light shines in the darkness," (Jn. 1:5) — and then instituted the Blessed Eucharist to restore more light to man. So now we draw man once again united to God, but inside a new triangle, because God has become man.

Though man never did, and never will, recover his first shining clarity of intellect, and though the propensity to sin and concupiscence remains as the result of original sin, God now gives the poor myopic creature greater light and grace than under the Old Law — and He gives it in a special way in the Eucharist. *Instituting the Eucharist, Christ prayed that all might be one as He and the Father are one.*

Mary's role, as we see, began before Christ was born, and we must love her because by bearing Christ, she gave

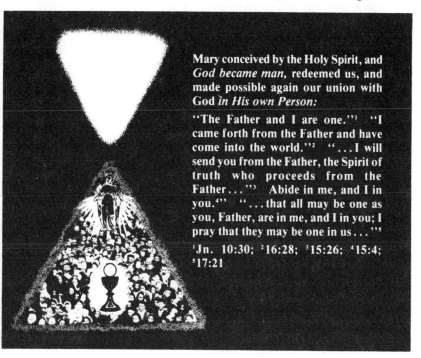

Mary conceived by the Holy Spirit, and *God became man,* redeemed us, and made possible again our union with God *in His own Person:*

"The Father and I are one."[1] "I came forth from the Father and have come into the world."[2] "...I will send you from the Father, the Spirit of truth who proceeds from the Father..."[3] Abide in me, and I in you.[4]" "...that all may be one as you, Father, are in me, and I in you; I pray that they may be one in us..."[5]

[1]Jn. 10:30; [2]16:28; [3]15:26; [4]15:4; [5]17:21

back to humanity the hope of salvation that the first mother lost for us. She is really our mother, *the mother of our supernatural life.*

Mary's role also continued through Calvary, and it continued afterward. Indeed, we should use the present tense, for it continues in the Eucharist.

We see that Christ loved her on Calvary and provided for her before He died by placing her in the care of St. John. We love her then, because He did.

Moreover, we love her because He gave her to us through John: "Son, behold your Mother."

Surely also we love her because everything that she did for human souls, she did with tremendous generosity. With wholehearted abandon she placed her life and her very being quite simply in God's hands to use as a tool or an instrument as suited His purposes. Whatever He wanted, she wanted with every fiber of mind and heart.

What does God want? What does God always will? St. Paul tells us succinctly: "This is the will of God, your sanctification."

Our Lord Himself emphasized this one day when someone interrupted Him with the announcement that His mother was outside. His love for her was well known. He had remained alone with her until He was thirty years of age, and He performed His first miracle, before His time, at her mere suggestion. Now He profited by this interrupton to show that He loved her not just because she was His mother, but *because she fulfilled God's will.*

"And who is my mother and who are my brothers?" He asked. "Those who do the will of my Father in heaven."

So Mary by all that she did brought Christ to the world and to souls. Today *she is still bringing Christ to the world and to souls, and souls to Christ, especially Christ in the Eucharist.* And this is demonstrable.

We can go to any one of her shrines throughout the world — to Pompeii, Fatima, Lourdes, Pontmain, to Guadalupe near Mexico City, and so on and on. In any of these places where she has appeared and a shrine has been established in her honor, *we find major activity centered on the same reality: the Mass and the Eucharist.*

So obviously Mary continues to lead man to one Person and to one place: to Christ in the tabernacle.

Strange? Not at all. We have seen that she herself was the first tabernacle. She was the first to carry the body of Christ (though it was not then called the Eucharist) on an errand of mercy when she went to her cousin, Elizabeth. As soon as she entered the house, Elizabeth cried out: "And how is it that the mother of my Lord should come to me?"

Saint Alphonsus de Liguori asks: "Why does Elizabeth not say, 'Why is it that the Incarnate God comes to me?' Why does she say, 'How is it that the *mother*... comes to me'?"

Alphonsus answers his own question by saying that Elizabeth knew that in welcoming the mother she was welcoming the Son; and the miracle of her own unborn child's presanctification* proved it.

If doubts about the Eucharist sometimes plague our minds, we can think of the tabernacle of the young mother of Nazareth. Is it any more remarkable that Jesus should be in a tabernacle than that He was in an embryonic state in Mary's womb? Is it any more remarkable that a box-like structure should contain Him than should a microscopic egg?

Just above we spoke of Mary's shrines and her role as guide-to-Christ in these places.

Today this is something that a person need not merely read about, or argue about or wonder about. Today anybody can see for himself. How far away are Lourdes and Fatima? Thanks to modern transportation facilities, these places are only hours away, and for some people reading these lines, perhaps less than an hour away, perhaps "minutes."

All of these places are filled with crowds who begin to pray at the spot where the Virgin supposedly appeared, but who end up before the Eucharist. We repeat that the acts of worship provided at all these so-called "Marian" shrines are the Eucharistic sacrifice or the Mass, and the Benediction of the Blessed Sacrament.

Among the crowds are invalids who arrive clamoring: "Lord, that I may walk! Lord, that I may see!" But (despite many miracles) comparatively few of these invalids receive physical help. Instead, they receive spiritual help. Suddenly, they are awakened as though from a drugged sleep. Their spirit soars. They know a new calm, and a joy, and a peace beyond understanding. Their lives are renewed. They feel like different people.

How? Why?

Even the casual observer can see that they have received an increase of faith and love and an indefinable glow which one can only call the light of the Eucharist.

Yes, that is what a visitor to a Marian shrine sees in others and experiences himself: light.

It is not the kind of light that we turn on when we flip a switch, but the kind of light which must have shone from the face of Moses when he descended from the mountain after talking with the Lord; Scripture says that his face appeared horned with rays of light. Or is it the kind of light which artists see aureating the face of a holy

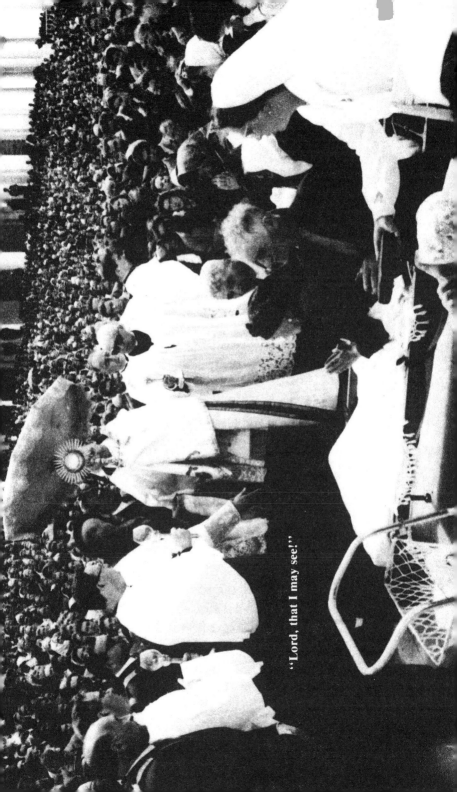

"Lord, that I may see!"

person and which they portray on their canvases as halos? A person who has never seen such light radiating from another's face has missed one of life's most memorable experiences.

"Oh, if only the sinner in the darkest, blackest night only knew enough to call on Mary!" exclaimed Saint Alphonsus. "He would at once find light."

This eminent churchman whose books have helped many a struggling Christian, avers that the whole world would change quickly enough if enough people would turn to Mary, our prime intercessor with Christ.

Other saints also recognize this role of Mary's. Before Communion St. Therese often pictured herself as a little girl with a soiled face and grimy clothes who ran to her mother asking to be made ready to meet the king.

Of course we too can always go to Mary and ask her to prepare us for Christ. We can do this even if we cannot visit her shrines. After all, few Christians, percentagewise, ever get to shrines. True, space is shrinking but that fact does not provide dollars for travel.

Fortunately, there are many ways of reaching Mary, and through her, her Son. Saint Louis de Montfort, author of *True Devotion to Mary,* tells us that the best way to adore Christ in the Blessed Sacrament is to place our hearts spiritually in the Immaculate Heart of Mary. In essence, this French saint says that the only *true devotion* to Mary is the one *which relates to Christ* and relates us through her to Him. He advocated devotion to Mary as a sure, easy, safe way to reach union with Christ. Any devotion to Mary for its own sake he labels "false."

Pope Paul VI made this thought the central message of his encyclical *Signum Magnum,* issued on May 13,

Saint Therese of Lisieux, whose autobiography thrilled over two million readers and whose spiritual feats caused Pius XI to call her the star of the Twentieth Century, said that before each Communion she ran to her Mother Mary like a child with soiled and dirty clothes so that she could be quickly made clean and beautiful for the visit of the King of Kings.

1967, when His Holiness went in pilgrimage to Fatima.

A wise and imaginative man who had the same notion expressed it this way: "Have you ever tried to drink water without a glass, or without putting it in a container? It is just as awkward and difficult to try to drink from the fountain of life without using Mary as a vessel." And that this was understood by the early Christians is confirmed by the tablet of Abercius.

Perhaps some of us are inhibited by the feeling that if we pray to Mary we may be taking some honor from God. But when we use the glass as a drinking vessel so that we won't spill any of the water, do we offend the water?

As we go to Communion we can ask Mary to lend us her Immaculate Heart in which to receive her Son; we can ask her to adore Him in us and for us and in union with us. Surely Christ, Who comes to us in the Eucharist, will be pleased to find not just sinful, unworthy creatures like ourselves, but at least our awareness and our love for His mother in our hearts.

At first to think of me and Mary and Christ simultaneously seems complicated, like learning to swim. To learn to swim properly we must learn separately how to breathe, how to move the arms and how to move the legs. When we first try to swim we may wonder if we are *ever* going to learn to coordinate the separate functions. Then suddenly the day comes when we roll for breath automatically, arms and legs fall into rhythm, and we are able to enjoy the sheer freedom of motion as we speed almost effortlessly through the water. We have conquered a new element.

So when we first start to pray as St. Louis de Montfort teaches us, and as we are instructed to do at Fatima, we may expect to feel slightly awkward.

When some persons first try to swim they may almost drown and be afraid to try again. Others may waste much time envying the swimmers who have mastered the technique but may never really try themselves. But in learning to go to Jesus through Mary we have a constant teacher: Christ. He gave us Mary. He set the example by obeying her Himself for thirty years. He performed His first miracle at her request. He gave her to the whole human race through John on Calvary.

Have we forgotten these truths?

The early Christians had them ever in mind. As we see in recent archeological excavations in the Mediterranean area, the early Christians frequently engraved in the stone walls of their subterranean havens the M along with the X and the P. The man who wanted to leave a memento of his faith spoke not only of the fish, but of the fish "which a holy Virgin drew with her hands from the fountain and ever gave its friends to eat, wine of great virtue, mingled with bread."

Is it any surprise that many who rejected Mary's intercession after the sixteenth century, ended up also by rejecting Christ in the Eucharist?

CHAPTER FIFTEEN

REPARATION

Perhaps one reason we have radically condensed the material in this book is because we wanted to speed to this moment when we are about to recall a little-remembered but most touching fact about the Last Supper during which Christ gave Himself to the world. It was illustrated, during a pilgrimage to Jerusalem, in a most graphic way.

A group of pilgrims had climbed Mt. Zion to visit the Cenacle in Jerusalem.

The room was very plain. The Jews, with more tolerance than we Christians might show if the holiest place of another religion were over the holiest place of our own, kept the room in repair and open to pilgrims. But the floor was covered with dust.

The priest who headed the group of twenty-one Christians asked them to gather in a circle in the approximate area where Christ washed the Apostles' feet, celebrated the Passover and instituted the Eucharist.

"The floor is too dirty for all of us to recline as the apostles did," he said, "but would one of you like to volunteer?"

Then the priest proceeded to recline in the dust himself, and a volunteer, following that lead, did likewise.

"That's right" Father said to his floor companion. "If Christ were in the center of the table you, at His side, would naturally recline just as you have done."

Then addressing the group, the priest went on: "Remember reading in the Gospels about the beloved disciple who reclined at table next to the Master? At one point in the meal he actually rested his head on the Lord's breast. Now as we two men lie here, our heads almost touch. If I slightly shift my position, as I would naturally do in the course of a long meal, it would be easy for the man next to me to rest his head on my chest."

Here he drew the volunteer's head into position to demonstrate.

"That was the first act of devotion to the Sacred Heart of Jesus," he declared.

Suddenly in that room of sacred memories the past sprang to life and became for the moment the pulsing present. The wonder of Christ's Sacred Heart beating with love for man beneath John's head became something that everybody there could almost feel and hear.

How near, how approachable, how lovable Christ is!

John acknowledged Christ as the Master, yet this apostle had dared to inch over and rest his head familiarly upon the Master's heart! John had evidence that Christ was the Miracle-Worker. John had been on Mt. Tabor when Christ, transfigured with dazzling light, had spoken with the prophets Moses and Elijah. John had heard the awesome voice from heaven saying, "This is my beloved Son." Indeed, John had heard Christ say, and had believed the words: "I and the Father are one." Yet this apostle dared such intimacy!

Yes, Christ was lovable and approachable. Every person in that room, gazing at the two men on the floor, was convinced.

But there we were after only a moment, slipping back

The room of the Last Supper on Mount Zion in Jerusalem as it is today. Here Christ instituted the Eucharist.

into the past tense!

Why are we mortals so prone to think of Christ as someone who lived in the long ago only? Why can't we always sustain our awareness of how approachable Christ *is?*

The *words* He used centuries ago are *for now* as well as for then and for every bit of time. *The things He did* centuries ago are for now as well as for then and for every bit of time. The life He lived centuries ago *He actually lives* in His eternal present at every moment in every tabernacle in the world. Today each of us, by the reception of Communion, *can in effect step into the place of the beloved apostle.* Each of us can rest his head on the Sacred Heart.

Is it any wonder then that in our own time we should be so forcefully reminded of the Eucharist as we were in the miracle at Fatima, and previously in the appearance of Christ — coming forth from the monstrance — to Saint Margaret Mary Alacoque* in a little chapel in France?

Is it any wonder, when so many millions of persons in the world today have refused His loving invitation to come to Him in the Eucharist that He appears out of the monstrance to complain?

"Behold the heart that has so loved men," He told the saint. "In return: ... ingratitude ... contempt in the Sacrament of Love."

Since saints crop up everywhere in these pages like dandelions in the spring, some readers may well ask how people who are not saints but who are at least struggling to keep a foothold on the straight and narrow should express devotion to the Eucharist. Aside from receiving Communion frequently, which is paramount, is there any special pious practice that they can cultivate?

When a certain man asked himself that question one day, it seemed to him that instantly he had a clear answer in the Sacred Heart Devotion,* a devotion of reparation to Christ for the indifference of so many Christians.

At the time, the man was in the little chapel in Paray-le-Monial, France, where three hundred years ago Christ appeared from the Eucharist to speak to the Visitation nun, Sister Margaret Mary. He told her of the love of His Heart for men and of their indifference to Him, and He asked for comfort and for reparation.

As this man was conjuring up the scene in his imagination, an old priest entered the sanctuary and held up the monstrance with the Host to give Benediction of the Blessed Sacrament to those in the chapel. Then, about to replace the Host in the tabernacle, he turned to the small knot of worshippers in the pews and, with tears in his eyes, said: "Why, oh, why would Our Lord have to appear to ask us to make reparation to Him?"

Why indeed!

The Sacred Heart devotion and devotion to the Eucharist are logically intertwined. No wonder that little chapel in Paray-le-Monial, where *formal* devotion to the Sacred Heart began, has become a center of Eucharistic devotion.

It seems appropriate that here in this same chapel was given the inspiration for two of the most dramatic Eucharistic practices of our day: To Emilie Tamisier, a humble laywoman, came the idea of Eucharistic Congresses;* to Father Mateo came the idea of the "Enthronement of the Sacred Heart"[1] in the home, and a

[1]The Enthronement of the Sacred Heart is the recognition of the sovereignty of Christ over the Christian family, affirmed outwardly by a ceremonious, solemn installation of an image of the Sacred Heart in a place of honor in any home, accompanied by a prescribed prayer of consecration.

Inscription over chapel door here in Paray-le-Monial, France, reads: "In this church Our Lord revealed His Heart to Saint Margaret Mary."

chain of a million hours of adoration of Christ in the Eucharist around the world.

It was in a confessional of this chapel that Margaret Mary first told Father Claude Colombiere, S.J.: "When I was kneeling in adoration before the Blessed Sacrament, *suddenly I saw Our Lord come from the monstrance and stand before the altar.* Through His robe I saw His heart surrounded by fire and He told me: 'Behold, the heart which has so loved men. It has spared nothing...In return I receive from most people only ingratitude by irreverence and sacrilege, by coldness, by contempt for me and the Sacrament of Love.'"

After long and exhaustive study, far more detailed perhaps than that of any court trial in which an accused person's life might be at stake, the Church finally and officially accepted the apparition as genuine. Over two centuries later, in our own day, the nun was canonized and the priest beatified.

The Eucharistic Christ Who had stepped from the monstrance asked Margaret Mary, among other things, to establish the practice of spending one hour before the Blessed Sacrament in prayer, the so-called Holy Hour. From then on she herself kept prayerful vigil from eleven o'clock to midnight on the eve of the first Friday of every month. She would meditate on the desolation that Christ felt when abandoned by His Apostles, when He suffered excruciating mental and physical anguish in the Garden of Gethsemane. Thus she prepared in a special way to receive a Communion of reparation on the following morning, the first Friday of the month.

The practice at least of the First Friday Communion (though not always of the Holy Hour) has become very widespread. On that day of the month the churches are

filled and the Masses well attended around the entire
globe.

After Christ's revelations to Saint Margaret Mary,
Saint Peter Julian Eymard founded the Congregation
of the Fathers of the Blessed Sacrament and launched
the Eucharistic League. The nation of France, in final
acknowledgment of St. Margaret Mary's revelation, built
the National Shrine of the Sacred Heart on the highest
hill in Paris, Montmartre, for perpetual adoration of the
Eucharist. The white sugar-loaf towers of Sacre Coeur
dominate the city. In Rome the practice of the Forty
Hours, another Eucharistic devotion, was extended to so
many churches that the act of homage to Our Lord in the
Blessed Sacrament begins in a different church somewhere in the city one right after the other, all year long.

Obviously this close association of the Eucharist with
the Sacred Heart devotion, which developed after the apparitions in Paray-le-Monial, does not imply that only
the Heart of Christ is present in the Blessed Sacrament.
Clearly "the Heart of Christ" is a metaphorical expression similar to the expression "I love you with all my
heart." In essence, Christ came from the monstrance at
Paray-le-Monial to whisper this to each of us.

Pope Pius XII, whose *Mediator Dei* is considered by
some a more precise modern definition of the Eucharist
than the decrees of Vatican Council II, also wrote *Hau-
rietis Aquas* (1956) on devotion to the Sacred Heart. A
Professor of Dogma at the University of Fribourg says:
"It should be made required reading for everybody who
feels enthusiasm for the liturgy for it is an example of
translating a popular devotion into terms of integral
Christian piety."[2] But presuming that the average reader

[2]O'Neill, *Meeting Christ in the Sacraments,* 1964, p. 368.

Left is the altar and tabernacle from the pre-Vatican II era in the chapel of Paray-le-Monial, surmounted by painting of the vision of Christ coming from the Blessed Sacrament. Below is the new altar in the same chapel, changed after Vatican II, when new emphasis was placed on the sharing of the congregation in the Eucharistic Liturgy by having the priest face the people as was the custom of the early Church. The original altar disappeared during the French Revolution.

is now learning of the Eucharistic Liturgy for the first time, we cannot go into the subject in detail.

But why was it ever necessary for Christ to have resorted to such a petty miracle as His appearance to Sister Margaret Mary to reaffirm the greatest love that the world has ever known?

Some readers might object to the word "petty" to describe the miracle of Christ's appearance out of the Eucharist. But by contrast to *the miracle of the Eucharist itself* this appearance (and others like it) is quite small, and *it is also a reproach.* He said:

"My daughter, I come into your heart. Through your person may you atone for the offenses which I received from lukewarm and slothful hearts which do not honor Me in the Sacrament."

He asked her to make known through her confessor that He promised to those who would make a Communion of reparation on nine consecutive First Fridays *the grace of a happy death.*

Several million Christians in the world today have made the nine First Fridays.* Often they now also make the First Saturdays* (a similar devotion predicted at Fatima and requested at Pontevedra), *and many go on to become daily communicants.* Although it is possible that a person can communicate thoughtlessly and without devotion, few people make the effort to communicate often without putting a certain amount of fervor into the act. Certainly it is logical to suppose that God will reward a person of fervor with more than enough grace at the time of death to save his soul. (Whether or not he accepts that grace, as is always the case, is of course up to him. We are free beings; we can either accept or reject God's gifts.) The Promises have provided the incentive

As the priest lifts the monstrance one can almost hear the words the Eucharistic Christ spoke at Paray-le-Monial: "Behold the Heart that has so loved men!"

many people need to go to Communion more often. As we said earlier, the First Friday devotion is very popular and the First Saturday devotion is growing.

It is lamentable that the Holy Hour devotion is not nearly so popular. Few hear the plaint of Christ still echoing from the Garden of Gethsemane on the night that He instituted the Eucharist, the night He made a stone prison a tabernacle, the night before He died. But His plaint can still touch a sensitive heart: *"Could you not watch one hour with me?"*

Has the Christian world forgotten those words He spoke to Peter, James and John as He prayed just a stone's throw from them and saw passing before His eyes the evil of all time, the murders, the deceits, the cruelties, the betrayals, the sacrileges, etc.?

Why did He rise from His knees after a time and go to the three who slept? Why did He awaken them to plead for their company? Why did He beg them to resist the lure of sleep?

Above all, why had He chosen the three who most certainly knew He was God, the three whom He had invited to witness Him transfigured on Tabor? And why did He go to them a second time, and a third time? He was the same Christ Who knew that Lazarus was dead and announced that fact to the Apostles before they came to Bethany. He was the same Christ Who told the Samaritan woman at the well about her five husbands. Yes, He knew that those chosen ones in Gethsemane would not be able to resist sleep: "The spirit is willing but the flesh is weak."

So what was the reason for accosting them as He did?

Are not we modern believers His reason, we who have lived or will live after that tragic night? In God's eternal present, were His words not meant to reach us chosen ones who share His Eucharistic life, the life He had just begun a few hours before the agony in Gethsemane, but a life which His disciples did not fully understand?

Pope John Paul II, in his encyclical *Dominicae Cenae* (On the Mystery and Worship of Holy Eucharist), said that worship of the Eucharist "must fill our churches also outside the timetable of Masses." The Pope added:

"Since the Eucharistic mystery was instituted out of love and makes Christ sacramentally present, it is worthy of thanksgiving and worship. And this worship must be prominent in all our encounters with the Blessed Sacrament, both when we visit our churches and when the Sacred Species are taken to the sick and administered to them.

"Adoration of Christ in this sacrament of love must also find expression in various forms of Eucharistic devotion: personal prayer before the Blessed Sacrament, hours of adoration, periods of exposition — short, prolonged, and annual (Forty Hours) — Eucharistic benediction, Eucharistic processions, Eucharistic congresses." [3]

Today there are some chosen ones who look at the empty churches where He is neglected and alone, as on the rock of Gethsemane, and who hear His plaintive words: "Could you not watch an hour with me?"

Some give an hour a day. Still others, following the saintly Father Mateo, give a prescribed hour a month from their own homes as they turn their minds to the nearest tabernacle. Some give an entire night to the morning of the First Saturday.

In 1960, the Bishop of Fatima conferred with Pope John XXIII, who had opened the famous "1960 secret"

[3]John Paul II, *Dominicae Cenae,* 1980, n. 3, 12.

the Visitation Chapel in Paray, contains the remains of the body of this saint to whom Our Lord revealed His Sacred Heart in "Final appeal for the love of men."

of Fatima, and then sent a letter to all bishops of the world asking for an All-Night Vigil of reparation to the Blessed Sacrament on October 12-13 of that year. Three hundred dioceses joined around the world. Pope John sent a cable of blessing and thanks to all who responded. Subsequently, the All-Night Vigil, promoted especially by The Blue Army of Our Lady of Fatima in the U.S., has been made by an increasing number of generous souls.

By 1980, *tens of thousands* were making the Vigils from the First Friday evening (beginning with Mass of the Sacred Heart) to First Saturday morning, closing with Mass of the Immaculate Heart. Concerning this the present writer has another book titled *Night of Love*.

There is one thing *everyone* can and certainly should do . . . something requiring no more than thirty seconds a day: *An offering* in the morning (preferably at the moment of waking) of all our works of the day *in union with the Eucharistic Sacrifice* taking place in every part of the world.

Pope John XXIII urged this practice on everyone. One of the last major things he did before his death was to grant the highest privilege in the Pope's power to those who would offer their sufferings daily, using any words they chose. A short time later he granted the same to those who would offer their works.

Some will be impatient to participate personally in the Liturgy, to "eat the bread of life." Some will add some hours of adoration. Some will give an entire night. Some may even become Eucharistic apostles like those mentioned in Chapter 13.

But all can make a half-minute beginning. (See *Blue Army*, pp. 268-69.)

CHAPTER SIXTEEN

THE SECRET TODAY

This book could just as well have been called "The World's Greatest Mystery." But we have preferred to refer to the Eucharist as the World's Greatest Secret because that is what It was when Christ first presented It to the world by the Sea of Galilee; this is what It remained during the early centuries of the Church; this is what It is to most persons outside of Christian Communion in the world today.

As was to be expected, Ecumenical Council Vatican II was enormously preoccupied with this Mystery, this Secret of Christian life. Perhaps few effects of the Council have been more palpable. The changes in the Eucharistic arrangements have been so great that if a person had been spirited out of this world before the Council and suddenly returned now, he might not know that he was in a Catholic church when he looked at the sanctuary. He might even have more doubts as the Mass progressed with the priest facing the congregation, prayers in the vernacular, lectern on the side of the altar, and even a different prayer used at the distribution of Communion.

The most notable change in the church itself would often be the location of the tabernacle, which up until the time of the Ecumenical Council was the most prominent feature in every Catholic church. Indeed it would seem that the altar was designed largely to support the tabernacle, and the ornamentation behind and around the altar used as a decoration or background to the tabernacle.

Now sometimes it might be difficult to know where the tabernacle is located. The altar is moved forward, standing like a table in the center of the sanctuary. It is possible that the small elevation on top of the table would hide a tabernacle beneath it. Or might it be that a simple structure, perhaps covered by a veil, off to one side, with little ornamentation around it, might be discerned as the repository of Christ physically present in our midst because of a lamp burning closer to this spot than to some other? Yes, in some churches it is like this.

In other churches the tabernacle remains central, with an ornate reredos to declare the splendor of its Royal Inhabitant, and another altar used for the Sacrifice of the Mass will have been erected some distance in front of it.

The reason for these variations, of course, will be the individual zeal and sense of artistry with which each pastor will have applied the rulings of the Ecumenical Council concerning the Eucharist and the Eucharistic Liturgy. But the reason behind all of these changes is simple.

The essence of the Eucharist, as the Council emphasized, is sacrifice. As a wonderful consequence of this sacrifice, the Presence of Christ is in our midst.

As was said earlier in these pages, the Eucharistic Liturgy *makes Calvary present*. The moment of consecration gives the participant an enamored moment of intimacy with the Divine.

The Psalmist said, "What shall I give to the Lord for all that he has given me?"

While the Psalmist could not answer this question in the days of the Old Testament, modern man can answer:

"I could give Him back His own Son, nailed to a cross in reparation for my sins and for the sins of the world." And this is the heart of the world's greatest Secret.

In the prayers said during and just after the consecration, we find the full meaning of the Eucharistic Liturgy:

The day before he suffered he took bread in his sacred hands and looking up to heaven, to you, his almighty Father, he gave you thanks and praise. He broke the bread, gave it to his disciples, and said:

Take this, all of you, and eat it: this is my body which will be given up for you.

When supper was ended, he took the cup. Again he gave you thanks and praise, gave the cup to his disciples, and said:

Take this, all of you, and drink from it: this is the cup of my blood, the blood of the new and everlasting covenant. It will be shed for you and for all so that sins may be forgiven. Do this in memory of me.

Father, we celebrate the memory of Christ your Son. We, your people and your ministers, recall his passion, his resurrection from the dead, and his ascension into glory; and from the many gifts you have given us we offer to you, God of glory and majesty, this holy and perfect sacrifice: the bread of life and the cup of eternal salvation.

Look with favor on these offerings and accept them as once you accepted the gifts of your servant Abel, the sacrifice of Abraham, our father in faith, and the bread and wine offered by your priest Melchisedech.

Almighty God, we pray that your angel may take this sacrifice to your altar in heaven. Then, as we re-

*ceive from this altar the sacred body and blood of
your Son, let us be filled with every grace and blessing. (Through Christ our Lord. Amen.)*

There is no doubt that since the Middle Ages the emphasis on Christ's Presence in our midst in the Eucharist
has sometimes come to be regarded with even greater
reverence than the essential *reason* for His Presence,
namely the Act of Sacrifice, the renewal of Calvary.

Many Christians were even receiving Communion
outside of the Eucharistic Sacrifice. Before the Ecumenical Council some steps were taken to curb this, in both
the Anglican Communion and the Church of Rome.

Extremes are usually to be avoided, and it might seem
to some that to have the tabernacle made inconspicuous
is an extreme. In some churches an excellent solution has
been found by giving a reverent location to the tabernacle in the apse of the church or in a special chapel. It
might be interesting to note that in the very special
Chapel of the Visitation Convent in Paray-le-Monial the
tabernacle has been very ingeniously incorporated into
the altar itself, but not receded so completely as to
appear of less importance than the altar. In this way it is
identified with the table of Sacrifice.

We have chosen to present a picture of this chapel of
Paray-le-Monial as it was up until the time of the Ecumenical Council and as it is now. Many Christians passed
through this period of change with various degrees of sub-
jective emotion. But the emotional adjustment is very
quickly made with the realization of the importance of constantly identifying Christ's Presence in the Eucharist with
the Sacrifice which gives us His presence. There is only one
return which Christ wishes from us, and that is sorrow
for our sins and prayer for the conversion of sinners. The

great lament to the world in the messages of Lourdes and Fatima were: "So many souls are lost because there is no one to pray and make sacrifices for them." And of what use is it for us to go and feel comfortable in the Presence of Christ in the Eucharist and miss the opportunity given to us in each Sacrifice of the Mass to bring to bear upon the world the enormous sacrificial force of Calvary?

It is thought that *any* Christian could make it possible for a thousand souls to be saved, who otherwise would be damned, by worthily participating *in even one single Sacrifice of the Mass.* It is a common belief that if any one of us could identify with the Heart of Mary as she kneels at the foot of the Cross and offers her Divine Son to the Father for the conversion of sinners, we would in that moment become a power like that of Therese of Lisieux, Francis of Assisi, Anthony of Padua.

For many of us the world's greatest Secret will remain a secret. For some, the Secret will yield Its meaning bit by bit, or perhaps even in one great flash of light.

Nevertheless, this Secret, this Mystery, will increasingly become the focal point of man on this planet. It may have grown in importance more in the last 500 years, during which Christians for the first time began to question It, than It did in the first 1,500 years when there was hardly any doubt.

Today no major city in Christian nations of the world is without a church where the Eucharist is reserved. Often it is the richest, most important structure in the entire city.

But there are two major places in the Holy Land that are not commemorated by churches: the place where the Eucharist was instituted and the place of the Ascension. Why?

Why is there nothing but a tiny room on the spot where Christ instituted the Eucharist? Why is there no great church on the spot where He ascended into heaven forty days after His resurrection?

There may be various reasons, but we like to think it is because God did not want to commemorate a spot where Christ seemed to be leaving the world.

The very emptiness of these sacred spots on Mount Zion and on the Mount of Olives recalls the truth that suddenly became clear to the Apostles at Pentecost: *He had not really left them at all.* He had been with them in the limited area of Palestine, but now He was to be with all men everywhere, physically, really.

When the early Christians received the Holy Spirit sent to them by Christ as He had promised just before the Ascension, they suddenly and wonderfully understood this. There in that same Cenacle room where He had given them the Eucharist for the first time *the Pentecostal light opened their eyes to the Eucharistic Christ more intimately present than He had ever been before.* They went forth to preach Him, to live for Him, to die for Him, to give Him to us today not in the Cenacle but *in churches in every corner of the world.* Only one of the twelve Apostles (excluding Judas) died in Jerusalem. All the others died establishing Christ's Church in different parts of the world. Even the one who was beheaded in Jerusalem had just returned from preaching the Eucharistic Christ in the farthest western limit of the known world.

But what about those of us who doubt?

Can we not, with just a thought, turn to the Mother of Christ, to ask her intercession that we, too, may realize this more fully? Can we not feel the need to tell the

Pilgrims gather at the place of the Ascension where Christ was last seen by the Church gathered together. There is no church here. The rings in the wall are for the tents where Liturgy is celebrated on the anniversary of the Ascension.

Truth-giving Spirit, Love Itself, that our minds are too small, our sins too great, our wills too weak, our habits too gross, our way of thought too careless and shallow to enable us to believe firmly without divine help? Can we not feel the need to pray for our own Pentecost, that His light may pierce the dark pall of our doubts and fears?

We may look upward toward that white disc which shines in the monstrance as toward the chink through which, for just a moment, shines the Light of the other world. For St. John writes: "Whatever came to be in him, found life, life for the light of men. The light shines on in darkness, a darkness that did not overcome it.... He was in the world, and through him the world was made, yet the world did not know who he was...."

He is in the world now. That fact cannot be insisted upon too often. But how many of us can really know Him? How many of us really acknowledge Him?

What about Christians, and even non-Christians, who have never actually received Communion? Do they have no "life" in them?

It was the special vocation of Pope John XXIII to emphasize to the world — even to apparent atheists — that God judges and visits men within the limits and lights of each. To Pope John, *most* were brothers. Who would not receive Communion if he knew and believed all that has been said of it in this book? Only *such* a man has no life in him.

All others have it as an object of desire, an unacknowledged center of their lives.

The tragedy of Christian disunity is never more evident than in the presence of this Sacrament of Unity. How much of that tragedy lies at the door of those who profess belief in It? And how great a responsibility lies upon those who possess It!

Sometimes we argue: But if He is here, why doesn't He do something to straighten out this mad, evil world? Why doesn't He sweep away slave-labor camps? Why doesn't He end wars, perfidy, conflicts and injustices of all kinds?

The answer is clear: These evils result from neglecting and rejecting Him. That was the Message of Fatima, confirmed by a pre-announced public miracle witnessed in our own day by some 100,000 witnesses! He makes Himself peculiarly available and accessible in the Eucharist, but He does not force us to accept Him.

We must reach out to Him if we are to increase the love among men which abolishes these evils and brings peace.

Cardinal Montini of Milan, who later became Pope Paul VI, said in a public speech: "We shall love our neighbors and those far afield. We shall love our country, we shall love other people. We shall love Catholics, the schismatics, the Protestants, the Africans, the indifferent, the Moslems, the pagans and the atheists. We shall love those who merit and those who do not merit being loved."

Where, oh, where can we find such love? A love that embraces such a conglomeration of human creatures?

After Cardinal Montini became Pope he told the world where he expected such love to be found. He wrote an encyclical on the Eucharist which we have appended to these pages.

In an earlier chapter we mentioned the Eucharistic vision of the Patriarch of Constantinople, first made public in March, 1967. After describing his vision of the Eucharist the Patriarch said: "I should like to visit the

Pope John Paul II blessing the sick at Fatima
May 13, 1982.

Pope in Rome as soon as possible. The Church and the world are surfeited with gestures and nice words. We must go straight to the point. Jesus said to Simon: *Put out into the deep and let down your nets for a catch. And Simon answered, Lord, we toiled all night and took nothing! But at your words I will let down our nets. And when they had done this, they enclosed a great school of fish.* Think of it, just think of it! With Saint Peter in the West and Saint John in the East, one vast net could be thrown into the sea of the world and encircle with love all those 900 million Christians." (See *Athenagoras,* p. 267-68 .)

Ultimately the secret of Christianity is Christ Himself *as a Living, Present Reality,* a Divine Love meeting human love.

It will always remain a secret in the sense that it is the secret of the fidelity of many Christians, the unrecognized source of their strength in the face of hardship and trial, and the wellspring of their holiness.

For others in our modern world it is a secret in the sense that they do not know about it, or if they know about it in some sort of cursory way, they ignore it or turn their backs upon it. And so they live in darkness, tragically miserable, not realizing that a remedy is at hand.

Today three small nations which claim to be Christian, but which are dominated exclusively by those who no longer believe in the Eucharist, are the world's unhappiest people. They have the highest suicide rate per capita of all nations on earth despite extremely high standards of living.[1] Currently they are plunged into an

---

[1]Denmark, Norway and Sweden.

agonized God-searching reminiscent of the Mycenean Age.

All Christians sooner or later must come to the realization that they cannot turn from Christ, as at Capernaum, shrug their shoulders and say: "This is hard to endure. Who can take it seriously?" (Jn. 6:60)

Whether they be the leaders of 214 divisions of the Church meeting in Geneva, or 2,500 bishops meeting in Rome, the voice they hear is from the same discourse the night before He died: "This is my Body; this is my Blood.... Father, I pray that they may be one as You and I are one."

Pope John Paul II, speaking at a seminary in the archdiocese of Milan on May 21, 1983, said:

"It is because of the Eucharist that the members of the Christian community are identified mystically with the Body of Christ, which is the Church, and become one among them.

"Therefore all the sacraments, as well as all the ecclesiastical ministries and works of the apostolate, are closely bound up with the Most Holy Eucharist and ordained to it. The Eucharist is truly the heart and the centre of the Christian world. In it is contained the Church's entire spiritual wealth, Christ himself, the living bread, who through his flesh, made vital and vitalizing by the Holy Spirit, offers life to men."[1]

The central reality of Christianity always will be unity with the submission of Christ's human will to His Father. And the Eucharistic Liturgy looms up to such vast importance because it makes the peak of Christ's submission (the sacrifice of Calvary) actually present.

[1]L'Osservatore Romano, 20 June 1983, p. 4.

"Christ is here!" were the often repeated words at the 1964 Eucharistic Congress in Bombay. Pope Paul VI came to celebrate the Eucharistic Liturgy in this global gathering to honor Christ among us.

Perhaps a lifetime of prayer and study would not suffice to plumb the depths of Christ's above statement. It certainly is not the intention of this book to try. But it is enough for the average Christian to know that any person can most easily enter into this sublime identification with the obedience of Christ by daily participation in the Eucharistic Liturgy.

All are obliged to participate once a week. But how much spiritual growth is possible if we limit ourselves to this minimum? And how much if we fail to prepare ourselves and bring to bear a maximum of attention?

Some cannot participate in the Liturgy each day, but all can meditate on the Liturgy of the Word and say the prayers, climaxed by spiritual communion, in union with the Eucharistic miracle taking place in every other part of the world "...not a new body, for He has only one; but an extension to His body, or better, a transposition of His body into a new dimension."

All that we have tried to say in this book may be summarized in a few paragraphs based on Saint Mark:

The world's greatest Secret began on a mountain in Palestine with the miracle of the loaves and the incredible words: "I am the bread of heaven...you must eat my flesh..." Pictures of this miracle became the most frequently used by early Christians as modern archeologists have discovered.

We used an entire chapter to describe this event almost at the very beginning. Everyone went away when Christ said that He would give His flesh to eat and His blood to drink, and that they would not live if they did not eat Him. But the Apostles themselves, though deeply shaken, did not leave.

Immediately after this Christ sent the Apostles across

Pope Paul VI prays in the Cenacle during the Ecumenical Council, recalling those words spoken here by Christ the night He instituted the Eucharist: "Father, that they may be one as you and I are One."

the Sea of Galilee.

A severe storm arose. They were rowing against heavy seas, fearfully straining to gain the shore, when suddenly a ghostly figure moved over the waves. It seemed to pass them. Saint Mark says:

"...He meant to pass them by. When they saw him walking on the lake, they thought it was a ghost and they began to cry out. They had all seen him and were terrified. He hastened to reassure them: 'Get hold of yourselves! It is I. Do not be afraid!'" (6:48-50)

Why did Christ put them to such a test? Their cries seem to indicate sheer terror. Why did He who loved them so much, pretend to go by in the storm?

Saint Mark (6:51-52) explains:

"And they were utterly beside themselves with astonishment, for they had not understood about the loaves, because their heart was blinded."

True, they had not gone away like the others. But like many Christians today, they had not remained because they truly believed they would one day eat His flesh but rather because, as Peter said, "Lord, to whom shall we go?" (Jn. 6:68).

After the terror-lesson of the storm, Christ calmed the wind. He proceeded to perform so many miracles that people began to forget the hard saying and again they wanted to proclaim Him King. Saint Mark says: *"And he got into the boat with them, and the wind fell.... And crossing over, they came to the land ... And wherever he went, into village or hamlet or town, they laid the sick in the market places, and entreated him to let them touch but the tassel of his cloak; and as many as touched him were saved"* (Jn. 6:51, 53, 56). Finally He called Lazarus from his grave in the presence of a host of witnesses, and they broke branches from the trees, laid cloaks in His path, and called Him King even up to the very gates of the Temple.

But it was to fulfill the hard saying that he had come. This was to be not only the secret of His Church but His greatest gift to men: Bread which would enable them never to die. So He chose a supper instead of a crown. He chose bread and wine to perform the first of innumerable transubstantiations and then performed the miracle of Lazarus in Himself as His final proof.

What a mystery and lesson ring out today in those incredible words of Saint Mark describing the frightened disciples in the endangered ship: *"They were utterly beside themselves... because they had not understood about the loaves."*

Millions of doubting, divided disciples of Christ have huddled through the storms of two global wars. Before the now-rising waves of the atomic armament race they seem to know, collectively, that this is a fateful hour for them. They strain at the oars with pleas for ecumenism.* Frightened cries rise from a building in New York City where they have been striving to establish unity under law, only to be thwarted again and again by waves of atheistic anarchism. The storm mounts.

So far the cries of fear do not have the shrill of sheer terror. And no one claims to have seen a specter moving over the waves, unless it might be the miracle of the sun at Fatima performed at a specified time and place "so that all may believe."

But if we are looking for one, profound explanation of the modern storm, might we not find it in that simple sentence of Saint Mark:

"They had not yet understood the miracle of the

loaves because they hearts were blind''?

Could it not be that too many have followed Christ simply because they know He has words of eternal life rather than because they recognize the world's greatest secret, *because they understand the miracle of the loaves?*

He could cure at a distance, but He preferred to be touched and to touch — even with as intimate an element as spittle. He preferred to give of Himself by touch — ''. . . and as many as touched him were saved.'' And He has remained through the mystery of transubstantiated bread *to touch and be touched. . now.*

Thus the world's greatest secret becomes the world's greatest hope. At this very moment another heart which might have passed by in the storm may be hearing His voice from a nearby tabernacle:

   "Do not be afraid. It is I." – Mk. 8:23

A PERSONAL MESSAGE
from the Author...

Sr. Lucia, the visionary of Fatima, with Pope John Paul II.

Dear Non-Believer:

I particularly had you in mind when I wrote this book.

You must have felt that for all these centuries the belief of millions of Christians in the true presence of Christ in the Eucharist had to be ridiculous.

I hope that the reading of these pages will show that it was not ridiculous, and perhaps open your own heart and mind at least to this incredible possibility: that Jesus indeed intended from the very moment that He came to this earth to give Himself to us as "the Bread of Life," and He longed for that moment "with great longing" until finally, on the night before He gave His life for us, He gave Himself to us — and abides with us and comes to us whenever we wish.

223

If you should be like Frances Allen, who took every occasion to mock the Eucharist, may you have the grace to visit Him in the tabernacle of a church near you and be favored as she was! Or if you were wondering or perhaps longing for such intimate contact, like St. Elizabeth Seton may you be inspired to direct your thoughts to a tabernacle and to say "Bless me, Jesus, if You are there!"

Perhaps you were given this book by a believer who loved you enough to want you to share this great secret of God's love. Certainly that same person is praying that you may have the gift of finding the Eucharistic Jesus.

If you do, do not forget so generous a friend.

Dear Apostle:

When I wrote this book, I already knew that there would be people like yourself who would be inspired to give or lend it to others so that, in our own day, more and more persons might come to know the living Jesus in our midst.

I hope you are a member of The Blue Army of Our Lady of Fatima. If not, I hope that at least you will have studied the great revelation of Fatima — which was so important that for the first time in history God permitted that a miracle be performed at a predicted time and place *"so that all may believe!"*

We are living in apocalyptic times.

Those of us who have the gift of faith must yearn to share it.

It is inspiring to contemplate that "final" vision of Fatima (the vision of June 13, 1929) which depicted the

Most Blessed Trinity, with Our Lord bleeding from head and heart to a Host and Chalice, while Our Lady stood beneath the cross showing her heart surrounded by thorns, and while words flowed from the left hand of Jesus "down over the altar": *grace* and *mercy.*

How are we to obtain graces and mercy for the world? How are we to see that the tremendous power of the sacrifice of the Mass and the coming to us of God Himself in the Blessed Sacrament is applied to the great spiritual needs of ourselves, our neighbors, our world?

Jesus will tell you. When you kneel before the tabernacle, and especially in those precious moments after Holy Communion, listen! And if you hear Him saying as He did to some fishermen on the shores of Galilee, "Follow me," do not hesitate! He probably will not ask you to "*leave* all" but rather to *use* something He has already given you.

One of the rather "new" messages of Vatican Council II was that this is an age when the laity are to play an increasingly important role. The Council spoke of the "priesthood of the laity." And one of the phenomena of our time is the action of the Holy Spirit in the souls of the individual lay persons, drawing them to become apostles of the Eucharistic Christ.

Pray to Our Lady, Queen and Mother of the Apostles, to enable you to hear His voice and to give you the loving strength to respond:

"Here I am, Lord, tell me what I should do!"

Dear Separated Christian:

As we gather together in the World Council of Churches (and in ecumenical services) the greatest sadness we feel — after the joy of common prayer — is that we are really not united.

And we cannot be united until we are all receiving the Sacrament of Unity, the Sacrament through which Jesus gives Himself, as He did at the Last Supper when He prayed: *"Father, that they may be one as You and I are one."*

Arguments will not serve. Only His own healing grace can bring us together in His Eucharistic banquet.

Each of us has something very precious to give to the other. Many deprived of Him in the Eucharist have still learned to identify with Him in a most personal way, while some others who have the Eucharist may take Him for granted or even worse, receive Him unworthily.

Let us pray for each other! Let us pray for an end to a divided Christianity! Let us not be content within the limits of our own faith. Let us desire earnestly for Communion together as Jesus Himself desired when He prayed that we might be one in Him!

Dear Believer:

When I went to Rome in 1962 to study the archeological findings for this book I already had with me two suitcases full of research material — enough to fill several books like this one!

I went to these lengths because there seemed a need for a book which could be placed in the hands of non-believers, and which at the same time might prove of value to all of us who, even after years of daily Communion, may feel the need to say: "Lord, I believe, help my unbelief!" (Mk. 9:23)

According to the Venerable Mary of Agreda's inspired

biography of the Blessed Virgin Mary, Our Lady had been told long in advance that the Eucharist would be instituted at the Last Supper and that she at once began to prepare herself during all those years for her first Communion, rejoicing once again she would possess Our Lord within her as she had at the moment of the Annunciation and for nine months.

In our own day we have the almost incredible story of Alexandrina of Balazar (Portugal), who longed for (but for several years did not receive) daily Communion, and who finally lived for thirteen years on absolutely nothing other than the Blessed Sacrament.

Alexandrina did not lose weight, even though she went through many sufferings, and this incredible and total fast for thirteen years (with no food whatever but the Blessed Sacrament) was verified as miraculous under scientific observation.

I wish for you the *longing* for the Eucharist which came to the most perfect of all human beings, the Blessed Virgin, and that *appreciation* of the "bread of life" which was manifest in the life of Alexandrina.

Let us rejoice with St. Elizabeth Mary Seton in our gift of faith in the Blessed Sacrament! Let us appreciate that there is nothing more precious possible to us than our very next Communion.

May Our Lady, Mother of the Eucharist, fill us all with her own great desire to have Jesus abide with us. May she impart to us the fullness of the faith, hope and love of her Immaculate Heart that we may respond with at least some degree of worthiness to this Sacrament of Love.

Dear Sufferer:

When you read Chapter Nine of this book, were you
surprised to find that most of the drawings of the early
Christians inscribed on the walls of the catacombs
referred to the Eucharist and miracles related to the
Eucharist? Most frequent of course were the pictures of
the "breaking of the bread." But the next greatest
number of pictures in order of frequency dealt with the
cure of the paralytic who was let down through the roof
of a house, the *resurrection* of Lazarus, the *cure* of the
woman with an issue of blood, and the *cure* of the blind
man whose eyes Jesus touched with spittle.

Why?

It is because Jesus who remains with us in the Eucharist, is the same Jesus described by Matthew in chapter
14, verse 14: "When he disembarked and saw the vast
throng, his heart was moved with pity, and he cured their
sick."

The very fact that Our Lord comes to us in the Eucharist is the greatest of all proofs of God's incredible love
for us. Why then do our own hearts remain cold? Why
do we bear our sufferings alone without carrying them to
Him? The woman with the issue of blood believed that if
she but *touched His robe,* she would be cured. And yet
we can do more than touch His robe! We can actually
receive Him, commune with Him, really and truly, spiritually and *physically* be *united* to Him!

Jesus reached out and *touched* people. He could have
said simply to the blind man: "See!" But He made a
little paste with His own spittle and rubbed it on the
man's eyes — so that the man *could actually feel a part
of Jesus* touching his affliction!

No wonder when the Christians gathered in the catacombs to receive the "secret Jesus" they were so aware that this was the Jesus who came in love and power, and who came to heal!

Of course, suffering is often a very great blessing from God. Our first instinct should be to make a return to the great love of Jesus by saying that we offer whatever suffering God may send us and we unite it to Him suffering in atonement for our sins and for reparation of the sins of the world.

But at the same time, we should ask for healing. We should *expect — without the slightest doubt* — one of two things:

1. That we shall be healed; or
2. We shall have an "inward healing" far greater than a healing of our actual illness which will turn our suffering into joy, as in the case of the amazing story of Alexandrina and some of the others like her!

If you are not a Catholic, and are not admitted to receiving Holy Communion, you can kneel before a tabernacle and meet the same Jesus there. And you can be sure that His Sacred Heart will overflow with compassion and love for you perhaps even more than for those who are privileged to receive Him every day!

Can you not hear Him saying: "Your faith has made you whole!"?

To obtain outward or inward healing, it will help greatly *to picture Jesus* to yourself as He comes to you.

Very few pictures of Jesus satisfy us because they would have to depict His authority and power, His singleness of purpose, and above all the greatness of His love — and this no picture can do. No artist could paint the eyes of Jesus as they really are as they gaze upon us from the Eucharist. But imagine those eyes full of love for us, and imagine that *power* of Jesus which compelled followers to say: "He speaks with authority," and caused fishermen and a tax collector to leave all at His simple request!

As we said in Chapter Twelve, *Jesus is performing more miracles today* all over the world *than He performed in Palestine 2,000 years ago!* But they are miracles received by individuals, sometimes slowly over a period of time, and sometimes in a few moments as in the case of Marie Ferrand or Arminda dos Campos. And no one knows.

The Eucharistic Liturgy itself teaches us to pray for healing.

One of the optional prayers of the penitential rite of the Mass (Option C8) reads:

"Lord Jesus, *You healed the sick:* Lord, have mercy!
Lord Jesus, You forgave sinners: Christ have mercy!
Lord Jesus, *You give Yourself to heal us and bring us strength:* Lord have mercy!"

And the second optional prayer before Communion asks for healing of mind and body:

"*Let it bring me...health in mind and body.*"

We can focus *on the love of Jesus,* and take Him at His word! He describes Himself in the Eucharist as *the bread of life.*

If you turn to Mary (remembering that *at her mere suggestion* Jesus worked His first and one of His greatest miracles) it will be easy. Ask her to pray for you. Ask her to show that she is your Mother, really and truly and that you want to believe in the Eucharistic Jesus with her faith, *you want to pray to Him with her confidence,* you want to respond to Him with the depth of love that fills her own Immaculate Heart!

For this reason the devotions of the Rosary and the Scapular are of greatest importance and assistance. Jesus promised that even a mountain would move if we asked it *with sufficient faith.* And Mary is the Mother of Faith as well as of Holy Hope!

O Mary, Mother of the Eucharist and our Mother, intercede for us!

The Bishops of the World, in the Second Vatican Council (1962-65), reaffirmed the doctrine of the true Presence of Jesus in the Eucharist. Two months after the promulgation of *Lumen Gentium*, (*The Constitution on the Church*), the Pope indicated the Rosary and the Scapular as the two principal Marian devotions for our time in keeping with paragraph 67 of that most important document of the Council.

THE MYSTERY OF FAITH
His Holiness, Pope Paul VI

Paul VI, by divine providence Pope, to our venerable brothers, the Patriarchs, Primates, Archbishops, Bishops and other local Ordinaries in peace and communion with the Holy See, and to all the clergy and faithful of the world: on the doctrine and worship of the Holy Eucharist. Venerable brothers and dear sons: Health and apostolic benediction.

The Catholic Church has always devoutly guarded as a most precious treasure the mystery of faith, that is, the ineffable gift of the Eucharist which she received from Christ her Spouse as a pledge of His immense love, and during the Second Vatican Council in a new and solemn demonstration she professed her faith and veneration for this mystery. When dealing with the restoration of the sacred liturgy, the Fathers of the council, by reason of their pastoral concern for the whole Church, considered it of the highest importance to exhort the faithful to participate actively with sound faith and with the utmost devotion in the celebration of this Most Holy Mystery, to offer it with the priest to God as a sacrifice for their own salvation and for that of the whole world, and to find in it spiritual nourishment.

For if the sacred liturgy holds the first place in the life of the Church, the Eucharistic Mystery stands at the heart and center of the liturgy, since it is the font of life by which we are cleansed and strengthened to live not for ourselves but for God, and to be united in love among ourselves.

To make evident the indissoluble bond which exists
between faith and devotion, the Fathers of the council,
confirming the doctrine which the Church has always
held and taught and which was solemnly defined by the
Council of Trent, determine to introduce their treatise
on the Most Holy Mystery of the Eucharist with the
following summary of truths:

"At the Last Supper, on the night He was handed
over, Our Lord instituted the Eucharistic Sacrifice of His
Body and Blood, to perpetuate the sacrifice on the cross
throughout the ages until He should come, and thus
entrust to the Church, His beloved Spouse, the memorial
of His death and resurrection: A sacrament of devotion,
a sign of unity, a bond of charity, a paschal banquet in
which Christ is received, the soul is filled with Grace and
there is given to us the pledge of future glory."[1]

In these words are highlighted both the sacrifice,
which pertains to the essence of the Mass which is
celebrated daily, and the sacrament in which the faithful
participate in Holy Communion by eating the Flesh of
Christ and drinking His Blood, receiving both grace, the
beginning of eternal life, and the medicine of immor-
tality. According to the words of our Lord: "The man
who eats my flesh and drinks my blood enjoys eternal
life, and I will raise him up at the last day"
(John 6, 55).

Therefore we earnestly hope that the restored sacred
liturgy will bring forth abundant fruits of eucharistic
devotion, so that the Holy Church, under this saving
sign of piety, may make daily progress toward perfect
unity (cf. John 17, 23) and may invite all Christians to a

[1]*Constitution on the Sacred Liturgy*, C. 2, N. 47, A.A.S. LVI, 1964, p. 113.

unity of faith and of love, drawing them gently, thanks to the action of divine grace.

We seem to have a preview of these fruits and, as it were, to gather in the early results not only in the genuine joy and eagerness with which the members of the Catholic Church have received both the Constitution on the Sacred Liturgy and the restoration of the liturgy, but also in the great number of well-prepared publications which seek to investigate more profoundly and to understand more fruitfully the doctrine on the Holy Eucharist, with special reference to its relation with the mystery of the Church.

All of this is for us a cause of profound consolation and joy. It is a great pleasure for us to communicate this to you, venerable brothers, so that along with us you may give thanks to God, the Giver of all gifts, who with His Spirit rules the Church and enriches her with increasing virtues.

Reasons for Pastoral Concern and Anxiety

However, venerable brothers, in this very matter which we are discussing, there are not lacking reasons for serious pastoral concern and anxiety. The awareness of our apostolic duty does not allow us to be silent in the face of these problems. Indeed, we are aware of the fact that, among those who deal with this Most Holy Mystery in written or spoken word, there are some who, with reference either to Masses which are celebrated in private, or to the dogma of transubstantiation, or to devotion to the Eucharist, spread abroad opinions which disturb the faithful and fill their minds with no little confusion about matters of faith. It is as if everyone were permitted to consign to oblivion doctrine already defined by the Church, or else to interpret it in such a way as to weaken the genuine meaning of the words or the recognized force of the concepts involved.

To confirm what we have said by examples, it is not allowable to emphasize what is called the "communal" Mass to the disparagement of Masses celebrated in private, or to exaggerate the element of sacramental sign as if the symbolism, which all certainly admit in the Eucharist, expresses fully and exhausts completely the mode of

Christ's presence in this sacrament. Nor is it allowable to discuss the mystery of transubstantiation without mentioning what the Council of Trent stated about the marvelous conversion of the whole substance of the bread into the Body and of the whole substance of the wine into the Blood of Christ, speaking rather only of what is called "transignification" and "transfiguration," or finally to propose and act upon the opinion according to which, in the Consecrated Hosts which remain after the celebration of the sacrifice of the Mass, Christ Our Lord is no longer present.

Everyone can see that the spread of these and similar opinions does great harm to the faith and devotion to the Divine Eucharist. [These and subsequent italics have been added.]

And therefore, so that the hope aroused by the council, that a flourishing of eucharistic piety which is now pervading the whole Church, be not frustrated by this spread of false opinions, we have with apostolic authority decided to address you, venerable brothers, and to express our mind on this subject.

We certainly do not wish to deny in those who are spreading these singular opinions the praiseworthy

effort to investigate this lofty mystery and to set forth its
inexhaustible riches, revealing its meaning to the men of
today; rather we acknowledge and approve their effort.
However, we cannot approve the opinions which they
express, and we have the duty to warn you about the
grave danger which these opinions involve for correct
faith.

The Holy Eucharist is a Mystery of Faith

First of all, we wish to recall something which is well
known to you but which is altogether necessary for
repelling every virus of rationalism, something to which
many illustrious martyrs have witnessed with their
blood, while celebrated Fathers and Doctors of the
Church constantly professed and taught it; that is, that
the Eucharist is a very great mystery. In fact, properly
speaking, and to use the words of the sacred liturgy, it is
the Mystery of Faith. *Indeed, in it alone,"* as Leo XIII,
our predecessor of happy memory very wisely remarked,
*"are contained, in a remarkable richness and variety of
miracles, all supernatural realities."* [2]
We must therefore approach especially this mystery
with humble respect, not following human arguments,
which ought to be silent, but adhering firmly to divine
revelation.

St. John Chrysostom, who, as you know, treated of
the eucharistic mystery with such nobility of language
and insight born of devotion, instructing his faithful on
one occasion about this mystery, expressed these most
fitting words:

"Let us submit to God in all things and not contradict
Him, even if what He says seems contrary to our reason

[2] Encyclical *Mirae Caritatis, Acta Leonis XIII,* Vol. XXII, 1902-1903.

APPENDIX

and intellect; rather, let His words prevail over our
reason and intellect. Let us act in this way with regard to
the (eucharistic) mysteries, looking not only at what falls
under our senses but holding on to His words. For His
word cannot lead us astray."[3]

The scholastic Doctors often made similar affirma-
tions: That in this sacrament are the true Body of Christ
and His true Blood is something that "cannot be appre-
hended by the senses," says St. Thomas, "but only by
faith which relies on divine authority. This is why, in a
comment on Luke 22, 19: ('This is My Body which is
given for you') St. Cyril says: 'Do not doubt whether this
is true, but rather receive the words of the Savior in faith,
for since He is the truth, He cannot lie.'"[4]

Thus the Christian people, echoing the words of the
same St. Thomas, frequently sing the words: "Sight,
touch, and taste in Thee are each deceived, the ear alone
most safely is believed. I believe all the Son of God has
spoken — than truth's own word there is no truer
token."

In fact, St. Bonaventure asserts: "There is no difficulty about Christ's presence in the Eucharist as in a
sign, but that He is truly present in the Eucharist as He is
in heaven, this is most difficult. Therefore to believe this
is especially meritorious."[5]

Moreover, the Holy Gospel alludes to this when it tells
of the many disciples of Christ who, after listening to the
sermon about eating His Flesh and drinking His Blood,
turned away and left our Lord, saying: "This is strange

Homily on Matthew, 82, 4, Migne, P.G. 58, 743.
[4]Summa Theologica, III, Q. 75, A. 1, C.
[5]In IV Sent., Dist X, P. I, Art. Un., Uq. I, Opera Omnia, tome IV, Ad Claras
Acquas, 1889, p. 217.

talk, who can be expected to listen to it?'' Peter, on the other hand, in reply to Jesus' question whether also the twelve wished to leave, expressed his faith and that of the others promptly and resolutely with the marvelous answer: "Lord, to whom should we go? Thy words are the words of eternal life" (John 6, 61-69).

It is logical, then, that we should follow as a guiding star in our investigation of this mystery the magisterium of the Church, to which the Divine Redeemer entrusted for protection and for explanation the revelation which He has communicated to us through Scripture or tradition. For we are convinced that *"what since the days of antiquity was preached and believed throughout the whole Church* with true Catholic Faith is true, even if it is not submitted to rational investigation, even if it is not explained by means of words."[6]

But this is not enough. Having safeguarded the integrity of the faith, it is necessary to safeguard also its proper mode of expression, lest by the careless use of words, we occasion (God forbid) the rise of false opinions regarding faith in the most sublime of mysteries. St. Augustine gives a stern warning about this in his consideration of the way of speaking employed by the philosophers and of that which ought to be used by Christians.

"The philosophers," he says, "speak freely without fear of offending religious listeners on subjects quite difficult to understand. We, on the other hand, must speak according to a fixed norm, lest the lack of restraint in our speech result in some impious opinion even about the things signified by the words themselves."[7]

---

[6]St. Augustine, *Contr. Julian,* VI, 5, 11, Migne., P.L. 44, 829.
[7]*City of God,* X, 23; P.L. 41,300.

The Church, therefore, with the long labor of centuries and, not without the help of the Holy Spirit, has established a rule of language and confirmed it with the authority of the councils. This rule, which has more than once been the watchword and banner of Orthodox faith, must be religiously preserved, and let no one presume to change it at his own pleasure or under the pretext of new science. *Who would ever tolerate that the dogmatic formulas used by the ecumenical councils for the mysteries of the Holy Trinity and the Incarnation be judged as no longer appropriate for men of our times and therefore that others be rashly substituted for them? In the same way, it cannot be tolerated that any individual should on his own authority modify the formulas which were used by the Council of Trent to express belief in the Eucharistic Mystery.* For these formulas, like the others which the Church uses to propose the dogmas of faith, express concepts which are not tied to a certain form of human culture, nor to a specific phase of human culture, nor to one or other theological school.

No, these formulas present that part of reality which necessary and universal experience permits the human mind to grasp and to manifest with apt and exact terms taken either from common or polished language. For this reason, these formulas are adapted to men of all times and all places. But the most sacred task of theology is, not the invention of new dogmatic formulas to replace old ones, but rather such a defense and explanation of the formulas adopted by the councils as may demonstrate that divine Revelation is the source of the truths communicated through these expressions.

It must be admitted that these formulas can sometimes be more clearly and accurately explained. In fact, the achievement of this goal is highly beneficial. But it would be wrong to give to these expressions a meaning other than the original. Thus, the understanding of the faith should be advanced without threat to its unchangeable truth. It is, in fact, the teaching of the First Vatican Council that "the same signification (of sacred dogmas) is to be forever retained once our Holy Mother the Church has defined it, and under no pretext of deeper penetration may that meaning be weakened."[8]

The Mystery of the Eucharist is Verified In the Sacrifice of the Mass

For the inspiration and consolation of all, we wish to review with you, venerable brothers, the doctrine which the Catholic Church has always transmitted and unanimously teaches concerning the Mystery of the Eucharist.

We desire to recall at the very outset what may be termed the very essence of the dogma, namely, that by means of the Mystery of the Eucharist, the Sacrifice of the Cross, which was once offered on Calvary, is remarkably re-enacted and constantly recalled, and its saving power exerted for the forgiveness of those sins which we daily commit.[9]

Just as Moses with the blood of calves had sanctified the Old Testament (cf. Ex. 24,8), so also Christ our Lord, through the institution of the Mystery of the Eucharist, with His own Blood sanctified the New Testament, whose Mediator He is. For, as the Evangelists narrate, at the Last Supper "He took bread, and blessed and broke it, and gave it to them, saying: 'This is My

[8]*Dogmatic Constitution on the Catholic Faith*, C. 4.
[9]cf. Council of Trent, *Teaching on the Holy Sacrifice of the Mass*, C. 1.

Body, given for you; do this for a commemoration of Me. And so with the cup, when supper was ended. This cup, He said, is the New Testament, in My Blood which is to be shed for you'''(Lk 22, 19-20; cf. Mt 26, 26-28; Mk 14, 22-24). And by bidding the Apostles to do this in memory of Him, He made clear His will that the same sacrifice be forever repeated.

This intention of Christ was faithfully executed by the primitive Church through her adherence to the teaching of the Apostles and through her gatherings summoned to celebrate the Eucharistic Sacrifice. As St. Luke carefully testifies, "These occupied themselves continually with the Apostles' teaching, their fellowship in the breaking of bread, and the fixed times of prayer" (Acts 2, 41). From this practice, the faithful used to derive such spiritual strength that it was said of them that "there was one heart and soul in all the company of believers" (Acts 4, 32).

Moreover, the Apostle Paul, who has faithfully transmitted to us what he had received from the Lord (1 Cor. 11, 23 ff.), is clearly speaking of the Eucharistic Sacrifice when he points out that Christians, precisely because they have been made partakers at the table of the Lord, ought not to take part in pagan sacrifices. "Is not the cup we bless," he says, "a participation in Christ's Blood? Is not the bread we break a participation in Christ's Body?...to drink the Lord's cup, and yet to drink the cup of evil spirits, to share the Lord's feast, and to share the feast of evil spirits, is impossible for you" (I Cor. 10, 16). Foreshadowed by Malachias (1, 11), this new offering of the New Testament has always been offered by the Church, in accordance with the teaching of Our Lord and the Apostles, "not only to atone for the sins of the living faithful and to appeal for their other needs, but also to help these who have died in Christ but have not yet been completely purified."[10]

Passing over other citations, we recall merely the testimony rendered by St. Cyril of Jerusalem, who wrote the following memorable instructions for his neophytes:

"After the Spiritual Sacrifice, the unbloody act of worship has been completed. Bending over this propitiatory offering we beg God to grant peace to all the Churches, to give harmony to the whole world, to bless our rulers, our soldiers, and our companions, to aid the sick and afflicted, and in general to assist all who stand in need; and then we offer the Victim also for our deceased holy ancestors and bishops and for all our dead. As we do this, we are filled with the conviction that this Sacrifice will be of the greatest help to those souls for whom prayers are being offered in the very presence of our holy and awesome Victim."

This holy Doctor closes his instructon by citing the parallel of the crown which is woven for the emperor to move him to pardon exiles: "In the same fashion, when we offer our prayers to God for the dead, even though they be sinners, we weave no crown, but instead we offer Christ slaughtered for our sins, beseeching our merciful God to take pity both on them and on ourselves."[11] St. Augustine testifies that this manner of offering also for the deceased "the Sacrifice which ransomed us" was being faithfully observed in the Church at Rome,[12] and at the same time he observes that the universal Church was following this custom in her conviction that it had been handed down

---

[10]Council of Trent, *Doctrine on the Holy Sacrifice of the Mass,* C.2.
[11]*Catecheses,* 23 (Myst. 5), 8-18; p.g. 33, 1115-1118.
[12]cf. *Confessions IX,* 12, 32; P.L. 32, 777; cf. Ibid. IX, 11, 27; P.L. 32, 775.

by the earliest Fathers.[13]

To shed fuller light on the mystery of the Church, it helps to realize that it is nothing less than the whole Church which, in union with Christ in His role as Priest and Victim, offers the Sacrifice of the Mass and is offered in it. The Fathers of the Church taught this wondrous doctrine.[14] A few years ago our predecessor of happy memory, Pius XII, explained it,[15] and only recently the Second Vatican Council enunciated it in its treatise on the People of God as formulated in its Constitution on the Church.[16]

To be sure, the distinction between universal priesthood and hierarchical priesthood is one of essence and not merely one of degree,[17] and this distinction should be faithfully observed. Yet *we cannot fail to be filled with the earnest desire that this teaching on the Mass be explained over and over until it takes root deep in the hearts of the faithful.* Our desire is founded on our conviction that the correct understanding of the Eucharistic Mystery is the most effective means to foster devotion to this Sacrament, to extol the dignity of all the faithful, and to spur their spirit toward the attainment of the summit of sanctity, which is nothing less than the total offering of oneself to service of the Divine Majesty.

We should also mention "the public and social nature of every Mass,"[18] a conclusion which clearly follows

[13]cf. *Serm.* 172, 2; P.L. 38, 936; cf. *On the Care to be Taken of the Dead,* 13; P.L. 40, 593.

[14]cf. St. Augustine, *City of God,* X, 6; P.L. 41, 284.

[15]cf. Encyclical *Mediator Dei,* A.A.S. XXXIX, 1947, p. 552.

[16]cf. *Dogmatic Constitution on the Church,* C. 2, N. 11; A.A.S. LVII, 1965, p. 15.

[17]cf. Ibid, C. 2, N. 10; A.A.S. LVII, 1965, p. 14.

[18]*Constitution on the Sacred Liturgy,* C. 1, N. 27; A.A.S. LVI, 1964, p. 107.

from the doctrine we have been discussing. For even though a priest should offer Mass in private, that Mass is not something private; It is an act of Christ and of the Church. In offering this Sacrifice, the Church learns to offer herself as a sacrifice for all. Moreover, for the salvation of the entire world she applies the single, boundless, redemptive power of the Sacrifice of the Cross. For every Mass is offered not for the salvation of ourselves alone, but also for that of the whole world. Hence, although the very nature of the action renders most appropriate the active participation of many of the faithful in the celebration of the Mass, nevertheless, that Mass is to be fully approved which, in conformity with the prescriptions and lawful traditions of the Church, a priest for a sufficient reason offers in private, that is, in the presence of no one except his server. From such a Mass an abundant treasure of special salutary graces enriches the celebrant, the faithful, the whole Church, and the entire world — graces which are not imparted in the same abundance by the mere reception of Holy Communion.

Therefore, from a paternal and solicitous heart, we recommend to priests, who bestow on us a special crown of happiness in the Lord, that they be mindful of their power, received through the hands of the ordaining bishop, of offering sacrifice to God and of celebrating Masses both for the living and for the dead in the name of the Lord,[19] and that they worthily and devoutly offer Mass each day in order that both they and the rest of the faithful may enjoy the benefits that flow so richly from the Sacrifice of the Cross. Thus also they will contribute most to the salvation of the human race.

[19]cf. Roman Pontifical.

In the Sacrifice of the Mass
Christ is Made Sacramentally Present

By the few ideas which we have mentioned regarding the Sacrifice of the Mass, we are encouraged to explain a few notions concerning the Sacrament of the Eucharist, seeing that both sacrifice and Sacrament pertain inseparably to the same mystery. In an unbloody representation of the Sacrifice of the Cross and in application of its saving power, in the Sacrifice of the Mass the Lord is immolated when, through the words of consecration, He begins to be present in a sacramental form under the appearances of bread and wine to become the spiritual food of the faithful.

All of us realize that there is more than one way in which Christ is present in His Church. We wish to review at greater length the consoling doctrine which was briefly set forth in the constitution "De Sacra Liturgica" [Vat. II, "Const. on the Sacred Liturgy"].[20] Christ is present in His Church when she prays, since it is He who "prays for us and prays in us and to Whom we pray as to our God."[21] It is He who has promised: "where two or three are gathered together in my name, I am there in the midst of them" (Mt. 18, 20).

He is present in the Church as she performs her works of mercy, not only because we do to Christ whatever good we do to one of His least brethren (cf. Mt. 25,40), but also because it is Christ, performing these works through the Church, who continually assists men with His divine love. He is present in the Church on her pilgrimage of struggle to reach the harbor of eternal life,

[20]cf. C. 1, N. 7; A.A.S. LVI, 1964, p. 100-101.
[21]St. Augustine, *On Psalm 85, 1*; P.L. 37, 1081.

since it is He who through faith dwells in our hearts (cf. Eph. 3,17) and, through the Holy Spirit whom He gives us, pours His love into those hearts (cf. Rom. 5,5).

In still another genuine way He is present in the Church as she preaches, since the Gospel which she proclaims is the Word of God, which is not preached except in the name of Christ, by the authority of Christ, and with the assistance of Christ, the Incarnate Word of God. In this way there is formed "one flock which trusts its only shepherd."[22]

He is present in His Church as she governs the People of God, since her sacred power comes from Christ, and since Christ, "The Shepherd of Shepherds,"[23] is present in the pastors who exercise that power, according to His promise to the Apostles: "Behold I am with you all through the days that are coming, until the consummation of the world."

Moreover, in a manner still more sublime, Christ is present in His Church as she offers in His name the Sacrifice of the Mass; He is present in her as she administers the Sacraments. We find deep consolation in recalling the accurate and eloquent words with which St. John Chrysostom, overcome with a sense of awe, described the presence of Christ in the offering of the Sacrifice of the Mass: "I wish to add something that is plainly awe-inspiring, but do not be astonished or upset. This Sacrifice, no matter who offers it, be it Peter or Paul, is always the same as that which Christ gave His disciples and which priests now offer: The offering of today is in no way inferior to that which Christ offered, because it is not men who sanctify the offering of today;

[22]St. Augustine, *Against the Letter of Petiliani*, III, 10, 11; P.L. 43, 353.
[23]St. Augustine, *On Psalm 86, 3;* P.L. 37, 1102.

it is the same Christ who sanctified His own. For just as the words which God spoke are the very same as those which the priest now speaks, so too the oblation is the very same."[24]

No one is unaware that the Sacraments are the actions of Christ, Who administers them through men. Therefore, the Sacraments are holy in themselves, and by the power of Christ they pour grace into the soul when they touch the body. The mind boggles at these different ways in which Christ is present; They confront the Church with a mystery ever to be pondered.

But there is yet another manner in which Christ is present in His Church, a manner which surpasses all the others; it is His presence in the Sacrament of the Eucharist, which is for this reason "a more consoling source of devotion, a more lovely object of contemplation, a more effective means of sanctification than all the other sacraments."[25]

The reason is clear; it contains Christ Himself and it is "a kind of perfection of the spiritual life; in a way, it is the goal of all the sacraments"[26]

This presence is called "real"—by which it is not intended to exclude all other types of presence as if they could not be "real" too, but because it is presence in the fullest sense; that is to say, it is a substantial presence by which Christ, the God-Man, is wholly and entirely present.[27] It would therefore be wrong to explain this presence by having recourse to the "spiritual" nature, as it is called, of the glorified Body of Christ, which is

[24]*Homily on the Second Episle to Timothy,* 2, 4; P.G. 62, 612.
[25]Aegidius Romanus, *Theoremata De Corpore Christi,* Theor. 50, Venetiis 1521, p. 127.
[26]St. Thomas, *Summa Theologica,* III, Q. 73, A. 3, C.
[27]cf. Council of Trent, *Decree on the Eucharist,* Ch. 3.

present everywhere, or by reducing it to a kind of symbolism, as if this most august Sacrament consisted of nothing else than an efficacious sign "of the spiritual presence of Christ and of His intimate union with the faithful, members of His Mystical Body."[28]

It is true that much can be found in the Fathers and in the scholastics with regard to symbolism in the Eucharist, especially with reference to the unity of the Church. The Council of Trent, restating their doctrine, taught that the Savior bequeathed the blessed Eucharist to His Church "as a symbol... of that unity and charity with which He wished all Christians to be most intimately united among themselves," and hence "as a symbol of that One Body of which He is the Head."[29]

When Christian literature was still in its infancy, the unknown author of that work we know as the "Didache or Teaching of the Twelve Apostles" wrote as follows on this subject: "In regard to the Eucharist, give thanks in this manner:... Just as this bread was scattered and dispersed over the hills, but when harvested was made one, so may Your Church be gathered into Your kingdom from the ends of the earth."[30]

The same we read in St. Cyprian, writing in defense of the Church against schism: "Finally, the sacrifices of the Lord proclaim the unity of Christians, bound together by the bond of a firm and inviolable charity. For when the Lord, in speaking of bread which is produced by the compacting of many grains of wheat, refers to it as His Body, He is describing our people whose unity He has sustained, and when He refers to wine pressed from many

[28]Pius XII, Encyclical *Humani Generis,* A.A.S. XLII, 1950, p. 578.
[29]*Decree on the Most Holy Eucharist*, Introduction and Ch. 2.
[30]*Didache*, 9:1, Funk, *Patres Apostolici,* 1, 20.

grapes and berries, as His Blood, He is speaking of our flock, formed by the fusing of many united together."[31]

But before all of these, St. Paul had written to the Corinthians: the one bread makes us one body, though we are many in number the same bread is shared by all (1 Cor. 10,17).

While the Eucharistic symbolism brings us to an understanding of the effect proper to this Sacrament, which is the unity of the mystical Body, it does not indicate or explain what it is that makes this Sacrament different from all others. The constant teaching which the Catholic Church passes on to her catechumens, the understanding of the Christian people, the doctrine defined by the Council of Trent, the very words used by Christ when He instituted the Most Holy Eucharist, compel us to acknowledge that "the Eucharist is that flesh of Our Savior Jesus Christ who suffered for our sins and whom the Father in his loving-kindness raised again."[32] To these words of St. Ignatius of Antioch, we may add those which Theodore of Mopsueta, a faithful witness to the faith of the Church on this point, addressed to the faithful: *"The Lord did not say: This is a symbol of My Body, and this a symbol of My Blood but: 'This is My Body and My Blood.' He teaches us not to look to the nature of those things which lie before us and are perceived by the senses, for by the prayer of thanksgiving and the words spoken over them, they have been changed into Flesh and Blood."* [33]

The Council of Trent, basing itself on this faith of the Church "openly and sincerely professes that within the

[31]*Epistle to Magnus*, 6; P.L. 3, 1189.
[32]St. Ignatius, *Epistle to the Smyrnians*, 7, 1; P.G. 5, 714.
[33]*Commentary on Matthew*, Ch. 26, P.G. 66, 714.

Holy Sacrament of the Eucharist, after the Consecration of the bread and wine, Our Lord Jesus Christ, true God and true Man, is really, truly and substantially contained under those outward appearances." In this way, the Savior in His humanity is present not only at the right hand of the Father according to the natural manner of existence, but also in the Sacrament of the Eucharist "by a mode of existence which we cannot express in words, but which, with a mind illuminated by faith, we can conceive, and must most firmly believe, to be possible to God."[34]

Christ Our Lord is Present in the Sacrament Of the Eucharist by Transubstantiation

To avoid misunderstanding this sacramental presence which surpasses the laws of nature and constitutes the greatest miracle of its kind[35] we must listen with docility to the voice of the teaching and praying Church. This voice, which constantly echoes the voice of Christ, assures us that the way Christ is made present in this Sacrament is none other than by the change of the whole substance of the bread into His Body, and of the whole substance of the wine into His Blood, and that this unique and truly wonderful change the Catholic Church rightly calls transubstantiation.[36] As a result of transubstantiation, the species of bread and wine undoubtedly take on a new meaning and a new finality, for they no longer remain ordinary bread and ordinary wine, but become the sign of something sacred, the sign of a spiritual food. However, the reason they take on this

[34]*Decree on the Most Holy Eucharist,* Ch. 1.
[35]cf. Encyclical *Mirae Caritatis, Acta Leonis XIII,* Vol. XXII, 1902-1903, p. 123.
[36]cf. Council of Trent, *Decree on the Eucharist, Ch. 4, and Canon 2.*

new significance and this new finality is simply because
they contain a new "reality" which we may justly term
ontological. Not that there lies under those species what
was already there before, but something quite different;
and that not only because of the faith of the Church, but
in objective reality, since after the change of the
substance or nature of the bread and wine into the Body
and Blood of Christ, nothing remains of the bread and
wine but the appearances, under which Christ, whole
and entire, in His physical "reality" is bodily present,
although not in the same way that bodies are present in a
given place.

For this reason the Fathers took special care to warn
the faithful that in reflecting on this most august
Sacrament, they should not trust to their senses, which
reach only the properties of bread and wine, but rather
to the words of Christ which have power to transform,
change and transmute the bread and wine into His Body
and Blood. For, as those same Fathers often said, the
power that accomplishes this is *that same power by which
God Almighty, at the beginning of time, created the world
out of nothing.*

"We have been instructed in these matters and filled
with an unshakeable faith," says St. Cyril of Alexandria, at the end of a sermon on the mysteries of the faith,
"that that which seems to be bread, is not bread, though
it tastes like it, but the Body of Christ, and that which
seems to be wine, is not wine, though it too tastes as
such, but the Blood of Christ...draw inner strength by
receiving this bread as spiritual food and your soul will
rejoice."[37]

St. John Chrysostom emphasizes this point, saying:

[37] *Catecheses*, 22, 9; *(Myst 4); P.G. 33, 1103.*

"It is not the power of man which makes what is put before us the Body and Blood of Christ, but the power of Christ Himself who was crucified for us. The priest standing there in the place of Christ says these words but their power and grace are from God. 'This is my Body,' he says, and these words transform what lies before him."[38]

Cyril, Bishop of Alexandria, is in full agreement with the Bishop of Constantinople when he writes in his commentary on the Gospel of St. Matthew: "Christ said indicating (the bread and wine): 'This is My Body,' and 'this is My Blood,' in order that you might not judge what you see to be a mere figure. The offerings, by the hidden power of God Almighty, are changed into Christ's Body and Blood, and by receiving these we come to share in the life-giving and sanctifying efficacy of Christ."[39]

Ambrose, Bishop of Milan, dealing with the Eucharistic change, says: "Let us be assured that this is not what nature formed, but what the blessing consecrated, and that greater efficacy resides in the blessing than in nature, for by the blessing nature is changed." To confirm the truth of this mystery, he recounts many of the miracles described in the Scriptures, including Christ's birth of the Virgin Mary, and then turning to the work of creation, concludes thus: "Surely the word of Christ, which could make out of nothing that which did not exist, can change things already in existence into what they were not. For it is no less extraordinary to give things new natures than to change their natures."[40]

[38] *Homily on Judas' Betrayal,* 1, 6; P.G. 49, 380; cf. *Homily on Matthew,* 82, 5; P.G. 58, 744.
[39] *On Matthew,* 26, 27; P.G. 72, 451.
[40] *On Mysteries* 9, 50-52; P.L. 16, 422-424.

However, there is no need to assemble many testimonies. Rather let us recall that firmness of faith with which the Church with one accord opposed Berengarius, who, yielding to the difficulties of human reasoning, was the first who dared deny the Eucharistic change. More than once she threatened to condemn him unless he retracted. Thus it was that our predecessor, St. Gregory VII, ordered him to pronounce the following oath:

"I believe in my heart and openly profess that the bread and wine which are placed upon the altar are, by the mystery of the sacred prayer and the words of the Redeemer, substantially changed into the true and life-giving flesh and blood of Jesus Christ Our Lord, and that after the Consecration, there is present the true Body of Christ which was born of the Virgin and, offered up for the salvation of the world, hung on the Cross and now sits at the right hand of the Father and that there is present the true Blood of Christ which flowed from His side. They are present not only by means of a sign and of the efficacy of the Sacrament, but also in the very reality and truth of their nature and substance."[41]

These words fully accord with the doctrine of the mystery of the Eucharistic change as set forth by the ecumenical councils. The constant teaching of these councils — of the Lateran, of Constance, Florence and Trent — whether stating the teaching of the Church or condemning errors, affords us an admirable example of the unchangingness of the Catholic Faith.

After the Council of Trent, our predecessor, Pius VI, on the occasion of the errors of the Synod of Pistoia, warned parish priests when carrying out their office of

[41]Mansi, *Collectio Amplissima Conciliorum*, XX, 524D.

teaching, not to neglect to speak of transubstantiation, one of the articles of the faith.[42] Similarly our predecessor of happy memory, Pius XII, recalled the bounds which those who undertake to discuss the mystery of transubstantiation might not cross.[43] We ourself also, in fulfillment of our apostolic office, have openly borne solemn witness to the faith of the Church at the National Eucharistic Congress held recently at Pisa.[44]

Moreover the Catholic Church has held on to this faith in the presence in the Eucharist of the Body and Blood of Christ, not only in her teaching but also in her practice, since she has at all times given to this great Sacrament the worship which is known as Latria and which may be given to God alone. As St. Augustine says: "It was in His flesh that Christ walked among us and it is His flesh that he has given us to eat for our salvation. No one, however, eats of this flesh without having first adored it...and not only do we not sin in thus adoring it, but we would sin if we did not do so."[45]

Latreutic Worship of the Sacrament of the Eucharist

The Catholic Church has always offered and still offers the cult of Latria to the Sacrament of the Eucharist, not only during Mass, but also outside of it, reserving consecrated Hosts with the utmost care, exposing them to solemn veneration, and carrying them processionally to the joy of great crowds of the faithful.

In the ancient documents of the Church we have many

[42]Const. *Auctorem Fidei,* 28 August 1794.
[43]Allocution of 22 Sept. 1956, A.A.S. CLVIII, 1956, p. 720.
[44]A.A.S. LVII, 1965, p. 588-592.
[45]*On Psalm 98, 9;* P.L. 37, 1264

testimonies of this veneration. The pastors of the Church in fact solicitously exhorted the faithful to take the greatest care in keeping the Eucharist which they took to their homes. "The Body of Christ is meant to be eaten, not to be treated with irreverence," St. Hippolytus warns the faithful.[46]

In fact the faithful thought themselves guilty, and rightly so, as Origen recalls, if after they received the Body of the Lord in order to preserve it with all care and reverence, a small fragment of it fell off through negligence.[47]

The same pastors severely reproved those who showed lack of reverence if it happened. This is attested to by Novitianus whose testimony in the matter is trustworthy. He judged as deserving condemnation anyone who came out of Sunday service carrying with him as usual the Eucharist, the Sacred Body of the Lord, "not going to his house but running to places of amusement."[48]

On the other hand St. Cyril of Alexandria rejects as folly the opinion of those who maintained that if a part of the Eucharist was left over for the following day it did not confer sanctification. "For," he says, "neither Christ is altered nor His Holy Body changed, but the force and power and vivifying grace always remain with it."[49]

Nor should we forget that in ancient times the faithful, harassed by the violence of persecution or living in solitude out of love for monastic life, nourished themselves even daily, receiving Holy Communion by their

[46]*Tradit. Apost.*, Ed. Botte, *La Tradition Apostolique De St. Hippolyte*, Muenster 1963, p. 84.
[47]*In Exod. Fragm.*, P.G. 12, 391.
[48]*De Spectaculis*, C.S.E.L. III, p. 8.
[49]*Epist. Ad Calosyrium*, P.G. 76, 1075.

own hands when the priest or deacon was absent.[50]

We say this not in order that there may be some change in the way of keeping the Eucharist and of receiving Holy Communion which was later on prescribed by Church laws and which now remain in force, but rather that we may rejoice over the faith of the Church which is always one and the same.

This faith also gave rise to the feast of Corpus Christi which was first celebrated in the Diocese of Liege specially through the efforts of the servant of God, Blessed Juliana of Mount Cornelius, and which our predecessor Urban IV extended to the Universal Church. From it have originated many practices of Eucharistic piety which under the inspiration of divine grace have increased from day to day and with which the Catholic Church is striving ever more to do homage to Christ, to thank Him for so great a gift and to implore His mercy.

Exhortation to Promote the Cult of the Eucharist

We therefore ask you, Venerable Brothers, among the people entrusted to your care and vigilance, to preserve this faith in its purity and integrity — a faith which seeks only to remain perfectly loyal to the word of Christ and of the Apostles and unambiguously rejects all erroneous and mischievous opinions. *Tirelessly promote the cult of the Eucharist, the focus where all other forms of piety must ultimately emerge.*

May the faithful, thanks to your efforts, come to realize and experience ever more perfectly the truth of these words: "He who desires life finds here a place to live in and the means to live by. Let him approach, let

[50]cf. Basil, *Epistle*, 93, P.G. 32, 483-486.

him believe, let him be incorporated so that he may receive life. Let him not refuse union with the members, let him not be a corrupt member, deserving to be cut off, nor a disfigured member to be ashamed of. Let him be a grateful, fitting and healthy member. Let him cleave to the body, let him live by God and for God. Let him now labor here on earth, that he may afterwards reign in heaven."[51]

It is to be desired that the faithful, every day and in great numbers, actively participate in the Sacrifice of the Mass, receive Holy Communion with a pure heaeart, and give thanks to Christ Our Lord for so great a gift. Let them remember these words: "The desire of Jesus Christ and of the Church that all the faithful receive daily Communion means above all that through the sacramental union with God they may obtain the strength necessary for mastering their passions, for purifying themselves of their daily venial faults and for avoiding the grave sins to which human frailty is exposed."[52]

In the course of the day the faithful should not omit to *visit the Blessed Sacrament,* which according to the liturgical laws must be kept in the churches with great reverence in a most honorable location. Such visits are a proof of gratitude, an expression of love, an acknowledgment of the Lord's presence.

No one can fail to understand that the Divine Eucharist bestows upon the Christian people an incomparable dignity. Not only while the sacrifice is offered and the Sacrament is received, but as long as the Eucharist is kept in our churches and oratories, Christ is truly the

[51]St. Augustine, *Treatise on John,* 26, 13; P.L. 35, 1613.
[52]Decree of the Sacred Congregation of the Council, 20 Dec. 1905, approved by St. Pius X; A.A.S. XXXVIII, 1905, p. 401.

Emmanuel, that is, "God with us." Day and night He is in our midst, He dwells with us, full of grace and truth (cf. John 1, 14). He restores morality, nourishes virtues, consoles the afflicted, strengthens the weak. He proposes His own example to those who come to Him that all may learn to be, like Himself, meek and humble of heart and to seek not their own interests but those of God.

Anyone who approaches this august Sacrament with special devotion and endeavors to return generous love for Christ's own infinite love, will experience and fully understand—not without spiritual joy and fruit—how precious is the life hidden with Christ in God (cf. Col. 3, 3) and how great is the value of converse with Christ, for *there is nothing more consoling on earth, nothing more efficacious for advancing along the road of holiness.*

Further, you realize, venerable brothers, that the Eucharist is reserved in the churches and oratories as in the spiritual center of a religious community or of a parish, yes, of the universal Church and of all of humanity, since beneath the appearance of the species, Christ is contained, the invisible Head of the Church, the Redeemer of the World, the Center of all hearts, "by whom all things are and by whom we exist" (I Cor. 8, 6).

From this it follows that the worship paid to the Divine Eucharist strongly impels the soul to cultivate a "social" love,[53] by which the common good is given preference over the good of the individual. Let us consider as our own the interests of the community, of the parish, of the entire Church, extending our charity to the whole world, because we know that everywhere there are mem-

[53] cf. St. Augustine, *On the Literal Interpretation of Genesis,* XI, 15, 20; P.L. 34, 437.

bers of Christ.

The Eucharistic Sacrament, venerable brothers, is the sign and the cause of the unity of the Mystical Body, and it inspires an active "ecclesial" spirit in those who venerate it with greater fervor. Therefore, never cease to persuade those committed to your care that they should learn to make their own the cause of the Church, in approaching the Eucharistic mystery to pray to God without interruption to offer themselves to God as a pleasing sacrifice for the peace and unity of the Church, so that all the children of the Church be united and think the same, that there be no divisions among them, but rather unity of mind and purpose, as the Apostle insists (cf. I Cor. 1, 10). May all those not yet in perfect communion with the Catholic Church, who though separated from her glory in the name of Christian, share with us as soon as possible with the help of divine grace that unity of faith and communion which Christ wanted to be the distinctive mark of His disciples.

This zeal in praying and consecrating one's self to God for the unity of the Church should be practiced *particularly by Religious, both men and women, inasmuch as they are in a special way devoted to the adoration of the Blessed Sacrament,* according to it homage and honor on earth, in virtue of their vows.

Nothing has ever been or is more important to the Church or more consoling than the desire for the unity of all Christians, a desire which we wish to express once again in the very words used by the Council of Trent at the close of its Decree on the Most Blessed Eucharist: "In conclusion, the sacred synod with paternal love admonishes, exhorts, prays and implores 'through the merciful kindness of our God' (Luke 1, 78) that each and

every Christian come at last to a perfect agreement
regarding this sign of unity, this bond of charity, this
symbol of concord, and, mindful of such great dignity
and such exquisite love of God our Lord who gave His
beloved soul as the price of our salvation and 'His flesh
to eat' (John 6, 48 ss.) believe and adore these sacred
mysteries of His Body and Blood with such firm and
unwavering faith, with such devotion, piety and veneration, that they can receive frequently that super-
substantial bread (Matt. 6, 11), which will be for them
truly the life of the soul and unfailing strength of mind,
so that fortified by its vigor (cf. Kings 19, 8) they can
depart from this wretched pilgrimage on earth to reach
their heavenly home where they will then eat the same
'Bread of Angels' (Ps. 77, 25) no longer hidden by the
species which now they eat under the sacred appearances.''[54]

May the all-good Redeemer who shortly before His
death prayed to the Father that all who were to believe in
Him would be one even as He and the Father were one
(cf. John 17, 20-21), deign speedily to hear our most
ardent prayer and that of the entire Church, that we may
all with one voice and one faith, celebrate the Eucharistic
Mystery and, by participating in the Body of Christ,
become one body (cf. I Cor. 10, 17), linked by those
same bonds which He Himself desired for its perfection.

And we turn with paternal affection also to those who
belong to the venerable Churches of the Orient, from
which came so many most illustrious Fathers whose
testimony to the belief of the Eucharist we have so gladly
cited in our present letter. Our soul is filled with intense

[54]*Decree on the Most Holy Eucharist, C. 8.*

joy as we consider your faith in the Eucharist, which is also our faith, and as we listen to the liturgical prayers by which you celebrate so great a mystery we rejoice to behold your Eucharistic devotion, and to read your theologians explaining or defending the doctrine of this most august Sacrament.

May the Most Blessed Virgin Mary from whom Christ Our Lord took the flesh which under the species of bread and wine "is contained, offered and consumed,"[55] may all the saints of God, specially those who burned with a more ardent devotion to the Divine Eucharist, intercede before the Father of mercies so that from this same faith in and devotion toward the Eucharist may result and flourish a perfect unity of communion among all Christians.

Unforgettable are the words of the holy martyr Ignatius, in his warning to the faithful of Philadelphia against the evils of division and schism, the remedy for which lies in the Eucharist: "Strive then," he says, "to make use of one form of thanksgiving for the flesh of Our Lord Jesus Christ is one and one is the chalice in the union of His Blood, one altar, one bishop."[56]

Encouraged by the most consoling hope of the blessings which will accrue to the whole Church and the entire world from an increase in devotion to the Eucharist, with profound affection we impart to you, venerable brothers, to the priests, Religious and all those who collaborate with you and to all the faithful entrusted to your care, the apostolic benediction as a pledge of heavenly graces.

[55] C.I.C., Canon 801, 1918.
[56] *Epistle to the Philadelphians*, 4; P.G. 5, 700.

Given at Rome, at St. Peter's, the third day of September, the Feast of Pope St. Pius X, in the year 1965, the third year of our pontificate.

— Paul VI, Pope

WORDS and REFERENCES

(marked in the text with an asterisk)

Accident: We use the word here in its philosophical meaning of *that which qualifies* a substance, such as color, size, shape, texture, or any quality or property of a thing *which is not essential to it.* (See *Substance.*)

Acrostic: A composition in which the first or last letter, taken in order, forms a word or phrase. If the acrostic is a word, as Christians used the Greek work for fish, each letter stands for another word.

Agape: This is actually a Greek word which we use because it cannot be translated. The closest single synonym in English would be *love.* But *agape* means divine love in all its dimensions. It means the love God has for us and the love we must have for Him, and for all our fellow men in Him. This love is expressed in the Eucharist, and hence the term is applied to the Eucharistic Liturgy, the "Lord's Supper."

Alacoque, Saint Margaret Mary: No one is bound to believe in the revelations made by this saint (see Chapter Fifteen) because we have only the word of the saint and confirmation of experience. But it is impractical, even irrational, to question them. There is evidence that the saint told the truth, and none that she lied. Papal encyclicals and bulls which affirm belief in these apparitions include Pius IX: *Brief of Beatification of Margaret Mary,* September 18, 1864; Leo XIII: encyclical *Annum Sacrum,* May 25, 1899; Benedict XV: *Bull of Margaret Mary's canonization,* May 13, 1920; Pius XI: encyclical *Miserentissimus,* May 8, 1928. But above all we see the benefits from the devotion, its universality, its fruits of holiness. Moreover, aside from the promises which Our Lord made when He appeared to Saint Margaret Mary out of the Eucharist, there is truly nothing new in the devotion but merely an appeal for reparation and love to Christ Who so loves us. Under obedience, Saint Margaret described the revelations in her own words published as "Life and Words." An edition with commentary by Msgr. Gauthey in three volumes was published in Paris in 1920: *Vie et Oeuvres de St. M. M.* Several miracles have been wrought through the saint's intercession as was proved when she was canonized. (See this word.)

Angel: The figure which appeared to the children of Fatima was radiant, and had appeared before. He identified himself as an angel. We do not concern ourselves with *how* the apparition took place. We have many scriptural precedents of angelic visitations: to Abraham, to Elijah, to the Virgin Mary. But for the "initiated" there are perhaps two other questions which arise: Where did the angel obtain the Host? And how can Divinity be offered to Divinity?

Rev. Messias Coelho, one of the world's greatest students of the subject, presumes that the Host was from some tabernacle. As for the second question: The angel does not offer just the Divinity of Christ to the Divinity of the Holy Trinity (which would indeed be offering Himself to Himself), but offers also Christ's Body, Blood and Soul. And this prayer which the angel taught to the children of Fatima, and which they found afterwards engraved in their memories so that each child remembered it word for word independently of the others, teaches us to offer Christ in the Eucharist to the Blessed Trinity (in adoration, reparation and petition) *even outside the Eucharistic Liturgy,* and thereby to a degree *extending the Eucharistic Liturgy throughout the day.* The entire prayer taught by the angel is as follows: *"O Most Holy Trinity, Father, Son and Holy Spirit, I adore Thee profoundly. I offer Thee the most precious Body, Blood, Soul and Divinity of Jesus Christ, present in all the tabernacles of the world, in reparation for the outrages, sacrileges and indifference by which He is offended. By the infinite merits of the Sacred Heart of Jesus and the Immaculate Heart of Mary* (see this word), *I beg the conversion of poor sinners."*

Archeologists: Students of antiquities, such as ancient relics, remains of buildings, old parchments or manuscripts, inscriptions, and the like. Historians deal primarily with facts and events, but archeologists are preoccupied by the things which bear witness to facts and events of ancient times.

Archeology: The science of antiquities. Once it was largely a guessing science, but in modern times it has become more precise due to comparative studies among experts in the field, carbon tests, spectrum analysis, and other modern aids. History usually gives archeology the clues for its discoveries.

Athenagoras I: Patriarch of Constantinople (now Istanbul, 262nd successor of Saint Andrew, was the spiritual leader of over 160 million members of the Orthodox (see this word) Church. He can be likened to Pope John XXIII, whom he knew intimately, and he is perhaps as revered in the Eastern Church as John is in the West. He spent eighteen years in the U.S. as Archbishop of the Orthodox in North and South America. The vision of the "Chalice of the Lord" which the Patriarch made

public in an interview with LIFE reporter Peter Dra-
gadze in March 1967, is a vision of the Eucharist.
Dimitrios I succeeded Athenagoras as Patriarch of the
Orthodox (1982). The Orthodox do not communicate
with a Host, as in the Church of Rome. They consecrate
bread, then drop the Eucharist into a chalice, and
communion is given with a little spoon from the chalice.
Many other Christians communicate in the same manner, receiving Christ simultaneously under both species.

Benediction: This is a paraliturgical Eucharistic service
which began in the time of the Black Plague, when the
Blessed Sacrament was exposed for public adoration.
Soon it became a custom before returning the Blessed
Sacrament to "hiding" in the tabernacle (see this word)
to lift It in benediction upon the adorers. Churches where
the Blessed Sacrament is reserved may have a lengthy
period of solemn exposition every year (e.g. Forty Hours
Devotion), or perhaps shorter periods every month. A
monstrance (see this word) is usually used.

Blue Army of Our Lady of Fatima: Founded in 1947 by
an American priest (Msgr. Harold V. Colgan) as a response to the conditions given at Fatima for the conversion of Russia and world peace. It was ultimately
adopted by the bishops of Portugal as the official Apostolate of Fatima. Its international center, next to the Basilica of Fatima, was dedicated by Pope Pius XII in 1956
through a Legate, Eugene Cardinal Tisserant, Dean of
the College of Cardinals. The "Army" is a movement that
is uniquely spiritual, with no dues or meetings required
except among promoters. Each member is required to pray
a morning offering and to renew this offering (at least by
a thought or intention) in moments of temptation. As aids
to remembering the offering, and for spiritual strength and

assistance, the members are also required to pray the Rosary and wear the Brown Scapular (for the importance of these sacramentals in reference to the Eucharist, see reference to Saint Thomas Aquinas on p. 124). These requirements fulfill the basic conditions of the Message of Fatima and by 1982 had been promised by over twenty-two million Blue Army members in 110 countries around the world. It remains a movement with diocesan supervision in most instances. Philadelphia's Cardinal O'Hara had said: "It is something which must come from the people." Its most evident fruit is the spirituality of its members from whom grew the international movement of the All-Night Vigil (see authors's book *Night of Love,* published by AMI Press, 1967). Cardinal Van Rooey of Belgium said: "It is the most completely spiritual movement of the Church today." For a history of the movement see the author's other books *The Brother and I, Meet the Witnesses,* and particularly *Dear Bishop!* (memoirs of the author). A free copy of the Blue Army morning offering may be obtained from any of its centers.

Note: The official name of The Blue Army preferred by the Holy See is *World Apostolate of Fatima.*

Bosco, St. John: This great saint of the last century, whose special vocation was helping wayward boys, made many prophecies which were fulfilled in his own lifetime, as well as many which have been fulfilled since. One of the most remarkable of these prophecies was made in 1862 foretelling the Ecumenical Council and the tempests which would precede and follow it. The saint said that when the Pope succeeded in fastening the bark of Peter to the pillars of the Eucharist and of Mary, the tempest would subside.

Canonized: A person is "canonized" when the pope makes an infallible declaration that the person is in heaven. This is the culmination of a lengthy period of critical investigation and examination of evidence which may take a hundred years or more. Through canonization the Church wishes to present the person's life to the faithful as an example to be imitated. Public veneration (special honor because of their union with God) may then be given throughout the Church by honoring them in the Church's liturgy.

The steps toward canonization begin with a detailed critical investigation under the direction of the person's local bishop (which is conducted by a postulator). Evidence is gathered from every conceivable source, including documents, witnesses and experts (such as theologians, historians, and physicians who examine alleged cures attributed to the person's intercession after death).

All evidence gathered by the local bishop is forwarded to the Sacred Congregation for the Causes of the Saints in Rome which examines and re-examines the evidence with the assistance of additional experts. The final opinions of the Congregation are reported to the pope who alone can make the final judgment.

Catacombs: Cemeteries underground. The most famous of these are in and around Rome. So far over a hundred miles of tunnels, with graves on both sides, have been opened there. More are being opened at the present time. Already overwhelming evidence of the predominance of the Eucharist in the lives of early Christians has been brought to light as various photographs in this book bear witness. We may expect still more. Detailed documentation is available from the Pontifical Institute of Christian Archaeology in Rome and from the Fabbrica di San

Pietro, to both of which we are indebted for the photographs in this book dealing with early Christian art.

Chalice: A cup used in the Eucharistic Liturgy, usually gold (at least inside). It may be of any shape. The original chalice used by Our Lord at the Last Supper was known as the "Holy Grail" and was the object of fabled search in the Middle Ages. It is most often shaped like a goblet. Communion is given from a chalice in many instances. *See Athenagoras.*

Church: See Fathers of the Church.

Communion: Naturally in discussing the Eucharist we must use this word frequently because it is the final purpose of the Eucharistic Liturgy. It comes from the Greek word *koinonia* and is one of the key words of the theology of the Church, of salvation, and of grace. (See J. M. Tillard's *The Eucharist: Pasch of God's People,* 1967, p. 295.) By the Covenant (see this word) and especially by the New Covenant concluded "in the Lord Jesus," we are united with God in all the dimensions of love, in *agape* (see this word). And this is what we mean by communion. By receiving the Eucharist we enter into union not only with God but also with each other in Him. The fruit of this "communion" is the Mystical Body (see this word), the Church.

Consecrated Bread: See Consecration.

Consecration: In the Eucharistic Liturgy this word has special meaning: It refers to the repetition of the actual words of Christ over bread and wine by a duly ordained priest so that transubstantiation (see this word) occurs. It is the most solemn moment in the Eucharistic Liturgy.

Corporal: A small square linen cloth on which is placed the chalice (cup) and paten (plate) which contain the Bread and Wine. The corporal is placed on the altar cloth as extra protection in the event that any consecrated Wine might be spilled or any particles of a consecrated Host might be dropped. It is carefully cared for because it may come into direct contact with the Body of Christ.

Council: See Trent and Vatican II.

Covenant: In Hebrew it is *berit;* in Greek *diatheke.* Our English word, from the Latin "to come together," means an agreement between two parties, or an agreement by one party based on certain conditions being fulfilled by the other. This latter is of course the meaning of the word in Scripture. First God made a covenant with the Jews on Mount Sinai, following the first Passover; then He made a new covenant with all men following the Passover (Last Supper) which became the Eucharistic Liturgy. In the first Covenant He offers Himself to man on conditions of Justice. In the new Covenant He offers Himself on conditions of agape (see this word), or love. The word "testament" is often used interchangeably with "covenant."

Cryptography: From the Greek word *kryptos,* for secret: The act or art of writing in secret characters. This was a principal art and also a means of communication among the early Christians. Some of the secret symbols have only recently been deciphered as we have noted in Chapter Four.

Deposit of Faith: The sum total of truths revealed by Christ, taught by the Church without error, and witnessed by Scripture and Tradition. Concerning the latter, we have the teaching of the Fathers. One of the marks of a Father of the Church, in addition to wisdom and a holy life and having lived in the early centuries, is that what he taught had the consensus of approval by all

Christians. *See Fathers of the Church.*

Eastern Rites: See Orthodox and Ecumenism.

Ecumenical Council: See Trent and Vatican II.

Ecumenism: Comes from a Greek word meaning "Inhabited world." We might translate it as "universalism." Until recent times it appeared only as an adjective (ecumenic, or ecumenical) but especially since Pope John XXIII the word has come to be very commonly used among all Christians as an attitude and effort towards unity of faith, hope and love among all who confess Christ, the Lord, and even more generally among all who confess the Fatherhood of God. The Eucharist remains at the heart of ecumenism not only because it is the sacrament (see this word) of unity, but because *at its institution* Christ prayed for all: *"Father, that they may be one as You and I are one."* All efforts at true Christian ecumenism remain peripheral until they arrive at the Eucharist, although that day of "arrival" may not be as close as many would like.

The late Patriarch of Constantinople, His Holiness Athenagoras I, a powerful figure in the ecumenical movement, said: "I often have a vision when I look from my bedroom window: I see a beautiful hand holding the chalice of Our Lord over a nearby hill, and I hear secret voices that speak of love between humanity and peace among men... The responsibility for starting toward unity lies with the Christians." (Interview published in LIFE magazine, March 31, 1967). The vision of the venerable Patriarch, who is as revered in the Eastern Orthodox Church as much as Pope John XXIII in the West, bears amazing similarity to the vision seen by the children of Fatima in 1916 described in Chapter Twelve of this book.

Embryo: The earliest formation of cells which will develop into a complete living being. When its external form clearly resembles the newborn, it is called a fetus.

Entelechy: From the Greek meaning *to complete.* Science at the present time does not know what properties in cells cause them to develop in a definite progress of complex multiplications to a single, whole, living being. Since the word entelechy designates a conception completely actualized, in distinction from mere potential existence, we apply this word to what nevertheless remains unknown.

Eucharist: From the Greek word *eucharistia:* thanksgiving. The name refers to Christ under the form of bread and wine and is derived from the thanksgiving which Christ made to His Father when on the night of the Last Supper He transformed an ordinary prayer of thanksgiving over bread and wine (a Hebrew tradition) into the Mass. The Sacred Liturgy is thus a "eucharist" (thanksgiving) through which the priest, in union with Christ, the High Priest, turns bread and wine into His Body and Blood by the power of the Holy Spirit.

Eucharistic Christ: This term is actually redundant because the Eucharist *is* Christ. It is something like saying "the Christly Christ." But we use it to emphasize Christ in His hidden, sacramental form as distinguished from Christ as He is in heaven or as He was in Palestine.

Eucharistic Congress: These international assemblies have grown in importance with each passing year. There is perhaps no demonstration on earth that draws more persons, from more nations, in a prolonged act of divine worship. Lasting several days (the one in Bombay, India in 1964 was attended by Pope Paul VI and lasted ten days) it consists of a series of Masses, hours and nights of adoration and reparation, sermons, studies and conferences, processions, etc., all aimed at honor to Our Lord in the Eucharist and of increasing Eucharistic devotion in the world. They have been held on every continent, and in most of the principal nations of the world. They take place every four years, as in Bogota, Colombia, in August, 1968, then in Melbourne, Australia, in 1972, in Philadelphia, Pa. in 1976, and in Lourdes in 1981.

Eucharistic Heart of Jesus: The heart of Jesus is a real part of His real body but it has been the object of special devotion through the ages, especially in modern times, *as representing the love of Christ for men.* For the history of the devotion, see Aug. Harmon, S.J., *Histoire de le devotion au Sacre-Coeur,* published in Paris 1923-1940, in five volumes. And for one of the best single works on the object, motives and practice of the devotion, see *Devotion to the Sacred Heart,* by Louis Verheylesoon, S.J., published in London by Sand & Co., Inc., 1955.

Faith: See Deposit of Faith.

Fathers of the Church: The Christian Church was completely united for the first thousand years, and even the political separation between the East and the West was not final until the fifteenth century. The doctrinal break came after Martin Luther in the sixteenth. So the "Fathers" of the Church are common to all Christians and the title is applied to those great Christian teachers of the first centuries when Christians dared to come out in the open after the persecutions. These were the men who explained what Christ had taught even more fully than the Gospels reported. John had said that if all they had learned from Our Lord were recorded, "I doubt there would be room enough in the entire world to hold the books to record them'' (Jn. 21:25). And churchmen like Justin, Aristides, Origin, Clement of Alexandria, said far more than had ever been preached in public. But even before them were others like Ignatius, Polycarp and Clement (the first two were actual disciples of Saint John) who had recorded explanation and facts received directly from the Apostles. And they all became witnesses (martyrs). Then as time passed there came Saint Augustine, Saint Gregory the Great (sixth century), and finally the last Father of the East: St. John Damascene (eighth century). We consider what was taught by the ''Fathers'' as belonging to the Deposit of Faith left by the Apostles.

Fatima: A town in central Portugal, 3000 feet above sea level, about 90 miles north of Lisbon in the Serra d'Aire Mountains. It was an obscure mountain parish comprised of a scattering of very small villages until 1917 when three shepherd children here had a series of nine apparitions: three of angels, in 1916; six of the Blessed Virgin in 1917, climaxed by a miracle at a time and place predicted by the children ''so that all may believe.'' The message given by these multiple visions is, in the words of Pope Pius XII, ''an affirmation of the Gospel.'' There was nothing new except the apparitions themselves, and the miracle. The message covered just about every gospel doctrine: Heaven, hell, sin, reparation, angelic messengers, the Eucharist, and above all, daily duty; the acceptance of God's will in all things. New stress was placed on devotion to the Blessed Virgin, as explained in Chapter Fourteen of this book, as a source of strength both for entering into the Gospel message and for living it. But the message itself was the Gospel message. Some say Fatima mi ht be likened to Sinai.

There was nothing new in the Ten Commandments, either, but the world had forgotten them. The Eucharistic character of the Message of Fatima was not completely known until August, 1967, when a vision like the diagram (see p. 278) was made public for the first time. The vision actually took place in June, 1929, and was communicated to Pius XI by letter. "It shows," says Rev. Messias Coelho, Portuguese authority who revealed this letter to Pius XI from Lucia, "that the Message of Fatima is essentially Eucharistic." The words communicated by Our Lady to the world at the time of this vision were: *"The moment has come when God asks the Holy Father, in union with all the bishops of the world, to make the consecration of Russia to my Immaculate Heart, promising to save it by this means."* Pope Pius XII made the consecration of the world to the Immaculate Heart in 1942, and ten years later, consecrated the peoples of Russia to Mary's Heart in an apostolic letter. Pope Paul VI renewed both consecrations of his predecessor at the close of the third session of the Ecumenical Council Vatican II, on November 21, 1964. Then, on May 13, 1982, at Fatima, Pope John Paul II not only renewed the consecrations of Pius XII but also said that he was renewing the consecration of the world and of Russia to the Immaculate Heart of Mary *in spiritual union with all his brother bishops, as a body and as a college.* Sister Lucia, sole surviving seer of Fatima, was seen to have tears of joy streaming down her face as the Holy Father made the consecration. The vision of June, 1929, which requested the "collegial" consecration, bears a striking resemblance to the first apparition of the angel at Fatima in 1916: Christ appeared on the cross all in light, surmounted by representations of the Holy Spirit and the

Father. Blood flowed from His side to a Host, and from the Host into a Chalice, while Our Lady stood on the opposite side interceding with outstretched hands, her Immaculate Heart shown surrounded by thorns.

First Fridays: They have to do with the most important of the promises made to Saint Margaret Mary Alacoque (see *Alacoque*) by Our Lord, when He appeared to her out of the monstrance (see this word) on July 2, 1674. He said: "First you are to receive Me in the Blessed Sacrament as often as obedience will allow, no matter what mortification or humiliation it may entail. Moreover, you are to receive Holy Communion on the first Friday of each month, and every night between Thursday and Friday I will make you a partaker of that sorrow unto death which it was My will to suffer in the Garden of Olives." Our Lord asked this in reparation (see this word) for the sins of men. Then, during the octave of the Feast of Corpus Christi, in 1675, He appeared again. He said: "Behold this Heart which has so loved men that I spared nothing... And in return I receive from the greater part of men nothing but ingratitude, by the contempt, irreverence, sacrileges and coldness with which they treat Me in this Sacrament of Love." To those who would receive Him in Communion on nine consecutive First Fridays He promised the grace of a happy death.

First Saturdays: Although Marian acts of reparation on First Saturdays were encouraged by the Church before the apparitions of Fatima, they were dignified in 1925 with a promise from Heaven similar to that attached to the First Fridays (see this word). The Blessed Virgin promised that those who would go to confession, pray five decades of the Rosary, spend fifteen minutes in meditation on the mysteries of the Rosary and receive

Holy Communion... all four acts with the intention of making reparation for the offenses committed against her Immaculate Heart... would enjoy *her presence* at the hour of death, and a happy death, if they made the devotion for five consecutive First Saturdays. Subsequently it has become a custom for many generous souls to begin with Mass of the Sacred Heart on First Friday night, spend the entire night in reparation before the Blessed Sacrament, ending with the Mass of the Immaculate Heart on First Saturday morning. Thus they reply generously to the appeals for reparation made by Our Lord at Paray-le-Monial and by Our Lady at Fatima and Pontevedra and they are sure to enjoy the fullness of the great promises made by the Hearts of Jesus and Mary to repair the sins (see this word) of the world. However, less than an hour is actually needed to complete the essentials of the devotion on each of the Five First Saturdays.

Fridays: See First Fridays.

God: We speak of Him so often in this book that it might be proper, if somewhat daring, to try to define Him. But since that is what most of the entire science of theology (see this word) is about, we need merely say that He is *Being.* He has no parts, as do creatures. But even geniuses have only a vague idea of what this *Being* is because He is different from our kind of being. He is absolute Being and we have merely "contingent being." We can rationalize that He does not exist because we cannot understand *how we* can exist outside of Him. Anyone who has seen a miracle needs no rationalizing. Those who have not seen miracles can know of them from reliable witnesses. And those without excuses, and with common sense, just "know" they came from this *Being,* Who is all Perfection, and that they are destined to enjoy Him.

Harris, Frank: A contemporary of de Maupassant, prominent in British journalism in the last century. The quotations here are from his autobiography published by Corgi, London, 1963, p. 306. One of the prominent quotes used by the publisher in the introduction of this book describes Harris as a "dirty old man." Because of extreme pornography, the book was banned in the United States, like Henry Miller's work, for many years. However, contrary to the opinion expressed by the Englishman, it was never put on the Church Index (see this word). Few books, which one's common sense warns against, ever were.

Heris, Charles V., O.P.: Author of *L'Eucharistie, Mystere de Foi,* published by Alsatia in Paris in 1967, 224 pp. This book distinguishes between physical substance and real substance, and Father Heris says it is a serious mistake to confound the two domains of physical science and of the creation-and-restoration, because the first is of the order of *human* science and the other introduces us to divine Science (capitalized) in which Christ places His word: "This is my body..." Nowhere will the layman have greater difficulty in discussing the Eucharist with the metaphysician, or theologian, than in this area where the difference in the meaning of words can become an almost insurmountable stumbling block. In our chapter on "Science and the Secret," we talk the layman's language, not the metaphysician's. And we do not attempt to explain the unexplainable. We merely show that, in the light of modern science, even if Christ's words were applied to matter *as it really is* there will be found to be *no contradiction* in the limitation of Christ's "extension" or Body within the apparent confines of absolute accidents of bread and wine. For a scientist's comment on this, see *Heyden* below. Abbe Andre Richard, a friend of the author, who sought criticism of the French translation of this book, says:

"The explanation regarding scientific conceptions of today can perhaps be indicated as showing that beneath the appearances which fall upon the senses there is a specific and mysterious reality which is the basis of being, from which arises this or that quality or manifestation which our senses perceive.

"I have often given to children in catechism class the following image:

" Suppose God might suddenly annihilate the sun exactly at noon. We know that the sun's rays, the sun's light, the sun's heat, would all continue to arrive upon the earth for eight minutes. We would say: 'What a beautiful sun!' and in reality the sun would no longer be in existence. Then, suddenly, all would be dark.

" However, even if He did destroy the sun, God could by a miracle preserve the rays of the sun, with their light and heat, accomplishing by His direct Power what the sun did of its own nature.

" In a similar manner the 'rays' of bread...that is its exterior qualities...can be preserved by God even though the substance of the bread has been removed and changed to the Presence of the Body of Christ. "

See the word Accident.

Heyden, S.J., Dr. Francis J: Director of Georgetown College Observatory and world famous scientist. He commented on Chapter Seven: "It is true that the physical concept of matter today identifies it with energy inasmuch as the relation $E = mc^2$ has been verified both by fusion and fission. While most physicists also feel that what we call matter in the universe did condense from energy, they have not yet been able to demonstrate the reversal of energy into mass.

"Treating atoms as point forces, of course, goes back to the philosophers of the last century, Palmieri and Boscovitch, who described atoms as *puncta inflata* or inflated points, their doctrine of extension, by which quantity is measured, called it virtual in contrast to formal.

"Since no one can question either doctrine in cosmology as far as the mystery of transubstantiation is concerned, there is nothing wrong one way or the other with Chapter Seven in *The World's Greatest Secret*. But since we speak of energy density as well as plain density for mass, some cosmologist might want to argue about formal and virtual extension. Call it either, you still have extension or *partes extra partes*.

"The chapter establishes with sufficient clarity the fact that faith alone provides us with the information that the Real Presence exists after consecration under the appearance of bread and wine.

"How small a quantity must one have before one can have the Real Presence in consecration? I have never figured that out. I have always believed that perhaps the angels have to gather up the tiny flecks that fall or blow away while a priest gives communion."

Holy Spirit: See Trinity.

Holy Thursday: Also called Maundy Thursday, from the Latin "to wash," referring to the washing of feet before the Eucharistic Liturgy. It takes place on the Thursday before good Friday and recalls how Christ opened the first Eucharistic Liturgy the night before He died.

Host: From the Latin word for *hostage,* applied to Christ as the victim for our sins. This usage appears in the prayers of the Mass. But then it was applied to the Eucharist and in particular to the consecrated bread. It is sometimes improperly used to refer to the bread used for the Eucharist even before consecration (see this word).

Immaculate Conception: Contrary to somewhat common belief, this term has *nothing* to do with the fact that Mary was a Virgin. It means that from the moment of her conception she was sinless *in anticipation* of the merits of Christ's redemption. In other words, she was redeemed by Our Lord like all other humans, *but God gave her special graces and preserved her from original sin* (since she was to provide us with the Body of Christ) *in virtue of the redemption which would follow.* She was born, like Adam and Eve, sinless and in union with God. Thus she could become "the new Eve," as several Fathers of the Church refer to her. See *Fathers of the Church.*

Immaculate Heart: Since the first drop of Christ's Blood came, in a manner of speaking, from the heart of Mary, it was fitting that her heart should have been all pure. But, as in devotion to the Sacred Heart (see this word), this term refers to the Blessed Virgin in her entirety. The word "immaculate" emphasizes what Mary means to us who lost grace through our first parents. She is, as the Protestant poet Wordsworth exclaimed: "Our tainted nature's solitary boast." Most of the world's population (including Mohammedans) believe that she was immaculate, or sinless. Devotionally (as we explain in Chapter Fourteen) we try to apply this immaculateness to ourselves that we may the more worthily, confidently, easily plunge ourselves into the Sacred Heart of Christ.

Incarnation: From the Latin meaning "to become flesh." This is the word for the belief expressed by Christians in the ancient Nicene Creed: "We believe in one Lord, Jesus Christ, the only Son of God, eternally begotten of the Father,...begotten, not made, one in Being with the Father.... For us men and for our salvation he came down from heaven: by the power of the Holy Spirit he was born of the Virgin Mary, and became man."

Index of Prohibited Books: A listing of books which Catholics were formerly forbidden, under pain of excommunication, to possess, read or sell. These books were banned by the Holy See after publication because they were judged to contain serious occasions of doctrinal error or grave dangers to morals. On June 14, 1966, the Congregation for the Doctrine of the Faith declared that the Index and its related penalties of excommunication no longer had the force of law in the Church. It noted, however, that persons still had to take normal precautions against occasions of doctrinal error and immorality.

Lateran, Saint John: When Christians emerged from the catacombs, Constantine gave to Peter's successor the so-called Lateran Palace to be converted to Church use and it thus became the first principal church of the Christian world. To this day, it is so designated. Over its main portal is inscribed the phrase: *Omnium urbis et orbis ecclesiarum mater et caput,* "The Mother and Head of all the churches of the city and of the world." Because of its venerable character and importance, the Pope celebrates the Eucharistic Liturgy here on Holy or Maundy Thursday. A major relic of the church is considered a part of the table of the Last Supper. For the Passover, the Jews did not sit at table as at ordinary meals, but reclined around it on low divans. The famous painting by da Vinci is not historically accurate.

Liturgy: From the Greek, *leitourgia,* a public service. It refers to the official worship of God through the Church accomplished in three major ways: 1) Through the Eucharistic Sacrifice; 2) the recitation of the Liturgy of the Hours or the "Divine Office" (a collection of psalms and prayers arranged to continue the spirit of dedication of the day to God); 3) the administration of the Sacraments and the annexed use of the sacramentals. The *Maryknoll Catholic Dictionary* (by J. Nevins, M.M., 1965, p. 342) says: "The culmination of the liturgy is the Eucharist because here the encounter with Christ is *personal and very real,* the closest contact that can be obtained with Christ and salvation." (Italics ours.) But an important aspect of *liturgy* is the word "public." It is not a solitary, individual act. We participate in the liturgy as members of the Mystical Body of Christ, as members of His Church. Not only do we share in the love of Christ for the Father, but there is a force in the liturgy which enables us to share in His love for mankind and to love our neighbor as we love God. This aspect was strongly emphasized in the *Constitution on the Sacred Liturgy* issued by Vatican Council II on December 4, 1963.

Luther, Martin: He was an Augustinian friar who on October 31, 1517, launched the Protestant Reformation. Many feel that if John XXIII had been Pope, or if it had been 1967 instead of 1517, Luther would not have separated from Rome. But he did, and he taught (in defense of his own divergence) the right of private judgment. So subsequent divisions in Christianity have come to be numbered in the hundreds. Dr. Kent S. Knutson, Director of Graduate Studies at the Luther Theological Seminary in Saint Paul, Minn., was consulted in reference to our quotation from Luther in Chapter Seven. The statement we quoted appears in *Wider Etliche Tollen Geister,* but Dr. Knutson says: "You might quote a better known and more substantial work, such as the confession concerning Christ's Supper, of 1528, of *This Is My Body* where he says that 'These words of Christ, *This is my Body, etc.* still stand firm against the fanatics', written in 1527. There is never a question in the mind of Luther about the doctrine of the real presence."

Makhlouf, Saint Sharbel: A Lebanese Maronite monk of the Monastery of Annaya, which is about a two-hour drive by private car from Beirut and over 4000 feet above sea level. He died in 1898, at seventy years of age, after a life of incredible austerity. During the last twenty-three years he lived in an unheated hermitage, even without glass at the window and with the stone floor as his bed although the temperature much of the year was below freezing. His devotion to the Holy Mass was so great that he finally asked permission to spend his entire life just in preparing for Mass and making thanksgiving each day. Through the most extraordinary miracles, including the miracle of the preservation of his body and the constant emission of fluid from the incorrupt body, the attention of the world was drawn to his Eucharistic life. The few details quoted in this book are known to the writer at first hand. He was present at the beatification of Saint Charbel in St. Peter's Basilica in Rome on May 12, 1965, and examined much of the documentation, garments, samples of blood, etc. in the company of Father Touvia Ciade, Superior of the Monastery at Annaya, on the Feast of Corpus Christi, 1967. The Saint was canonized by Pope Paul VI in 1977.

Martyr: From the Greek word meaning "witness." We

use it to refer to a person who has died for his faith. But the early Christians used it to denote a person who, by giving his life, bore witness to the proof of Christ's resurrection and of the Eucharist and other doctrines He had taught them. *See Witness.*

Mary: See Immaculate Conception and Immaculate Heart.

Mass: From the Latin word "missa," at the end of the Eucharistic Liturgy. Because of its brevity the word has been commonly applied to the entire Eucharistic Liturgy but new stress has been placed on the full title since Vatican Council II. The words *Ite, missa est* at the end of the liturgy mean, "Go, it is finished."

Messiah: In Hebrew it means "Anointed," and it was used in Israel to designate the expected king (the Anointed One) who would deliver Israel and be the Savior of his people. *See Savior.*

Miller, Henry: Materialistic writer, contemporary of de Maupassant, whose books were a wide source of controversy because of pornographic passages. His own best-selling book he described as a "kick in the pants of God." It often reflects sloughs of despondency into which materialists logically fall and to which we refer here.

Miracle: The word here is used in its strict sense — not of something which is merely surprising, but something *above and beyond the powers of nature.* Some say that there are no miracles, just no explanations. But that shows a lack of understanding of what we mean by the word: We mean an act above and beyond the *known* and *explained* laws of nature, such as five thousand men being fed with food that was insufficient for five, or the instantaneous appearance of dry scars where there had been open, draining fistulas one moment before. By the word "miracle," we mean something which any rational person, with adequate knowledge of cause and effect, can attribute to God.

Monstrance: From the Latin "to show." This is a sacred vessel used to display the Eucharist for adoration. It is usually of precious metal, with rays emanating from a glass in the center beneath which the Sacred Host is reserved. During Forty Hours Devotion (see reference to Saint John Neumann, pp. 163-64) the monstrance is used, as well as for other periods of adoration (sometimes perpetual) and for the ceremony of blessing with the Eucharist known as Benediction. In recent years, thousands of persons have been spending entire nights before the Blessed Sacrament exposed in a monstrance in petition and reparation. This is called the "All-Night Vigil."

Mount Zion: Also known as Mount Sion, this is the mountain on which Jerusalem was first built and on which King David was buried. Here Jews and Christians have holy places in common: The traditional location of the tomb of King David is beneath the "upper room" or "cenacle" where Christ celebrated the Passover the night before He died and instituted the Eucharist. It is also the room in which the Paraclete came upon the disciples.

Mystery: This book uses this word in its restricted sense of something which cannot be wholly understood. Some mysteries of life are only temporary; we may get to understand them with increased knowledge. But the Eucharist is a mystery which we not only cannot understand now, but will never wholly understand because to do so we would have to understand the Incarnation (see this word) and this would in turn require an understanding of the nature of God Himself which is beyond our scope. There arrives a point at which, in the words of the great scholastic genius, Thomas Aquinas, we must say: "I believe because Christ, Who is Truth, told me." We believe not because we understand, but because it is unreasonable not to believe. Despite all the facts and all the miracles, the mystery remains. Still we can be dazzled by passages of the *Summa Theologica* of Saint Thomas Aquinas, especially in Part III, questions 79 and 80, of which Tillard says: "Here the great optimism of living Tradition about the redemptive value of the Eucharistic body and blood vibrates to the fullest."

Mystical Body: It is important not to mistake the word "mystical" which means *hidden,* with the word "mythical" which means *fable.* Christ, at the first Eucharistic Liturgy, said that now Christians, united to each other by commmunion with Him (in the actual consumption of Him under the forms of bread and wine), were like branches of a vine: "I am the vine, you are the branches." (Jn. 15:5) Now all Christians become joined in His Body into one body. This body cannot be seen, except in its individual members. But it is a *real* body. The doctrine was explained by Pope Pius XII in a magnificent encyclical: *Mystici Corporis.*

Mysticism: Communion between two lovers is visible in sighs, words, deeds. Communion between the soul and God is often invisible, and is therefore called "mystic" or secret. "Mysticism" refers primarily to the very highest form of communion with God. It means a very real experience of God's presence in the soul which often results in definite physiological or psychological manifestations, such as freedom from gravity (levitation), radiance, inexplicable fragrances, stigmata, etc. Such manifestations are not always present, but in modern usage a "mystic" is usually thought to be a person in such close communion with God that such manifestations are evident. Therese Neumann, to whom we refer here and who lived for years solely on the Eucharist, was a well-known mystic of recent times. All the mystics of Christian history seem to have centered their lives on the Blessed Sacrament.

Neumann, Theresa: See Mysticism.

Nicene Creed: This is the common ground of almost all Christians. It was composed in the Council of Nicaea in A.D. 325, immediately after the age of persecutions, to publicly state the major truths of the Church which might be called into question. Since the Eucharist was still the "Christian Secret," and perhaps also because it was the unquestioned center of the Christian faith, it was not included in the Creed. At the time of the Council of Nicaea, the Eucharist was universally the center of Christian life and faith.

Orthodox: When we use this term we are referring to the Eastern Church not in union with Rome. It was a collective name for self-governing churches of Eastern Europe and western Asia. Most of these churches, under the Patriarch of Constantinople, separated from Rome in 1054 largely because of political differences. Their manner of celebrating the Eucharistic liturgy differs from most western churches (as it has from earliest times), but doctrinal differences are few. The Patriarch of Constantinople in 1967 referred to the Patriarch of the West, the Pope, as "My brother Paul," and said: "We must now eliminate through ecclesiastical acts those elements which divide us." Most Russians are to be counted among the more than 160 million Orthodox. They have a valid priesthood, valid sacraments, and consequently the true Eucharist.

Our Lady of the Blessed Sacrament: This is the title of an excellent booklet of prayers published by St. Peter Julian Eymard's congregation (Fathers of the Blessed Sacrament). Although the prayers are especially written for the nine days preceding May 13, Feast of Our Lady of the Blessed Sacrament, they may be used at any time. In the United States this booklet is published by the Sentinel Press (194 E. 76th St., New York, NY 10021). There are three major reasons cited for the devotion to "Our Lady of the Blessed Sacrament": 1) The body of Our Lord, received in Communion, was born of Mary; 2) Grace comes through Mary, and especially the greatest of all graces, the Eucharist; 3) The life of the Blessed Virgin after the ascension of Our Lord (when she lived with Saint John) models for us the relationship we should have in our own lives to Christ in the Eucharist.

Pasch: The Hebrew word is *pesah,* or passover. It is a Jewish feast commemorating the deliverance of the Israelites from Egyptian slavery. *See Passover.*

Passover: From the words *pass* and *over,* referring to the fact that the Angel of Death passed over those houses which were sprinkled with the blood of the lamb and thus led to the great *passage* of the Jews from the slavery of Pharaoh to freedom and the promised land. Aphraates, a Greek Father of the Church and also called "the Persian Sage," draws the comparison between the original Passover, the Last Supper, and the New Covenant: "On the Passover the Jews escaped from the slavery of Pharaoh; on the day of the Crucifixion we were delivered from the slavery of Satan. They sacrificed a lamb whose blood saved them from the exterminator; we were delivered by the blood of the well-beloved Son from our works of corruption. They had Moses for a guide; we have Jesus for Head and Savior. For them Moses divided the sea and had them cross; our Savior opened the depths and broke their gates when, descending into the depths he opened them and forged the way at the head of all those who were to believe in him" (*Demonstrations,* 12, 8, 1902-07). J. M. Tillard, O.P. in *The Eucharist: Pasch of God's People*, 1967, develops this point at length.

Presanctification: This refers to the passage described by Saint Luke: "When Elizabeth heard the greeting of Mary, the baby leapt in her womb. Elizabeth was filled with the Holy Spirit and cried out in a loud voice: 'Blest are you among women and blest is the fruit of your womb. But who am I that the mother of my Lord should come to me? The moment your greeting sounded in my ears the baby leapt in my womb for joy'" (Lk. 1:41). It is understood that this was, in a sense, the moment of baptism for the child of Elizabeth who was himself to become the baptizer, the herald of Christ. Hence the word "presanctification," or sanctification before birth.

Reformation: See Luther.

Reparation: This is an important word in the modern world. Great stress was placed on it in the messages of Fatima and Lourdes. If enough good persons make reparation, the world was told at Fatima (see this word) that God will obtain peace among all men. But if reparation is not made (obviously by those who believe for those who do not believe), communism and allied errors will spread through the entire world and provoke further wars, ultimately "entire nations will be annihilated." To understand it we need merely to understand the meaning of sin (see this word).

Rosetta Stone: Despite years of effort to decipher the hieroglyphics of ancient Egypt, no one succeeded until a trilingual stone was found in the town of Rosetta. This stone gave archeologists the key to understanding hieroglyphics and thus unlocked countless facts of the ancient world, facts previously unknown altogether or else the object of mere guesswork.

Sacrament: Originally the Latin word meant any "sacred thing," but in the Church today, a sacrament means only those seven things made particularly sacred by Christ: Marriage (at Cana); the Eucharist and the Priesthood (at the Last Supper and after the Resurrection); Anointing of the Sick, for the sick or dying (as on Calvary); Baptism and Confirmation (sending of the Paraclete); Penance ("If you forgive men's sins, they are forgiven them. . . . "). And these seven sacred things bear the Presence of Christ within them, although He is physically present only in the Eucharist which is therefore called the *Blessed Sacrament.* Other instruments of God's help, not directly instituted by Christ and not containing grace as it were within themselves, are called "little sacraments" or "sacramentals." Among the most celebrated of the latter are rosaries, scapulars, representations of Christ and the saints, and so on. In Catechism, a sacrament is defined as *an outward sign of inward grace, instituted by Christ.*

Sacred Heart: This is an endearing and reverential term *for Christ Himself,* even as the term "dear heart" might refer to any beloved person. The term refers to the entire Christ because the heart is the symbol of love and Christ is Love Itself (Cardinal Franzelin, S.J., *De Verbo Incarnato,* cap. vi, tesis xiv, 1874). The great Arthur

Vermeersch, whom we have delighted to quote in other of our books, points out that the Heart of Christ is not taken like a metaphor but as the real and natural *symbol* of Christ's love *(Pratique et doctrine de la devotion au Sacré Coeur,* vol. 2., pub. by Casterman, France, 1930, p. 33.

Sacrifice: The Eucharist must be seen in two lights: As a Sacrament (see this word), and sacrifice, which means an offering of expiation. As we explain in the text, the Eucharistic Liturgy *makes the sacrifice of Calvary present.* But neither aspect (sacrament or sacrifice) is *ever actually separate.* "Communion," says Tillard (op. cit., p. 313), "with the consecrated bread is intended only to render us participants in the sacrifice of the Pasch of Jesus; the bread and wine are consecrated to render sacramentally present this pascal sacrifice." We perhaps can appreciate this if we place ourselves in the position of Saint John at the Last Supper — resting his head on the very breast of Christ, feeling His Heart beat — and within a matter of hours standing at the foot of His cross. To us a single Communion is all this. The very word "host" means a victim. The Eucharist unites me to my Savior, and my Savior to me.

Saint: See **Canonized.**

Saturdays: See **First Saturdays.**

Secret of the Mass: That part of the Mass just after the recitation of the Nicene Creed which prepares for the consecration (see this word) when transubstantiation (see this word) will occur. In the early Church, anyone who had not been baptized and confirmed was not allowed to remain in church when this sacred part of the Liturgy began. Some writers suggest that this part was called "Secret" because the priest said the prayers in a low voice. But, as we have shown extensively in these pages, this sacred part of the Eucharistic Liturgy was indeed a secret — which means, of course, something hidden from the uninitiated. The use of the term lost meaning after the early centuries of persecution, but to this day, many (especially non-Christians) are amazed to discover this "Secret" of Christians. Vatican Council II removed the word "Secret" and substituted the words "Liturgy of the Eucharist." The sacred prayers previously said "secretly" are now said aloud and in the vernacular so that all may join their hearts with that of the priest and the entire Church in offering the Eucharistic Sacrifice.

Sin: Can be described in various ways, but essentially it is disobedience to God Who is All Goodness. It is the free choice of personal indulgence in a matter contrary to the law of God, whether that law be manifest through legitimate authority or through principles evident in creation. Its gravity depends especially on the knowledge and motivation of the sinner. An act wrong in itself is not a sin if the person performing it does not recognize it as sinful, i.e., as contrary to the will of God. The extent of the evil in the first sin, committed by a man and a woman who enjoyed intimacy with God and an abundance of intelligence and light, can hardly be understood by those who have never enjoyed such divine intimacy. It required a supreme act of love on the part of God to restore man to the intimacy which the first man and woman had voluntarily renounced. The Eucharist is the perpetuation of that supreme act of love: the Incarnation. It follows (as taught by the angel of Fatima) that the best way of repairing for the sins of men is adoration, love and offering of the Blessed Sacrament to the Most Holy Trinity.

Substance: From Latin words meaning *stand under.* We use it in this book, in reference to transubstantiation, in a restricted sense of "that which makes a thing what it is," or rather that which is *real* rather than that which is *apparent*. It is the abiding part of any existence as distinguished from visible parts which may change, like color, shape, texture, etc. A table, for instance, is a table regardless of how many legs it has, what color or size it is, etc. The *substance* of a table is *that which makes it what it is. See Accident and Heris, Charles V., O.P.*

Tabernacle: Between celebrations of the Eucharistic Liturgy, the Eucharist, or Sacred Species, is reserved in a boxlike structure known as a tabernacle. The word comes from ancient times. During the Exodus it was a portable box, with curtains, in which the Jews put the tablets of the commandments. This became the sacred place in the great temple of Jerusalem and was considered *the place of God's most intimate presence among His people.* Today there are churches all over the world where Christ is present Eucharistically in tabernacles, before which the sanctuary lamp burns as a sign of His presence. The orignal tabernacle from the time of Moses has been lost.

Testament: See Covenant.

Theologians: Those who study theology (see this word) professionally, whether ascetical, mystical, dogmatic, moral, positive (eg., scripture and tradition), pastoral or natural. Usually we think of the theologian as a student of all branches, but particularly *dogmatic*, which deals with truths of what we must believe about God. It is complex and requires a vast amount of other knowledge as well as spiritual sensitivity. Hence there are very few *great* theologians. They classically came from two schools: the Alexandrian and Antiochan, the first growing out of Platonic philosophy, the second from Aristotle. In the debates which raged between them during the early centuries, a clearer view of God began to emerge. Today the leading theologian of the past who is most invoked as an authority in reference to the matter of this book is Saint Thomas Aquinas. Some new, great theologians are arising today out of the ferment of thought exposed by Vatican Council II. The writer of this book skimmed many relevant theological works. He wanted to retain the simple layman's point of view while at the same time ascertaining that this view should not be without consciousness of the best professional opinions. (See *Substance*.)

Theology: Many have the false notion that theology is just a study of religion. Actually theology is a science, and perhaps the highest of all sciences because its object is the highest: God (see this word). Like any science, it is a study that proceeds from the known to the unknown and its primary method is to doubt and question and to seek incontrovertible answers. Because of its scientific method, theologians in general tend to be disputatious. There is so little about God of which we *are* certain that, as in philosophy, we find ourselves following the best minds or the majority of minds on those questions which are not dogmatic. It is the right of the theologian, the scientist of God, to question. It is perhaps also a right for simple layfolk to be spared their arguments. See *Theologians*.

Tradition: See Fathers of the Church.

Transubstantiation: This is a key word to understanding the Eucharist. It was formally developed by St. Cyril in the fourth century and strongly confirmed by the Council of Trent. (See St. Cyril's *Mystogogic Catechesis,* 4, 2 and 5, 7 and *Enchiridion Symbolorum* published in Freiburg by Denzinger, 1953, pp. 877, 884. Pope Paul VI also strongly confirmed it in the encyclical published in this book. It is a word which means literally what it implies: a transfer of substances. What was the substance of bread becomes the substance of Christ, whole and entire, Body and Blood and Soul and Divinity. All that remains of the bread are the absolute accidents of color, size, texture: that which is visible. See *Substance* and *Accident.*

Trent: At the height of the Protestant "revolt" the bishops of the world assembled in this Austrian town to answer questions which had never before been seriously raised by Christians. There had been earlier councils, but this was the most important because the divisions of Protestantism brought about the first major break in the doctrinal unity of Christians. The bishops, who met in December, 1545, were convened off and on for eighteen years. They confirmed the Nicene Creed and "defined" the Real Presence and Transubstantiation as its mode. They also declared that holy communion in both kinds was necessary only for those celebrating because Christ is whole and entire under both species. They based their definitions on what had been taught since the time of Our Lord, as well as on reason and universality of belief among Christians transmitted by tradition and documents. Convened only 28 years after Martin Luther nailed his ninety-five theses on the doors of the church in Wittenberg, the Council affirmed (at least on the Eucharist) what nearly all Christians, *including Martin Luther,* had believed up to this time.

Trinity: From Latin meaning Three-One. It is an aspect of the nature of God which we would not know if Christ had not told us during the first Eucharistic Liturgy. This revelation was a further testimony of His love. He wanted us to know, in a sense, what God is like inside: Love so powerful that in loving Himself He becomes Himself again; returning the love He again becomes Himself. Loving, He is the Father; loved, He is the Son; loving between Father and Son He is the Holy Spirit. Yet He remains One, Simple, Absolute Being. As the Father He sent Himself into the world; as the Son He saved men and transubstantiated Himself to remain with us in the Eucharist; as the Paraclete He comes to enable us to return His love. *See God.*

Vatican II, Ecumenical Council: Opened October 11, 1962, by Pope John XXIII with 2,540 Council Fathers. It ended December 8, 1962, and reconvened under Pope Paul VI on September 29, 1963, during which the *Constitution on the Sacred Liturgy* was adopted. The third session closed on November 21, 1964 with a consecration of the world, and in particular of Russia, to the Immaculate Heart of Mary by Pope Paul in the presence of all the Council Fathers. (See *Fatima*, p. 276.) The final sessions of the Council in 1964 and 1965 dealt with the nature of the Church and ecumenism. The author wrote this book in Rome during most of the Council, and was present in St. Peter's on December 7, 1965, when the last votes were cast and a Legate of Patriarch Athenagoras I, head of the 160 million-member Orthodox Church, read in the presence of the Council the lifting of the interdict against Rome, while the Secretary of the Council read a similar proclamation lifting the interdict against the Eastern Church. All the bishops of the world broke into spontaneous applause as the Legate of the Eastern Church walked in solemn procession around the tomb of Peter. Our only quotation in this book from the *Constitution on*

the Sacred Liturgy is from Rush, which is an early translation, but we used it because it coincides with the quotation
in the encyclical of Pope Paul VI which we quote in full
in the Appendix; several fine translations of the Vatican
Council II documents are now available like the paperback
published by America Press *(The Documents of Vatican
II,* ed W. Abbott, S.J., 1966), with notes and comments
by Catholic, Protestant and Orthodox authorities, and
Vatican II: The Conciliar and Postconciliar Documents
(ed. A. Flannery, O.P., 1975). The sixteen texts pro-
mulgated by the Council run to 103,014 words. Many of
them may be forgotten but the effect of the Council on
the union of the Eastern and Western Churches and the
final union of all Christians is materializing as the Council's (and Pope John's) twentieth century "miracle."

Virgin: It seems to have become customary among all
Christians to refer to the Mother of Christ as "the Virgin,"
or the "Blessed Virgin," perhaps because such
was the first reference to her by Saint Luke: "... *to a
virgin* betrothed to a man named Joseph.... (Lk. 1:27);
and in Matthew: "All this happened to fulfill what the
Lord had said through the prophet: 'The virgin shall be
with child and give birth to a son, and they shall call him
Emmanuel,' a name which means 'God is with us.'"
(Mt. 1:22) Devotionally it is more proper to refer to her as
"Mother" because in consenting to become the Mother
of Christ she became the mother of His whole body, and
His Mystical Body (see this word). She has appeared on
earth several times in the past century as a concerned and
caring mother.

Witness: Comes from an Anglo-Saxon word meaning
"to know." It means attestation of a fact or event, or
testimony to a truth. Many witnesses of the past are

inert, like the inscriptions on the tombs of the first Christians. Other witnesses, equally silent but eloquent, are those who gave their lives rather than expose the truth to ridicule (like Tarcisius, see Chapter Thirteen).

Prophecy of Padre Pio
Concerning this Book

Perhaps never before has any one ever tried to write a popular book on this difficult subject, not merely because of the theological and scientific details, but because of the sublime, often ineffable nature of the Secret itself.

But there can be no Christian Ecumenism until this "hard saying" of Jesus is understood.

Even when Our Lord Himself first made it known, all around Him found it incredible. A moment before they had wanted to make Him a King, and now they all withdrew from Him. Even those closest to Him were confused. But He insisted on the "hard saying" and asked even whether they also wanted to go away. They could not understand it either. But Peter spoke for them:

"Where shall we go? You alone have the words of Eternal Life."

Because of the difficulties involved, an advance edition of this book was printed and sent to *over five hundred critics of all faiths.* The manuscript was also translated in French and Italian for criticism by European scholars.

Not one criticism from any source was overlooked.

The result is one of the most important books of our time. An Anglican housewife in Edmonton, Ont., wrote to say that she found it more uplifting than any book she had ever read — except for the Bible.

Many persons make an apostolate of buying the book in quantities for wide distribution.

Padre Pio, famous Capuchin whose cause for beatification has been entered, prayed for the book's success and prophesied: "It will succeed while the author is living, but will have its greatest success after his death."

Hearing this, the author quipped:

"I want to hurry up and die, because we may have a new world soon if enough people learn the secret!"